Value Added Tax and the Digital Economy

EUCOTAX Series on European Taxation

VOLUME 46

Series Editors

Introduction

EUCOTAX (European Universities Cooperating on Taxes) is a network of tax institutes currently consisting of eleven universities: WU (Vienna University of Economics and Business) in Austria, Katholieke Universiteit Leuven in Belgium, Corvinus University of Budapest, Hungary, Université Paris-I Panthéon-Sorbonne in France, Universität Osnabrück in Germany, Libera, Università Internazionale di Studi Sociali in Rome (and Università degli Studi di Bologna for the research part), in Italy, Fiscaal Instituut Tilburg at Tilburg University in the Netherlands, Universidad de Barcelona in Spain, Uppsala University in Sweden, Queen Mary and Westfield College at the University of London in the United Kingdom, and Georgetown University in Washington DC, United States of America. The network aims at initiating and coordinating both comparative education in taxation, through the organization of activities such as winter courses and guest lectures, and comparative research in the field, by means of joint research projects, international conferences and exchange of researchers between various countries.

Contents/Subjects

The EUCOTAX series covers a wide range of topics in European tax law. For example tax treaties, EC case law, tax planning, exchange of information and VAT. The series is well-known for its high-quality research and practical solutions.

Objective

The series aims to provide insights on new developments in European taxation.

Readership

Practitioners and academics dealing with European tax law.

Frequency of Publication

2-3 new volumes published each year.

The titles published in this series are listed at the end of this volume.

Value Added Tax and the Digital Economy

The 2015 EU Rules and Broader Issues

Edited by

Marie Lamensch
Edoardo Traversa
Servaas van Thiel

Wolters Kluwer

Published by:
Kluwer Law International
PO Box 316
2400 AH Alphen aan den Rijn
The Netherlands
Website: www.wklawbusiness.com

Sold and distributed in North, Central and South America by:
Aspen Publishers, Inc.
7201 McKinney Circle
Frederick, MD 21704
United States of America
Email: customer.service@aspenpublishers.com

Sold and distributed in all other countries by:
Turpin Distribution Services Ltd
Stratton Business Park
Pegasus Drive, Biggleswade
Bedfordshire SG18 8TQ
United Kingdom
Email: kluwerlaw@turpin-distribution.com

Printed on acid-free paper.

ISBN 978-90-411-6612-8

Printed and Bound by CPI Group (UK) Ltd, Croydon, CR0 4YY.

Contributors

Emanuele Ceci is Assistant at the Université Catholique de Louvain and a practising lawyer in Brussels.

Sophie Claessens is Senior Manager, Indirect Tax, at PwC Belgium (Antwerp). She has extensive experience on B2C industries (including telecom and e-commerce) and is a driver of PwC's Business Working Group on the EU 2015 VAT changes.

Walter Hellerstein is Distinguished Research Professor & Francis Shackelford Distinguished Professor in Taxation Law at the University of Georgia, US.

Oskar Henkow is Associate Professor at the Department for Business law at Lund University School of Economics and Management in Sweden.

Charléne Herbain teaches Value Added Tax at the University of Luxembourg and Tax Law at the University of Lorraine and is post-doctoral researcher at the Catholic University of Louvain. She has been a VAT practitioner for ten years and serves as a tax advisor to several law firms in Luxembourg.

Marie Lamensch is Professor in 'International and European Taxation' at the Institute for European Studies (Free University Brussels) and Lecturer in 'Value Added Tax' at the Catholic University of Louvain. She participates in the OECD Working Party 9 Technical Advisory Group on Consumption Taxes.

Ine Lejeune is Attorney at Law and Partner Tax Policy, Dispute Resolution and Litigation practice with the Brussels law firm 'Law Square'. She is a member of the European Commission's VAT Expert Group and lectures at the Vienna University of Economics and Business (WU).

David O'Sullivan is Official of the Irish Revenue and a Seconded National Expert to DG TAXUD, European Commission.

Donato Raponi is Head of Section at DG TAXUD of the European Commission.

Pernilla Rendahl is Associate Professor (Docent) in Tax Law at the School of Business, Economics and Law of the University of Gothenburg.

Ben Terra is Professor at the Universities of Amsterdam and Lund.

Edoardo Traversa is Professor of Tax Law at the Université Catholique de Louvain and at the Katholieke Universiteit Leuven and Of Counsel at Liedekerke in Brussels.

Cristina Trenta is Senior Lecturer in Tax Law at Örebro University.

Servaas van Thiel is Professor in International and European Taxation at the Institute for European Studies of the Free University Brussels and works for the European External Action Service.

Summary of Contents

Table of Contents

Preface

In the spring of 2014, academic and professional experts from different disciplines and nationalities gathered together at the 'Vrije Universiteit Brussel' to discuss the large number of issues that arise when jurisdictions attempt to apply value added tax or general sales tax to the digital economy. Subsequently the associated annual International PhD seminar on VAT and other Indirect Taxes was organised in Louvain-la-Neuve by the Universities of Durham (Prof. Rita de la Feria), Münster (Prof. Joachim Englisch), Lund (Prof. Oskar Henkow and Ben Terra) and Louvain (Prof. Edoardo Traversa). The fundamental starting point of these open and creative discussions was that the digital economy has taken shape, and is rapidly growing, in a virtual reality which works with completely new concepts, and in which suppliers and consumers conclude numerous transactions in anonymity, and unrestrained by time and place. The contrast with traditional sales tax systems, which are based on a physical supply between parties who (often know and) meet each other in person at a certain place and time, could not be more evident.

A general part of those discussions focused on the European VAT rules on 'electronically supplied services' (which entered in force in January 2015) and related issues such as the problem of combating e-commerce fraud and the Mini One Stop Shop. Another part centred on VAT questions that arise specifically in a digital environment, such the digital fixed establishment and VAT aspects of internet search engines, virtual currencies (bitcoins) and cloud computing.

Subsequently, the reflection process continued and top experts agreed that it would be important for all public and private sector VAT professionals to have a crystal clear overview of the relevant VAT rules that apply in the European Union since January 2015, as well as a critical analysis of these rules and of the issues that are still outstanding. Contributions from those experts have now been collected in this book, which first sets out the general EU VAT framework for 'electronically supplied services', before tackling those more specific issues.

We would like to thank in particular all the contributors for the time and intellectual energy which they have placed at the disposal of this project, and the 'Université Catholique de Louvain' and the Institute for European Studies of the 'Vrije

Universiteit Brussel' for providing the premises for the initial discussions and the resources for the subsequent research.

Marie Lamensch
Edoardo Traversa
Servaas van Thiel
Brussels, 29 July 2015

CHAPTER 1

VAT on Online Supplies: A Brief Outline of Current Issues

*Servaas van Thiel**

1.1 THE VAT SUCCESS-STORY

Value added tax (VAT) was proposed in the beginning of the twentieth century by Von Siemens and Adams[1] and it was first introduced by France in 1954.[2] Since then it has been successfully applied in around 150 countries worldwide and it usually ranks first or second as a source of tax revenue in those countries.[3]

VAT systems were designed in times when most transactions consisted of physical supplies between parties who (often knew and) met each other in person at a certain place and time. If at all, services were supplied within single jurisdictions between parties that often acted within the framework of a regular 'business' relationship. This changed rather fundamentally with the appearance of the Internet, which allows for 'online', 'digital' or 'electronic' supplies (i.e., supplies of digital content against electronic payment) that take place instantaneously and in anonymity, between suppliers and consumers who are not constrained by time and place. Although it is difficult to determine with precision the volume and thus the economic importance of online supplies (official statistics generally do not account for e-commerce as a

* Prof. van Thiel teaches international and European taxation at the Institute for European Studies of the Free University Brussels and works for the European External Action Service. The views expressed in this contribution and purely personal and cannot be attributed to any of the organizations mentioned.

1. See C.F. von Siemens (1919): 'Veredelte Umasatzsteuer' (published in 'Siemenstadt') and Th. S. Adams (1921): 'Fundamental Problems of Federal Income Taxation' 35 Quarterly J. of Econ. at p. 527. See also R. Van Brederode (2009): 'Sales Taxation', Kluwer.
2. Introduced by Act No. 54-404 of 10 Apr. 1954. 'Journal Officiel' of 11 Apr. 1954 and 'Rectificatif Journal Officiel' of 20 May 1954.
3. See A. Tait (1988): 'Value-added-tax: International Practices and Problems', IMF. See also R. Van Brederode (2009): 'Sales Taxation', Kluwer.

separate category of trade),[4] it is widely believed to be a rapidly growing part of international trade which has been remarkably resistant to economic downturns and is responsible for ever increasing shares of corporate profits.[5] The resulting 'e-commerce' has proven to be an engine for economic growth and jobs in many developed and developing countries, and a fast-growing portion of overall taxable consumption is now realized via online supplies.[6]

In these circumstances, it is crucial for national governments as well as for competing businesses that VAT is effectively assessed and collected by all suppliers who are active in this sector. At the same time, it is crucial for businesses not to be faced with disproportionate compliance burdens or international double taxation. Unsurprisingly, therefore, tax professionals have been discussing the VAT aspects of e-commerce since the early 1990s,[7] and the European legislator was the first to pioneer

4. See for an extensive analysis Ch. 4 in Marie Lamensch (2015): 'European Value-Added Tax in the Digital Era: A Critical Analysis and Proposals for Reform', IBFD, Amsterdam, Doctoral Series (expected vol. 36).
5. According to the BEPS report on the digital economy (http://www.keepeek.com/Digital-Asset-Management/oecd/taxation/addressing-the-tax-challenges-of-the-digital-economy_9789264218789-en#page77): '*The Internet facilitates transactions such as ordering goods and services. This means that many transactions that would have taken place without the Internet can be conducted more efficiently and at less expense. In addition, the Internet has expanded the reach of smaller businesses, enabling them to reach markets that would not have been possible to reach without its existence. As a result, the number of firms carrying out business transactions over the Internet has increased dramatically over the last decade. For example, e-commerce in the Netherlands has increased as a share of total company revenue from 3.4% in 1999 to 14.1% in 2009. Similarly, between 2004 and 2011, this share increased from 2.7% to 18.5% in Norway and from 2.8% to 11% in Poland. Based on comparable data, as illustrated in the chart below, e-commerce is nearing 20% of total turnover in Finland, Hungary, and Sweden, and 25% in the Czech Republic.*'
6. In 2012, B2C e-commerce sales were estimated to exceed USD 1 trillion for the first time. During 2013, they are estimated to grow an additional 18.3% to USD 1.298 trillion, with the Asia-Pacific region surpassing North America as the top market for B2C e-commerce sales. It is worth mentioning that at the moment B2C e-commerce represents a small fraction of overall e-commerce, which is mainly made up of B2B transactions. Global B2B e-commerce, particularly among wholesalers and distributors, was estimated to be approximately USD 12.4 trillion in 2012. According to other estimates made by the International Data Corporation, the size of total worldwide e-commerce, when global business-to-business and consumer transactions are added together, equated to USD 16 trillion in 2013 (see point 4.1.2.4 at p. 75 and 76 of the BEPS report on the Digital Economy: http://www.keepeek.com/Digital-Asset-Management/oecd/taxation/addressing-the-tax-challenges-of-the-digital-economy_9789264218789-en#page77).
7. See for instance, A. Cockfield, W. Hellerstein, R. Millar and Ch. Waerzegers (2013): 'Taxing Global Digital Commerce', Kluwer; D.J.B. Svantesson (2007): 'E-Commerce Tax: How the Taxman Brought Geography to the Borderless Internet', 17 Revenue L. J. 1 of 2007; R. Bird (2005): 'Taxing electronic commerce: the end of the beginning', Paper 0502 University of Toronto series International Tax Program Papers; Ch. Mc Lure (2002): 'Thinking Straight About the Taxation of Electronic Commerce: Tax Principles, Compliance Problems, and Nexus', National Bureau of Economic Research (Tax Policy and the Economy), MIT Press, p. 122; W. Hellerstein, Ch. Mc Lure (2001): 'Sales taxation of Electronic Commerce: What John Due Knew All Along', Tax Analysts of January 2001. R. Doernberg and L. Hinnekens (1999): Electronic Commerce and International Taxation, Kluwer Law International; F. Dittmar and H-J Selling (1998): 'How to control Internet Transactions? A contribution from the point of view of German Tax Inspectors', 26 Intertax 3 of 1998 at 88; L. Hinnekens (1998): 'The Challenges of Applying VAT and Income Tax Territoriality Concepts and Rules to International Electronic Commerce' in 26 Intertax 3 at 54; P. Jenkins (1995): 'VAT and Electronic Commerce: The Challenges and Opportunities', 10 International VAT Monitor of January/February 1995 at 3.

with VAT rules applicable to 'electronically supplied services'.[8] But the question is whether tax administrations have been successful in adapting their regulatory and administrative frameworks in such a way as to ensure an effective assessment and collection of indirect taxes on electronic supplies, while simultaneously avoiding unnecessary administrative costs for tax administrations and excessive compliance burdens for taxable persons who act as tax collectors in the indirect tax area.

This book first gives a broad and up to date overview of the general European Union (EU) regulatory framework for VAT on electronically supplied services as it applies since January 2015, with a clear analysis of the gradual steps towards realizing the principle of taxation at destination, improving the fight against fraud and simplifying compliance obligations by means of the Mini One Stop Shop (MOSS) (see 1.2 and Chapters 2–6). It subsequently discusses a number of topical issues that arise when the indirect taxman tries to get to grips with the increasingly complex virtual dimension of the international market place (see 1.3 and Chapters 7–11).

1.2 THE EU VAT FRAMEWORK FOR ONLINE SUPPLIES: NEUTRALITY CONCERNS, COMPLIANCE BURDENS AND COMBATING FRAUD

The EU VAT framework for online supplies is based on the OECD's 1998 'Ottawa Framework' recommendations on e-commerce, which emphasized the need to ensure taxation at destination and to achieve fiscal neutrality between online suppliers and traditional sectors of the economy.[9] It consists of a number of EU legal texts which are, to the extent relevant and for the convenience of the reader, reproduced at the end of this book in the Appendices section.[10]

8. Council Directive 2002/38/EC of 7 May 2002 amending and amending temporarily Directive 77/388/EEC as regards the value-added-tax arrangements applicable to radio and television broadcasting services and certain electronically supplied services, OJ L 128, 15.5.2002, p. 41–44 (see Appendix I).
9. The 1998 OECD Ottawa Ministerial endorsed the report: 'Electronic commerce: taxation framework conditions'. Implementing guidelines were issued in 2001 and 2003 by OECD Working Party 9 ('Consumption tax aspects of electronic commerce', http://www.oecd.org/ctp/consumption/2673667.pdf) and in 2003 by the OECD Center for Tax Policy and Administration ('Electronic Commerce Simplified Registration Guidance', http://www.oecd.org/tax/consumption/5590980.pdf, 'Verification of Customer Status and Jurisdiction', http://www.oecd.org/tax/consumption/5574687.pdf, 'Facilitating Collection of Consumption taxes on B2C E-commerce', http://www.oecd.org/tax/consumption/34422641.pdf).
10. Council Directive 2002/38/EC of 7 May 2002 amending and amending temporarily Directive 77/388/EEC as regards the value-added-tax arrangements applicable to radio and television broadcasting services and certain electronically supplied services, OJ L 128, 15.5.2002, p. 41–44. Council Directive 2008/8/EC of 12 Feb. 2008 amending Directive 2006/112/EC as regards the place of supply of services, O.J. 20 Feb. 2008, L44/11. Council Regulation 282/2011 of 15 Mar. 2011 laying down implementing measures for Directive 2006/112/EC on the common system of value-added-tax, O.J. 23 Mar. 2011, L 77/1. Council Regulation 967/2012 of 9 Oct. 2012 amending Implementing Regulation (EU) No. 282/2011 as regards the special schemes for non-established taxable persons supplying telecommunications services, broadcasting services or electronic services to non-taxable persons, O.J. 20 Oct. 2012, L 290/1.Council Regulation 1042/2013 of 7 Oct. 2013 amending Implementing Regulation (EU) No. 282/2011 as regards the place of supply of services, O.J. 26 Oct. 2013, L 284/1.

In Chapter 2 of this volume, Donato Raponi and David O'Sullivan give a historic overview of the gradual steps taken by the European Union to ensure that the destination principle would also apply to e-commerce (now more generally the 'digital economy'), as suggested by the 1998 OECD Ottawa Framework. They recall the 2003 E-Commerce Directive, which, as a first step, introduced the destination principle in relation to third countries, thus ending the distortion that intra-Community (intra-EU) electronic supplies were subject to VAT, while inbound electronic supplies (into the EU from a third country) were not. In a second step, the 2008 VAT package provided that, by 2015, the place of supply rules for intra-EU supplies to non-taxable persons (B2C supplies) of telecommunication-, broadcasting- and electronic services would change from the place of establishment of the supplier to the place of establishment of the customer. This ended the intra-EU distortion of competition resulting from VAT rate differentials, which had induced electronic suppliers to locate their businesses in low VAT jurisdictions, such as Luxembourg. These key steps were accompanied by the introduction of a MOSS which allows suppliers to account for their EU-wide VAT obligations in their own Member State. Raponi and O'Sullivan also provide a roadmap of possible next steps to ensure a more neutral and efficient VAT for B2C supplies. Proposed measures include the extension of the MOSS to all intra-EU B2C supplies of goods and services, the removal of the distance sales thresholds, the application of home country and/or standardized rules on VAT compliance, the introduction of home country auditing and revenue sharing, and the abolition of the VAT exemption of small consignments.

In Chapter 3, Charlène Herbain recalls that the pre-2003 distortion (VAT on intra-EU supplies, but not on inbound supplies) induced EU suppliers to relocate outside the EU (thus eroding the EU VAT base). She adds that after 2003, inbound suppliers of broadcasting and electronic services, though taxable (destination principle), had the advantage that they could benefit from the MOSS, which streamlines the collection process, but that it was even more advantageous for them to relocate or set up a subsidiary in the lowest EU VAT jurisdiction (Luxembourg) in order to be able to charge VAT at origin, at the lowest available rate, irrespective of the customers' residence (just like intra-EU suppliers, who also had an incentive to locate in the lowest VAT jurisdiction). This was then remedied by the VAT package which gradually introduced the destination principle for all inbound and intra-EU supplies and extended the MOSS to intra-EU suppliers. But Herbain argues that further difficulties subsist in the case of electronic supplies, including in particular as regards determining the location (where does the consumer consume) and status (taxable or non-taxable person) of a customer as a prerequisite for being able to use the MOSS, and as regards the identification of the supplier. The author, finally, touches on the proposals to generalize the MOSS and to carry out simultaneous and multilateral audits and on the unanimity rule for adopting EU tax legislation.

In Chapter 4, Marie Lamensch discusses the challenges that businesses, who act as tax collectors, face in identifying the status and the location of their customers, for tax assessment and collection purposes, in the specific e-commerce context (high volume of low value real-time transactions with anonymous customers; significant cross-border trade). She notes that under the 2015 EU rules (Council Regulation

282/2011 as amended by Council Regulation 1043/2013 and Commission Explanatory Notes, see Appendices III, IV and V) EU and non-EU businesses are required to collect information that cannot be obtained in the timeframe of an electronic transaction and is hard to verify and therefore prone to manipulation, while nevertheless costly to obtain. Lamensch gives a detailed analysis of these rules from a 'compliance burden' and 'legal certainty' perspective. She essentially concludes that the rules on customer identification are unworkable, both for outbound B2B supplies (third countries may not issue usable certificates or VAT numbers for taxable persons and 'any other proof' may not be available), and for intra-EU and inbound B2B supplies (VAT number may not be available or reliable, if available what to do if it is not verifiable in VIES, what is the supplier's obligation 'in case of doubt'). Likewise the rules on customer location are unworkable, not only for intra-EU B2B supplies (self-identification information from customers may not be available and reliable, what are normal commercial security measures relating to identity or payment checks, what to do with customers located in multiple jurisdictions, how to determine that the fixed establishment has permanence and actually enjoys the service), but in particular also for inbound and intra-EU B2C supplies (self-identification information cannot always be verified by the supplier, how to determine the rule that best ensures taxation as the place of consumption or the place where the online supply is effectively used and enjoyed).

Lamensch also analyses the presumptions which the supplier should use if it is extremely difficult to determine the customer's location (Council Regulation 1042/2013 and explanatory notes) and concludes that these are overly complicated for electronic suppliers (the exact scope of some of these presumptions is unclear, how can suppliers know whether customers use a fixed land-line and where it is located, or when and how to apply the 'other circumstances' and 'abuse' presumptions) or do not provide a satisfactory proxy (the wi-fi hotspot presumption is a real consumption test rather than a proxy for customer location). The general conclusion is that the very definition of electronically supplied services ('automated' and 'with minimal human intervention') is at odds with the requirement that online suppliers proceed to transaction based verifications.

In Chapter 5, Edoardo Traversa and Emanuele Ceci note that VAT fraud in the EU is significant enough (the 2014 EU VAT gap has been estimated at EUR 177 billion) to raise fundamental issues of efficiency and neutrality. The sheer size of the phenomenon illustrates the structural weaknesses of a common VAT system that was designed decades ago and explains why combating VAT fraud has become the focal point of EU digital VAT policy. In a destination type system, fraud-proof location rules are key to the implementation of a robust VAT system, but the exponential growth of digital transactions has had a twofold disruptive effect on traditional ways of addressing VAT fraud. On the one hand, digitalization has triggered the adoption of legislative reforms, whether specific, such as the adoption of anti-fraud and avoidance mechanisms, or more encompassing, such as the modification of location criteria used to allocate taxing powers between Member States as regards supplies of electronic services. However, these reforms could prove to be insufficient to cope with the pace of the changes observed in the business world. On the other hand, the digitalization of the economy and the progress made in the area of information and communication technology open new opportunities, which could substantially enhance the effectiveness of the control of taxable persons and transactions by administrations, namely through the use of 'digital' solutions and a more efficient and timely cooperation between EU Member States and even third countries.

While most of the above authors critically assess the new EU rules, on the positive side, credit is due to the EU legislator for having designed a revolutionary simplified VAT registration and in Chapter 6, Ine Lejeune and Sophie Claessens discuss the details of the MOSS. They give a description of the system and an overview of the first six months of its application since the EU 2015 VAT go-live for B2C telecoms, broadcasting and electronic services. In addition, the authors comment on the implications and challenges for tax administrations and businesses, and address these in the context of the Digital Single Market Strategy for Europe and the announced 2016 proposals from the European Commission to extend the One Stop Shop system to other B2C transactions

1.3 THE EU VAT FRAMEWORK FOR ONLINE SUPPLIES: TOPICAL ISSUES

In addition to the broader questions surrounding the introduction of the 2015 EU VAT rules on electronically supplied services, a number of topical issues have arisen in practice and several authors examine the relevance of existing indirect tax rules and case law for finding possible solutions to those topical issues such as defining the digital fixed establishment and taxing internet search engines, virtual money such as bitcoins and cloud computing.

In Chapter 7, Ben Terra, discusses the October 2014 decision of the European Court of Justice in Case C-605/12 Welmory, on the question of whether a Polish company which provides services (advertising services, provision of information and data processing) to and puts technical equipment at the disposal of a Cypriot company to run an 'auction website' in Polish, is providing those services to the Cypriot company (supply not subject to Polish VAT) or to a Polish fixed establishment of the Cypriot company (supply subject to Polish VAT).[11] The Polish tax authorities were of the opinion that the Cypriot company was making use in Polish territory of the Polish company's technical and human resources, so that the Polish company was to be treated as a fixed establishment of the Cypriot company in Poland. The Court essentially decides that its previous VAT case law (on Article 9.1 of the Sixth VAT Directive) is relevant for the new VAT Directive and subsequently decides, on that basis, that the primary point of reference for determining the place of supply of services is the place where the taxable person receiving them has established his business. In addition it recalls that for the Cypriot company to be considered as having a fixed establishment in Poland, that establishment must be characterized by a sufficient

11. Interesting further elements are that the Polish company itself was selling its products through the website, that it received not only the price obtained for those products through the auction but also part of the money which clients paid to the Cypriot company in order to be entitled to place bids during the auction, and that the Cypriot Company ultimately became the parent of the Polish Company.

degree of permanence and a suitable structure in terms of human and technical resources to enable it to receive and use the services supplied to it for its own needs.

In Chapter 8 in this volume, Christina Trenta looks at the VAT aspects of Internet search engines, such as Google, which provide services free of charge, but earn their money by making advertising space available to companies, which may or may not induce the search engine users to buy products and services from those companies. She notes that search engines allow users to search the web and allow companies to advertise their supplies. She also notes that advertising messages on websites (banner ads) are considered electronically supplied services, but that the VAT relevant relation (direct link) is between the search engine and the advertisers. If the search engine user buys an advertised product from the advertising company, the two VAT relevant relations are between the search engine and the advertiser, and between the user and the advertiser. There is, however, no VAT relevant link between the search engine and the user because there is no remuneration and no direct link between the search engine service to the user and the remuneration received from the advertising company.

In Chapter 9, Oskar Henkow asks the question how virtual currencies should be treated for VAT purposes. After separating traditional supplies (content is supplied physically) from e-commerce supplies (content is delivered electronically or shared between consumers on peer to peer platforms) he distinguishes three types of virtual currencies: closed virtual money which does not leave its specific context (e.g., monopoly money), unidirectional virtual money that can be bought with (but not changed back into) regular currency (e.g., Facebook credits), and bi-directional virtual money that can be bought with and changed back into regular currency (e.g., cryptocurrencies such as bitcoins).

In the absence of a clear definition of 'money' and 'currency' in EU legislation, Henkow believes that cryptocurrencies can be considered neither as electronic money (under the Electronic Money Directive), nor as a voucher (under the ECJ VAT case law), but that they do satisfy the typical functions of money (store of value, unit of account and means of payment) even though they are not legal tender. He notes that the Swedish Supreme Administrative Court has asked the ECJ whether the exchange of virtual currency for traditional currency and vice versa constitutes a VAT relevant supply of a service,[12] and he leans towards considering cryptocurrencies as any other (VAT exempt) debt instrument, because of their money like functions and also in the interest of neutrality. He also notes, however, that legally speaking, cryptocurrencies should probably not be treated as exempt financial transactions (and that taxing these unwelcome and unauthorized currencies could be favoured by governments).

In Chapter 10, Walter Hellerstein looks at the lessons that can be learned from the US subnational Retail Sales Tax (RST) experience when assessing and collecting consumption taxes on 'cloud computing' (i.e., on demand remote access to a network where resources are pooled between multiple consumers and access is elastic according to need). After notes of caution over the parallel between VAT and RST (which is a single stage tax, partly on business and only on tangibles and some services), and the

12. Case *C-264/14 Hedqvist* available at http://curia.europa.eu/juris/recherche.jsf.

dangers of trying to apply existing rules by analogy, he recalls the US constitutional limits on state taxation (physical presence or 'nexus' required) and the ensuing emergence of the odd combination of sales and use taxes.

On the first question for US states, i.e., whether they have personal jurisdiction over (or nexus with) the provider or purchaser to the cloud computing transaction, Hellerstein notes that if purchasers or suppliers own or lease servers in a state they can be assumed to have physical presence there, but if they merely purchase or use software application services (from an unrelated party) this is unlikely to establish the required de minimis physical presence in the state where the software is hosted. Guidance offered by a handful of US States goes along these lines.

On the second question, i.e., whether the transaction is taxable in a state, Hellerstein notes that US States have generally inquired whether there is a 'sale or use' of a 'taxable good, service or intangible' 'in the state'. On the first issue (sale or use) States differ on whether a cloud computing transaction involves a transfer of possession or title and can thus be seen as a 'sale' (New York, Utah) or not (Tennessee), and if not, whether it can nevertheless be considered as a lease of tangible personal property (Arizona, Wisconsin). Even if the provider of cloud computing is not making a taxable sale the purchaser could still be making a taxable use (Nebraska). On the second issue (taxable sale of tangible property or non-taxable sale of a service), Hellerstein recalls that this depends on the 'true object', 'dominant purpose' and 'essence of the transaction', and briefly discusses state practice, while expressing concern over the ease with which some states consider cloud computing as taxable 'canned prewritten software'. On the third issue (location of the sale or use), Hellerstein argues that it is not easy to apply the traditional location test of 'the place of delivery' (used for tangible personal property) in the case of cloud computing (remotely accessed hardware and software). He indicates that several states locate hosted software transactions at the place of the server on which the software is stored (administrative advantages but no taxation at destination), while others attribute hosted software transactions to the location of the consumer (taxation at destination principle but not without compliance problems for sellers). His overall conclusion is that applying existing consumption tax rules by analogy to cloud computing may be doomed to failure and that states may be compelled to take a simpler approach by choosing a practical proxy for the location of the transaction.

In Chapter 11, Pernilla Rendhal identifies and systematizes some methodological notes related to VAT and electronic commerce. She recalls one of the main differences between electronic and traditional commerce, i.e., that digital supplies are instant and that therefore the decision on the right amount of tax needs to be built into an automatic system. In general it is crucial for taxable persons to predict the right amount of tax to each supply, and since many e-transactions are cross-border and involve more than one jurisdiction, there is risk of double taxation or unintentional non-taxation. To avoid this, increased international coordination has been suggested as a solution. Such international coordination involves soft law measures both at an international level (OECD) and a regional level (EU). Rendahl discusses the use of soft law measures from a methodological perspective, systematizing the measures into proxy methods and presumption methods, to create a basis for further discussion. She notes that even though soft law may constitute a useful interpretative tool and have positive effects on certainty and efficiency, it may also have negative effects, decreasing certainty and efficiency, in particular if presumptions are complex in themselves, leading to different interpretations of legal concepts and legal facts.

1.4 OUTLOOK

From the contributions to this book, it is clear that the EU has come a long way in trying to ensure taxation of online supplies at destination with the least possible administrative costs for tax administrations and the lowest possible compliance burdens for taxable persons. It may also be clear that the full realization of this objective is work in progress and it is safe to predict therefore that further steps will be made in the future to improve the EU rules on the assessment and collection of VAT on online supplies.

Though we have no crystal ball, this is likely to include steps to further reduce the compliance burden and the red tape for taxable persons and thus to improve the European business climate. Interesting in this respect is that, on 6 May 2015, the European Commission announced reforms of the EU VAT system in its 'Strategy for the EU Digital Single Market'[13] indicating that it will make a legislative proposal in 2016 to modernize the VAT for cross-border e-commerce and reduce the burden on businesses arising from different VAT regimes. Such a proposal is likely to include the extension of the One Stop Shop to intra-EU and third country online sales of tangible goods to private consumers, the introduction of a common EU-wide simplification measure (VAT threshold) to help small start-up e-commerce businesses, allowing for home country controls including a single audit of cross-border businesses for VAT purposes and removing the VAT exemption for the importation of small consignments from suppliers in third countries. Preliminary data for the MOSS indicate that EUR 3 billion in VAT will be paid through the system in 2015 which represents approximately EUR 18 billion of cross-border sales of telecommunications, broadcasting and electronically supplied services to private consumers.[14]

Further in the future, the EU and the tax administrations of the Member States may pick up on the suggestions that were initially made by the OECD,[15] to develop technology based solutions for the assessment and collection of VAT on online supplies. This would be logical because it may well be an illusion to continue to try to fit online supplies within assessment and collection rules that were developed forty years ago when trade was tied to place and time and carried on between parties that knew each other and often acted within established business relationships. Interesting in this respect are recent suggestions that a software program be developed that would allow banks and other financial intermediaries to correctly assess and collect VAT on

13. http://ec.europa.eu/taxation_customs/taxation/vat/digital_single_market/index_en.htm.
14. European Commission statement in a BBC interview, at http://www.bbc.co.uk/programmes/b05xch5f (accessed on 28 Jul. 2015).
15. OECD (2001): 'Consumption tax aspects of electronic commerce', A report from WP 9 on consumption taxes to the Committee on Fiscal Affairs', pp. 7, 8, 9, 13, 14, 17, 18 and 20 and OECD (2003): 'Implementation of the Ottawa Taxation Framework Conditions', The 2003 report, pp. 20 and 23.

online supplies at the moment the customer makes the electronic payment for the online supply through that bank or credit card company.[16] Further research on the feasibility of these technology based solutions would be a good investment.

16. See further Ch. 4 in Marie Lamensch (2015): 'European Value-Added Tax in the Digital Era: A Critical Analysis and Proposals for Reform', IBFD, Amsterdam, Doctoral Series (expected vol. 36).

CHAPTER 2

VAT and Taxation of the Digital Economy from the Perspective of the EU Policy Maker

*Donato Raponi & David O'Sullivan**

2.1 INTRODUCTION

The issue of taxation of the digital economy has moved centre stage in the media and in national parliaments in recent years, with reports that large enterprises exploited elaborate tax planning techniques resulting in very low levels of corporate income tax. Governments are now forced to respond, by a general public that has been subjected to austerity and increased taxation as a result of the crisis. While the discussions have predominately focused on direct tax issues, there is a general consensus on the importance of VAT in ensuring the correct taxation of the digital economy, and specific VAT measures are likely to be included in the recommendations by the OECD Task Force on Taxation of the Digital Economy. That important role of VAT has also been recognized in the EU, where the Commission Expert Group on Taxation of the Digital Economy[1] (chaired by the former Portuguese Minister for Finance and current Fiscal Affairs Director of the IMF, Vítor Gaspar), concluded that: '*VAT has a significant role to play in ensuring that appropriate tax revenues accrue from businesses operating in the digital economy*'.

* Donato Raponi is Head of Section at DG TAXUD, European Commission. David O'Sullivan is an Official of the Irish Revenue and a Seconded National Expert to DG TAXUD, European Commission. The views in this chapter are those of the authors and should not be interpreted as representing the views or policies of the European Commission or the Irish Revenue.

1. See report of the Expert group http://ec.europa.eu/taxation_customs/resources/documents/taxation/gen_info/good_governance_matters/digital/report_digital_economy.pdf.

For VAT experts, the digital economy is not a new issue and indeed, experience gained in the VAT area with the application of the destination principle can provide some early wins for the Base Erosion Profit Shifting (BEPS) process. Ensuring taxation at destination, i.e., at the place of consumption, has been under discussion since the 1990s. Significant progress has been made and there is a clear roadmap ahead on how to progress. The EU has been at the forefront of developing VAT rules to ensure that the destination principle is applied and that tax revenue accrues to the EU Member State of consumption. Nevertheless, as will be illustrated in this contribution, it has been and still is a gradual process. Some progress has been made, but the recent discussions demonstrate that more has to be done and that the EU can continue to take the lead globally. It also has to be recognized, upfront, that businesses act as tax collectors for VAT, and that policy makers therefore need to ensure that the compliance burden for businesses is minimized.

2.2 THE FIRST STEPS TOWARDS THE DESTINATION PRINCIPLE

The issue of VAT and the digital economy has been discussed within the OECD and the EU since the mid-1990s. This resulted in an initial agreement between OECD Member States gathering in Ottawa in 1998, that consumption taxes (like VAT) should result in taxation at the place of consumption. The adoption of the EU e-commerce Directive in 2002 (which took effect in 2003) put this principle into practice (for the text see Appendix I).[2] Effectively this meant that the place of supply for electronic services by a supplier located outside the EU changed to the place of the customer so that the supply would be taxed in the Member State of consumption. This was supported by vendor registration and remittance rules under which a non-established trader could account in a single Member State for the tax payable in respect of his supplies to all Member States. The responsibility then fell on that Member State to transfer the tax to the Member State of consumption. As such the EU was the first tax jurisdiction to tax electronic services in line with the OECD principles, and indeed the EU has continued to lead in this area, and Norway and South Africa have, since, implemented similar systems.

The 2003 changes were an important milestone in EU VAT law because they constituted a statement of intent for future developments. It can be safely assumed that failure to have implemented these changes would have resulted in a loss of competitiveness for EU businesses, a loss of tax revenue for EU Member States and a loss of employment opportunities for EU workers, simply because the digitalization of the economy allowed for the delivery of e-services without any physical presence in the EU. With average VAT rates in the EU of approximately 21%, there would have been a clear incentive for a business to locate outside the EU and thus to supply these services VAT free to EU consumers. The 2003 changes remedied this issue, but at the same time created their own problems, because the place of supply rules for supplies made intra-EU still provided that these were taxed at the place of the supplier rather

2. Directive 2002/38/EC adopted 7 May 2002 http://eur-lex.europa.eu/LexUriServ/LexUriServ.do?uri=OJ:L:2002:128:0041:0044:en:PDF.

than at the place of the customer. This meant that businesses could realize considerable gains by simply locating in a Member State with low VAT rates. The importance of this issue is illustrated by the wide variance in VAT rates within the EU (with standard rates of between 15% and 27%), and also by the possibility in some Member States to supply certain services, such as broadcasting, at super-reduced rates as low as 3%.

As a result, non-EU businesses located themselves in a low EU VAT jurisdiction, and EU businesses also relocated to a low EU VAT jurisdiction, which led to an erosion of the VAT base in certain (higher VAT) Member States. It is important to recognize that the gains were in respect of revenues (and not just profits) and could thus go up to 20% of the consumer price of the service. As a result, it quickly became apparent to the Commission and the Member States that there needed to be a move to a destination based VAT system also for intra-EU B2C supplies of electronic services, broadcasting and telecommunications.

It is relevant also to mention that, in 2003, digital services were still, in many respects, in an embryonic stage. At that time, people were generally buying their music in stores, renting movies on DVDs and buying physical books in bookstores. Profound changes have taken place since then, which can be illustrated by the fact that Apple opened the iTunes Store only in 2004, that in the first year, it sold 100 million songs globally, and that by 2013, Apple had sold 25 billion songs.[3] Apple, and indeed others such as Amazon, cable TV operators and telecommunication companies, have now expanded their offer to TV shows, movie sales and rental, and software applications. Likewise, in 2008, books were revolutionized with the arrival of the Amazon Kindle and eBooks, to the point that today traditional bookshops are disappearing from the high street. There is no doubt that this presents challenges for business in the traditional economy, but, in terms of taxation, it is also clear that the step taken by the EU in 2003, to move towards the destination system for supplies of electronically supplied services, was the correct one.

2.3 FURTHER PROGRESS: ADOPTION OF THE VAT PACKAGE IN 2008

As outlined above, the 2003 changes to the place of supply rules presented challenges within the EU. Taxation of electronic services supplied B2C within the EU took place in the Member State in which the supplier was established (and thus not at destination), while in relation with third countries, taxation in the Member State of destination was already the rule. This resulted in clusters of businesses establishing themselves in Member States with the lowest rate of VAT, from where they supplied electronic services across the EU at more advantageous VAT rates than those applicable to a business established in the Member State of the customer. This threat to fair competition and to the tax base of higher VAT Member States called for further reform of the place of supply rules based on the destination principle.

3. http://www.apple.com/pr/library/2013/02/06iTunes-Store-Sets-New-Record-with-25-Billion-Songs-Sold.html.

In 2005, the Commission proposed new place of supply rules to ensure that the principle of taxation at destination would also apply to the intra-EU supply of e-services. After a number of years of negotiation, new place of supply rules were indeed agreed by the Council as part of the 2008 'VAT package' compromise (for the text see Appendix II). As a result of this compromise, from 1 January 2015 onwards, the place of supply of telecommunication-, broadcasting- and electronic services to private individuals has been the Member State in which the customer is located, rather than the Member State in which the supplier is established. The same principle will therefore apply to intra-EU supplies and to inbound supplies from third countries.

In 2004, the European Commission proposed a 'one-stop' mechanism allowing a trader to fulfil all his VAT obligations for EU-wide activities in the Member State in which he is established.[4] While agreement on this proposal stalled (and indeed it subsequently was formally withdrawn), the principles of this vendor registration and remittance model were integrated into the VAT package, under which a Mini One Stop Shop (MOSS) would be introduced in 2015 to support the new place of supply rules. The MOSS, in place since 1 January 2015, allows the supplier to register, declare and pay the VAT due on supplies of electronic services to final consumers in all Member States via a web portal in his own Member State (rather than obliging him to register for VAT in each Member State in which he has a customer). The supplier will therefore submit, once a quarter, a single VAT declaration to his home administration.

2.4 THE SUCCESSFUL INTRODUCTION OF THE 2015 PLACE OF SUPPLY RULES AND MOSS

The 2011 Commission Communication on the Future of VAT considered that:

> The implementation of the mini OSS is seen by many Member States and by business as a major milestone. Its smooth functioning should pave the way for a more general use of this concept...The Commission remains convinced that, in a VAT system based on taxation at destination, an OSS is a crucial instrument to facilitate access to the single market, in particular for SMEs.[5]

The need for the successful implementation of the 2015 rules and the MOSS was also recognized by the Council in its May 2012 conclusions on the Commission Communication in which it supported: '*work to ensure the timely implementation of the mini One-Stop-Shop in 2015 as a key priority action*'.[6] The significance of the 2015 rules

4. COM(2004) 728 final, 29 Oct. 2004: 'Proposal for a Council Directive amending Directive 77/388/EEC with a view to simplifying value added tax obligations – Proposal for a Council Directive laying down detailed rules for the refund of value added tax, provided for in Directive 77/388/EEC, to taxable persons not established in the territory of the country but established in another Member State – Proposal for a Council Regulation amending Regulation (EC) No. 1798/2003 as regards the introduction of administrative cooperation arrangements in the context of the one-stop scheme and the refund procedure for value added tax.'
5. See http://ec.europa.eu/taxation_customs/taxation/vat/future_vat/index_en.htm.
6. See http://www.consilium.europa.eu/uedocs/cms_data/docs/pressdata/en/ecofin/130257.pdf.

and the MOSS was also recognized by the Commission Expert Group: '*The Group urges the Commission and Member States to continue their efforts to ensure the successful introduction of the MOSS and the new rules, which will lay the foundations for further developments.*'[7]

The successful implementation of the new place of supply rules and MOSS has been the highest priority for the Commission services and preparatory work proceeded in the following respects:[8]

- Legislative framework.
- Guidance for Member States and business.
- Communication.
- IT implementation.
- Auditing and mutual assistance.

2.4.1 Legislative Framework

To prepare for the 2015 changes and the MOSS, it was essential to put in place a clear legal structure to fully support this significant development. The Commission proposed three implementing regulations to this effect, which have been agreed by Member States. A Council Regulation relating to the obligations under the MOSS was adopted in October 2012 (for the text see Appendix VI),[9] along with a Commission Regulation relating to the standard forms and returns to be used.[10] In addition, a further Council Regulation was adopted on 7 October 2013, and it laid down measures that should help to identify correctly the place of supply of certain services and customer location, and that provided for a number of proxies in that respect (for the text see Appendix IV).[11] In particular, it clarifies the issue of customers having multiple locations, or using devices to buy electronic-, telecommunication- or broadcasting services in a Member State in which they are not established. Based on this new legal framework, there are now clear and very detailed definitions of electronic-, broadcasting- and telecommunication services.

---

7. See Report of the Expert Group at: http://ec.europa.eu/taxation_customs/resources/documents/taxation/gen_info/good_governance_matters/digital/report_digital_economy.pdf.
8. The description of the preparatory work for the new place of supply rules and MOSS has been adapted from material prepared for and included in Annex 6 of the Report of the Expert Group on Taxation of the Digital Economy.
9. Council Regulation (EU) No. 967/2012 of 9 Oct. 2012 amending Implementing Regulation (EU) 282/2011 as regards the special schemes for non-established taxable persons supplying telecommunications services, broadcasting services or electronic services to non-taxable persons (OJ L 290, 20.10.2012, pp. 1–7).
10. Commission Implementing Regulation (EU) No. 815/2012 of 13 Sep. 2012 laying down detailed rules for the application of Council Regulation 904/2010, as regards special schemes for non-established taxable persons supplying telecommunications, broadcasting or electronic services to non-taxable persons (OJ L 249, 14.9.2012, pp. 3–10).
11. Council Implementing Regulation (EU) No. 1042/2013 of 7 Oct. 2013 amending Implementing Regulation (EU) No. 282/2011 as regards the place of supply of services (OJ L 284, 26.10.2013, p. 1). See Appendix IV or the relevant provisions of this Regulation.

2.4.2 Guidance for Member States and Business

The 2011 Communication on the Future of VAT included a clear recommendation that the Commission should publish guidance in order to inform and guide businesses so as to promote a more consistent application of the common rules. This is seen by the Commission services as fundamental for the success of the new rules and the MOSS.

2.4.2.1 Explanatory Notes on the Place of Supply Rules

Following agreement on the Implementing Regulation in Council, the Commission in collaboration with Member States and business representatives prepared extensive Explanatory Notes which were published in April 2013 (for the text see Appendix V).[12] These 'Explanatory Notes' are intended as a guidance tool that can be used to clarify the practical application of the new place of supply rules for telecommunications-, broadcasting- and electronic services. They are currently available in English but will soon be translated in all other EU languages, as well as in Japanese, Chinese and Russian.

2.4.2.2 MOSS Guidelines

The Commission services also drafted a comprehensive Guide to the MOSS, which was adopted by the Standing Committee on Administrative Cooperation (SCAC) in October 2013.[13] This Guide gives detailed information on how the MOSS will work in practice and covers areas such as registration, deregistration, making returns, the payment process and record keeping. The guidelines have been published in the EU languages, Japanese, Chinese and Russian.

2.4.3 Communication

The Commission recognized the need to further inform business, both in the EU and in third countries, on the 2015 changes and the MOSS. Therefore the Commission, in collaboration with Member States and business organizations, participated in a number of seminars during 2014 to explain to business how the new rules would work, and what it could offer them in terms of simplicity. Such events have, to date, taken place in Brussels, Warsaw, London, Luxembourg and Berlin. In recognition of the global market place, the Commission has also participated in events in the USA and Japan. In addition, the Commission has prepared a dedicated web page with all the relevant information on the 2015 changes and MOSS.[14]

---

12. http://ec.europa.eu/taxation_customs/resources/documents/taxation/vat/how_vat_works/telecom/explanatory_notes_2015_en.pdf (see Appendix V).
13. http://ec.europa.eu/taxation_customs/resources/documents/taxation/vat/how_vat_works/telecom/one-stop-shop-guidelines_en.pdf.
14. http://ec.europa.eu/taxation_customs/taxation/vat/how_vat_works/telecom/index_en.htm#new_rules.

2.4.4 MOSS IT Implementation

The success of the MOSS is dependent on the development of appropriate IT systems. While responsibility primarily lies with Member States to ensure that the MOSS portals are fully functional for registration (as from October 2014), and for live operation (as from January 2015), the Commission worked very closely with Member States to ensure that the systems were ready in time. Technical specifications have been prepared by the Commission and the Standing Committee on Information Technology (SCIT) and agreed at the SCAC. It was fully expected that Member States would fulfil their legal obligations by delivering the MOSS on time.

2.4.5 Coordination of Audits

One important issue which is not yet fully resolved is the audit of the businesses under the MOSS. On the positive side, Member States have developed audit guidelines in order to promote the principle of coordination of audits, with the aim of reducing burdens on business, promoting voluntary compliance and raising the efficiency of audits. These guidelines have been published by the Commission and indicate those Member States that have agreed to them (See Appendix VII for the text of these guidelines).

On the negative side, EU legislation on the MOSS still foresees that controls and audits are to be carried out by the Member State of consumption, although several tools are available to Member States to enhance coordination of audits. For both EU and non-EU companies, this may involve up to twenty-eight different tax administrations auditing the same company without any coordination and leading to information requests in multiple languages. Not only could this create disproportionate administrative burdens on business, but it could also put at stake the efficiency of the audits themselves as well as the level of voluntary compliance (which is particularly sensitive where non-EU companies are involved). Appropriate new tools, such as joint audits, to enhance the efficiency of audits in this sector may be useful, provided Member States can agree on the legal basis. Delivering a successful MOSS as a precursor to the broader One Stop Shop (OSS) requires full trust by each Member State that taxes will be collected and that the necessary auditing (on the principle of risk) will take place.

2.5 A ROADMAP TO A DESTINATION BASED VAT SYSTEM FOR B2C TRANSACTIONS

Since 2003, the EU has been at the forefront of pursuing the destination principle for B2C supplies together with simplification measures for businesses as regards vendor registration and remittance. Because of the newly introduced rules, 2015 is a significant milestone in itself, but it is also important in terms of determining where we go next. Preparations are nearly completed following an unprecedented engagement with business. Member States, in general, have endorsed the approach of the Commission – formally through the May 2012 Council conclusions on the Communication on the

Future of VAT and most importantly through constructive engagement at Council and in the framework of the Commission committees. However, it is also clear that further work is needed. In spite of the 2015 changes, the VAT system, in terms of B2C transactions in particular, does not fully respect the principle of neutrality. This becomes even more important when one realizes the growth in e-commerce.

In short, it should not be easier and more tax advantageous for non-EU business to operate in the EU than it is for EU business. However, this is the case, in many instances, for B2C transactions. In terms of the importation of small consignments for instance, EU businesses are at a disadvantage as non-EU businesses, particularly from our close neighbours, can make B2C supplies VAT free. In contrast, the requirement for EU businesses to register and to account for VAT in each Member State in which it makes supplies is a clear barrier to fulfilling the single market. This is particularly problematic for SMEs who are the lifeblood of the European economy.

It is therefore clear that further change is needed. The VAT system has to become more efficient and fit for purpose for the technological age in which we live. While some may argue that we need to wait for a number of years to progress the destination system further, there are many arguments that suggest that we need to progress on this now. First, with new technologies, business can increasingly make supplies without any physical presence in markets. Second, we have seen evidence that the weaknesses and loopholes in the VAT system are being exploited with the ensuing tax losses for Member States and an uneven playing field for EU business. Third, as unanimity for VAT files is required under Article 113 of the Treaty, the legislative cycle from inception to implementation for a VAT file can be up to five years.

It is also relevant that the recent report of the Commission Expert Group on Taxation of the Digital Economy (May 2014) made a general proposal that the EU should pursue the destination principle for all supplies of goods and services on an incremental basis. The recommendations of the Expert group are broadly in line with the objectives set out in the 2011 Commission Communication on the Future of VAT. However, the report has highlighted that the broader OSS to cover all distance B2C supplies of goods and services needs to be pursued as a priority. The report also foresees the abolition of the VAT exemption for the importation of small consignments.

Taking account of existing Commission policy, the recommendations of the Expert Group, the OECD BEPS discussions as well as interactions with business representatives and Member States in respect of the existing rules, it is considered that the following represents a credible and achievable strategy to a neutral and efficient VAT regime for B2C transactions within the EU:

- *Extension of the MOSS:* The logical next step is to extend the MOSS to all intra-EU B2C supplies of goods and services. This can be a win-win for business and tax administrations. This measure also has the potential to deliver a true single market for consumers with particular benefits for SMEs.
- *Removal of the distance sales thresholds:* With a simplification regime in place, it is clear that the current distance sales registration thresholds are no longer

necessary. This simplifies business obligations and equally ensures that all businesses charge the same VAT rate to customers in the same Member State.

- *VAT compliance – Home country or standardized rules:* As recognized by the Commission Expert group and in interactions with many Member States and business representatives, the expansion of the One Stop Shop will require further simplification, although this will not apply to rates and exemptions, which will always follow the destination principle. Two options can be considered. The first is that home country rules apply i.e., as regards invoicing, bad debt relief etc. The second and most efficient option is to apply common rules in all twenty-eight Member States. While some may argue that this will impede the principle of subsidiarity, there is a stronger argument that this will cut down red tape and make rules easier to apply in practice for both business and tax administrations. In any case, the applicable rules must be clear, simple and accessible to all businesses through a central VAT Web portal where all the necessary and relevant information is easily obtainable.
- *Home country auditing and revenue sharing:* The expert group made a clear recommendation that for the One Stop Shop to be most effective there needs to be home country auditing. The current situation whereby a business can be audited by twenty-eight tax administrations is conducive neither to the single market nor to a good business environment. Therefore, the responsibility for auditing has to lie with the home Member State. Auditing should be carried out on the basis of risk analysis to ensure that non-compliant businesses are targeted. Home country auditing could be supported by revenue sharing whereby the home Member State retains a proportion of the tax revenues. This can ensure that the auditing activities are fully funded and provide a measurable 'yield' for auditors. Revenue sharing has been in place for the collection of customs duties for some time, and is also in place during the initial period of the MOSS.
- *Removal of the VAT exemption for the importation of small consignments and inclusion of B2C supplies of goods from third countries in the One Stop Shop:* The VAT exemption for small consignments should be abolished because it provides a clear and unfair advantage to non-EU businesses that are making inbound supplies into the EU. It also provides room for abusive tax planning to the detriment of EU business. The abolition of the exemption can be supported by simplification measures such as inclusion within the One Stop Shop and the provision of a fast track mechanism for customs clearance. These simplification measures will ensure that the burden on business as well as tax and customs administrations is not increased while contributing to a high degree of compliance. There is also a strong case to include consignments below the customs threshold (currently EUR 150), as this will ensure a major simplification for business and administrations.

The roadmap to a truly destination based VAT system for B2C transactions is a continuation of existing policies which have served the EU well.

A further, perhaps more long term objective, is to roll out the OSS to countries outside the EU through bilateral agreements based on reciprocity. For instance, rather than a non-EU business choosing, say Denmark, as the EU Member State in which to register and declare VAT due throughout the EU, the EU could cooperate directly with the authorities of the non-EU country so that the business would be able to account for VAT through its own tax administration which would transfer those revenues to the relevant EU Member State. The same arrangements for supplies to that third country would apply within the EU. Such a change, which may include revenue sharing, could improve compliance and facilitate trade.

Clearly further work is needed in terms of administrative cooperation with third countries, and the process may take some time, but equally there is a clear advantage both for businesses and tax authorities in improving tax compliance through simpler obligations.

2.6 CONCLUSIONS

The recent report of the Commission Expert Group on taxation of the digital economy clearly recognized that VAT is part of the solution to ensure taxation of the Digital Economy in Europe and elsewhere. A very important milestone was reached in the EU on 1 January 2015 with the entry into force of the new place of supply rules under which B2C supplies of electronic-, broadcasting- and telecommunication services will be taxed in the Member State of the consumer rather than in the Member State of the supplier. However, the EU must go further and provide that all B2C supplies of goods and services should be taxed in the Member State of consumption, supported by a broader One Stop Shop.

A destination based VAT system for B2C transactions which ensures neutrality for EU business is essential for the delivery of the digital single market, and there needs to be early buy-in by Member States. The roadmap outlined above, which reflects existing Commission policy and the recommendations of the Commission Expert Group, is a credible way to proceed.

It is relevant that the new Commission has recognized the importance of the digital single market with the appointment of a dedicated Commission Vice-President to coordinate the delivery on this as a priority for the Commission. The June 2014 European Council also prioritized the digital economy in its: '*Strategic Agenda for the Union in Times of Change*'.[15]

15. http://www.consilium.europa.eu/uedocs/cms_Data/docs/pressdata/en/ec/143478.pdf.

CHAPTER 3

Value Added Tax 3.0

Charlène Adline Herbain[*]

3.1 INTRODUCTION

Member States subject services consumed within their territories to VAT. This VAT rule on the place-of-supply dates back to the early days of the introduction of the European VAT, and therefore already existed in the Second VAT Directive.[1] The practical implementation of this rule, however, has not remained straightforward over the last sixty years. Taking twists and turns, the place of supply of services has evolved from the place of performance of the service, to the place of establishment of the supplier and, eventually, to the place of establishment of the customer.

Fifteen years ago, neither electronically provided services nor digital products were very developed. Consequently, they were not a specific category for the purposes of VAT and were subject to the standard VAT location regime. The modern age has seen the expansion of digital technology throughout all aspects of society, integrating cyberspace into everyday life. As a consequence of this development, the taxation of electronically provided services has evolved. The European VAT legislation has

* Charléne Herbain teaches Value Added Tax at the University of Luxembourg and Tax Law at the University of Lorraine in France, and is post-doctoral researcher at the Catholic University of Louvain in Belgium. She has been a VAT practitioner for ten years and serves as a tax advisor to several law firms in Luxembourg.

1. Council Directive 67/228/EEC of 11 Apr. 1967 on the harmonization of legislation of Member States concerning turnover taxes – Structure and procedures for application of the common system of value added tax (OJ 71 14 Apr. 1967, pp. 1303–1312) (hereinafter 'Second Directive') was adopted jointly with Council Directive 67/227/EEC of 11 Apr. 1967 on the harmonization of legislation of Member States concerning turnover taxes OJ 71 14 Apr. 1967, p. 1301–1303) (hereinafter 'First Directive'). The aim was the introduction of the common VAT system in the Community. See Article 3 of the Second Directive; See Article 5 of Council Directive 2006/112 of 28 Nov. 2006 on the common system of value added tax OJ L 347 11 Dec. 2006, p. 1–118 (hereinafter the 'VAT Directive').

identified and applied a special rule for the purpose of determining the place-of-supply, that is the place where VAT is due, of certain: '*services which are delivered over the Internet or an electronic network and the nature of which renders their supply essentially automated and involving minimal human intervention, and impossible to ensure in the absence of information technology*'.[2] The ordinary law concerning the place-of-supply of services was profoundly changed by the 2008 VAT Package,[3] and, subsequently, the expansion of cyberspace into the field of the 'Internet of Things', as well as the ever constant increase of digital exchanges, has led to further changes. A new era has come, that of VAT 3.0. This contribution intends to trace and analyse the path taken by the VAT from the beginning of the digital era to 2015.

3.2 ACROSS THE OCEAN

From the introduction of the common VAT system, the goal, in line with the consumption tax nature of VAT, has been to ensure that VAT would accrue to the country of consumption. In fact, the Member States chose this VAT system as the best way forward because, with its neutrality towards consumption patterns, it was expected to create a level playing field within the internal market.[4]

In the early stages, the rule that prevailed to ensure that VAT was levied at the place of consumption was to locate the services where they were used.[5] The application of this rule did, however, lead to some serious practical problems. In the face of these challenges, the adoption of the Sixth Directive[6] saw the rules on the place of taxation for services amended.[7] Aside from some exceptions, services became taxable for VAT purposes at the suppliers' location. Since the suppliers were in proximity to the clients, this new rule resulted in VAT accruing (mostly) to [...] the country of consumption.[8] It was, however, not broad enough to encompass digital exchanges.

---

2. Council implementing regulation (EU) No. 282/2011 of 15 Mar. 2011 laying down implementing measures for Directive 2006/112/EC on the common system of value added tax, Article 7. Distance sales of goods on a physical medium such as CD/DVD or video games are not covered, even if they are concluded on the Internet.
3. The VAT Package changes to the location of services are included in Council Directive 2008/8/EC of 12 Feb. 2008 amending Directive 2006/112/EC as regards the place-of-supply of services (OJ L 44 20 Feb. 2008, 11), (hereinafter 'VAT Package'). A thorough description of the VAT package measures affecting the location of services can be found in W. van den Corput (2008): 'Amendments to the EU VAT system', 19 International VAT Monitor 1 of 2008 at p. 6–12.
4. Charlène Herbain (2015): 'VAT neutrality', Promoculture-Larcier, 2015 at 31–36.
5. Article 6, paragraph 3 of the Second Directive stipulated that: '*the place of the provision of services shall, as a general rule, be regarded as being the place where the service provided, the right transferred or granted or, the object hired is used or enjoyed*'.
6. Sixth Council Directive 77/388/EEC of 17 May 1977 on the harmonization of the laws of the Member States relating to turnover taxes – Common system of value added tax: uniform basis of assessment [1977] OJ L145/1 (hereinafter the 'Sixth Directive').
7. COM(1973)950, OJ C/1973/80/1, Proposal for a Sixth Council Directive on the harmonization of Member States concerning turnover taxes Common system of value added tax: Uniform basis of assessment – explanatory memorandum, Article 10: ' ... *This choice was made mainly for reasons of simplicity and for the avoidance of difficulties of interpretation which might arise from notions such as the place of utilization or exploitation of the services...* '.
8. COM(2003) 822 final, JO C 96 du 21 Apr. 2004, Proposal for a Council Directive amending Directive 77/388/EEC as regards the place of supply of services, 2.

This contribution examines the consequences of this dysfunction and, particularly, how it affects the realization of the internal market goal.

3.2.1 The Sixth Directive

From 1977 until 2003, the general rules of location applied to radio and television broadcasting services as well as to most electronic services. To ensure that taxation occurred at the place of consumption,[9] these rules stipulated that the supply of services, and therefore their taxation, was deemed to be realized in the Member State from which the services originated, i.e., the place of establishment of the services provider.[10]

As a result of the application of the general rules, electronic services supplied from an EU operator were subject to EU VAT, regardless of the place of consumption (i.e., the VAT applicable in the Member State of establishment of the operator). Similar services from a non-EU operator, however, were free of any EU VAT. Therefore sales by non-EU operators to EU customers were not subject to any EU VAT, while similar sales by EU operators were subject to EU VAT and furthermore, sales by EU operators to non-EU customers were also subject to EU VAT. All in all, EU operators were facing an acute disadvantage.

The European legislator created these rules in an age when e-commerce had not yet become commonplace, but in which business-to-consumer (hereinafter 'B2C') transactions took place primarily within national boundaries. Consequently, the basic assumptions on which the VAT taxation rules were based were not adapted to e-commerce. Therefore, the drafters of the Sixth Directive supposed that imposing VAT at the supplier's location would ensure taxation at the place of consumption. Considering the geographic proximity between service providers and recipients within traditional trade environments, the drafters assumed that the consumer was most commonly in the 'neighbourhood' of the supplier, and that the need to travel would put the brakes on a massive development of inter-jurisdictional trade. E-commerce, however, presupposes a distance between the trader and the customer and makes such location rules inadequate to ensure taxation at the place of consumption. The application of the general VAT location rules '*produced perverse and discriminatory results*'[11] for EU e-traders and Member States.

---

9. Such principle being at the core of VAT, see OECD (2014): 'International VAT/GST guidelines' at 7: '*... the core features of a VAT: as a tax on consumption, the revenue should accrue to the jurisdiction where the final consumption takes place.*'
10. The rules of location implemented by the Second Directive (Article 6(3)) under which VAT was principally levied at the place of use of the services were amended by the Sixth Directive which organized in its Article 9(1) that the supply is deemed to take place of origin, that is the place of establishment of the supplier.
11. 'VAT: special arrangements applicable to services supplied electronically' (Europa Portal last update 20 Feb. 2007) http://europa.eu/legislation_summaries/information_society/other_policies/l31044_en.htm accessed 5 Mar. 2015.

3.2.2 Outcome versus Intentions

The application of the general place-of-supply rules lead to various undesirable consequences.

In the global playing field, taxing at origin lead to VAT free inbound supplies of international e-services, whereas similar intra EU and outbound transactions were subject to EU VAT. Practically, this meant that non-EU e-traders could sell their services in the common market at a price discount (free of EU VAT), whereas Community e-traders had to charge VAT on their services even when sold outside the Community. Such a system was giving rise to discrimination against EU e-traders, both at the Community and international level. This hurdle has been summarized by D. Raponi, head of the VAT unit at the European Commission, in 2000:

> the existing rules do not ensure that electronically delivered services can, in all cases, be exported free of charge and that a sufficient legal base exists for charging VAT on services supplied to EU private consumers by foreign operators. These have the potential to constitute a major distortion of competition and to place EU service providers at a competitive disadvantage compared to non-EU suppliers.[12]

The situation was also inducing an erosion of the Community tax base: in order to retain their competiveness, European e-traders were manipulating their place of establishment so as to be deemed outside the Community for VAT purposes. This was allowing them to lower their prices with an amount equivalent to the VAT.

In case of EU business-to-business transactions, the recipient of the e-supply was obliged to first pay the VAT charged by the supplier, after which he could request a refund. The refund procedure, however, was cumbersome and often made businesses abandon their claim, triggering tax accumulation and impeding the achievement of fair competition within internal market.

Moreover, under the given pattern of consumption, the taxation at origin contravened the core VAT principle that VAT should be imposed in the jurisdiction of consumption,[13] leading to the misallocation of VAT revenue among the Member States and subsequent non-taxation. Faced with this situation, the July 2000 European

12. D. Raponi (2000): 'VAT treatment of electronically delivered services', 9 EC Tax Review 3 at p. 188 (188–189). See also B.A.Van der Merwe (2004): 'VAT in the European Union and Electronically Supplied Services to Final Consumers' 16 SA Tydskrif vir Handelsreg 4 at p. 577 and 578 (577–588): '*...electronic deliveries from an EU supplier were taxed where the supplier was established, whether the consumer was in the EU or elsewhere. This gave rise to a number of undesirable consequences...This gave a tremendous competitive advantage to non-EU suppliers who could deliver goods electronically VAT free, while their EU competitors had to charge VAT when they supplied final consumers in the EU and elsewhere. For example, European exporters to the United States had to pay EU VAT, whilst American exporters were not under a similar obligation*'.
13. The issues linked to the application of the general location rules for digital services were notably underlined by a communication from the Commission of June 1998, (COM(1998) 374 final 'electronic commerce and indirect taxation' guideline no. 3); then by the conclusions of the July 1998 ECOFIN Council and also by the OECD conference in Ottawa in October 1998.

Commission Communication made the modernization of the VAT rules for [...] e-commerce a priority.[14]

3.3 IN LUXEMBOURG

In 2003, the European legislator stepped in to adapt the VAT regime to the important specificities of e-commerce. Council Directive 2002/38/EC on VAT arrangements for certain services supplied by electronic means, radio and television broadcasting services (hereinafter the 'E-commerce directive, see Appendix I'),[15] brought in new location rules with the purpose of ensuring a clear and fair VAT regime, and restored conditions of effective trade competition while ending the incentive for e-traders to relocate outside the Community.

3.3.1 The E-Commerce Directive

The E-commerce Directive provided an institutional framework, a definition of e-services,[16] and new place-of-supply rules, under which customers located in the EU[17] were charged EU-VAT, irrespective of the location of the trader.[18]

In cases of inbound international supplies, the practicalities of charging VAT varied depending on the VAT status of the e-service recipient. If the recipient was a VAT taxable person, the e-trader would not charge VAT but the recipient would self-assess and pay the VAT under the so-called reverse charge mechanism. Discharged from the obligation to charge VAT, the non-EU established e-trader would not have to register for VAT. If the recipient was not a VAT taxable person, the e-trader was required to charge VAT (in compliance with the rate and other requirements of the national VAT regime in the country where the recipient was established)[19] and for this, it was obligatory for the e-trader to be registered for VAT purposes in each Member State in which it provided e-services to EU non-taxable persons. For convenience,

14. Communication from the Commission to the Council and the European Parliament – A strategy to improve the operation of the VAT system within the context of the internal market, COM (2000) 348 final, appendix 1.2.
15. Council Directive 2002/38/EC of 7 May 2002 amending and amending temporarily Directive 77/388/EEC as regards the value-added tax arrangements applicable to radio and television broadcasting services and certain electronically supplied services [2002] OJ L 128/41.
16. The European Commission prides itself to be: '*...the first significant tax jurisdiction in the world to develop and implement a simplified framework for consumption taxes on e-services in accordance with the principles agreed within the framework of the Organisation for Economic Co-operation and Development (OECD).*' See 'http://ec.europa.eu/taxation_customs/taxation/vat/how_vat_works/e-services/index_en.htm' (Last update: 4 Feb. 2015) 26 Feb. 2015; See also M. Lamensch (2014): 'The Treatment of Digital products and Other E-Services Under VAT', conference 'The Future of VAT in a Digital Global Economy', Vienna, 24–26 Sep. 2014, in M. Lang and I. Lejeune (eds.): 'VAT/GST in a Global Digital Economy', to be published (Kluwer).
17. As of 1 Dec. 2009, the EU replaces and succeeds the European Community. The E- commerce Directive successively applied within the Community and within the EU. For clarity, this contribution refers only to the EU in the context of the E-commerce Directive.
18. Recital 3 and Article 1 of the E-commerce Directive; recitals 23 and Article 58, Article 59a(b) and 59b of the VAT Directive.
19. Articles 359, 364 and 367 of the VAT Directive.

however, an e-trader was given the opportunity to register only once, in a Member State of its choice.[20] Initially, the Commission had suggested that non-EU e-traders would charge VAT at the rate applicable in the Member State in which they had chosen to register,[21] but during the Council negotiations it was decided that VAT should be charged at the applicable rate in the Member State where the recipient was established. This simplification, according to which non-EU operators, undertaking inbound B2C activities into the EU, would only have to deal with a single tax administration within the EU, was maintained. Therefore, the non-established e-traders were reporting and paying any VAT collected on behalf of other Member States, to their Member State of identification.[22] This mechanism has functioned until end of 2014.[23]

When the recipient of the e-service was an EU taxable person, the establishment of the e-trader within or outside the EU was irrelevant. This level playing field was achieved by applying the reverse charge mechanism, making the person, to whom the supplies of e-services are made, liable for the payment of VAT, hence releasing the e-trader from the obligation to charge VAT on the supply.[24] This was, however, different in cases in which the recipient was a taxable person established in the same Member State as the e-trader. In this scenario, the e-trader was invoicing, collecting and paying VAT to the treasury in the same manner as if it would have been supplying to a non-taxable recipient.

The rules applicable to e-services supplied within the EU in B2C situations had not been amended by the E-commerce Directive. The place of taxation for VAT remained the place where the e-trader was located.[25] What did change, however, was the place of taxation in the case of outbound international supplies of e-services: regardless of the VAT status of the recipient, e-services for consumption outside the EU were no longer subject to EU VAT.[26]

The measures of the E-commerce Directive relating to the place of taxation of e-services and the facilitation of VAT compliance were due to expire on 30 June 2006. Unless new rules were implemented, the EU would have reverted to the rules prevailing before 2003. The Commission considered that the shortcoming of the pre-2003 rules had been rectified by the measures of the E-commerce Directive and that the slow rate of legislative progress in the Council was making the adoption of any amendments improbable before the end of 2006.[27] Therefore, it proposed an extension

20. Council regulation (EC) No. 792/2002 of 7 May 2002 amending temporarily Regulation (EEC) No. 218/92 on administrative cooperation in the field of indirect taxation (VAT) as regards additional measures regarding electronic commerce subsequently included in Regulation (EC) 1798/2003, introduced specific measures relating to the VAT registration of non-EU established e-service traders and for distributing the VAT receipts to the Member States entitled to it.
21. IP/00/583 Brussels, 7 Jun. 2000.
22. Article 1.3 of the E-commerce Directive.
23. Article 357 of the VAT Directive. On 1 Jan. 2015, the mini One-Stop Shop (MOSS) was launched, it continues these arrangements. See L. Grençon, J. Denton (2014): '2015 VAT changes: the details and the practicalities', 6 ACE of 2014 at p. 19 (13–21).
24. Article 44 of the VAT Directive.
25. Article 45 of the VAT Directive.
26. Article 1.1(a) of the E-commerce Directive; Articles 44 and 59 of the VAT Directive.
27. The Commission had proposed new provisions on the place of supply of services (to generalize the taxation of services in the Member State of the recipient) and on a more general electronic

of these measures to the end of 2008.[28] The approval of the extension materialized in Directive 2006/58/EC,[29] adopted just a few days before the expiry date of the previously mentioned measures of the E-commerce Directive, extending them until December of the same year. Afterwards, Council Directive 2006/138/CE ensured the arrangements would continue until 31 December 2008.[30]

3.3.2 Outcome versus Intentions

The dysfunctioning of the Sixth Directive within the digital environment prompted the adoption of the E-commerce Directive. Already in 2000, the recitals of the proposed directive underlined the practical weaknesses of the Sixth Directive:

> In the interests of the proper functioning of the internal market, such distortions should be eliminated and new harmonised rules introduced for this type of activity. Action should be taken to ensure, in particular, that such services where effected for consideration and consumed by customers established in the Community are taxed in the Community and are not taxed if consumed outside the Community.[31]

The E-commerce Directive was seeking to remove: '*a significant competitive handicap*',[32] therefore helping EU e-traders to develop clients in markets outside the EU, without the hassle of having to choose between not passing the VAT on to retail [...] prices (thus bearing the cost of it) or relocating outside the EU. It was also foreseen that the measures facilitating the administration of the VAT would induce non-EU traders active within the EU to comply with the EU rules in force.

---

mechanism (to cut the VAT red [...] tape on e-traders not established in the Member States where they supply their services). See COM(2005)334 Amended proposal for a Council Directive amending Directive 77/388/EEC as regards the place of supply of services CNS 2003/0329 and (COM(2004)728) Proposal for a Council Directive amending Directive 77/388/EEC with a view to simplifying value added tax obligations, CNS 2004/0261.

28. COM(2006) 210 final Proposal for a Council Directive amending directive 2002/38/EC as regards the period of application of the value added tax arrangements applicable to radio and television broadcasting services and certain electronically supplied services, CNS 2006/0069 and COM(2006) 0739 final Proposal for a Council Directive amending Council Directive 2002/38/EC as regards the period of application of the value added tax arrangements applicable to radio and television broadcasting services and certain electronically supplied services, CNS 2006/0245.
29. Council Directive 2006/58/EC of 27 Jun. 2006 amending Council Directive 2002/38/EC as regards the period of application of the value added tax arrangements applicable to radio and television broadcasting services and certain electronically supplied services [2006] OJ L 174, 28 Jun. 2006, p. 5.
30. Council Directive 2006/138/EC of 19 Dec. 2006 amending Directive 2006/112/EC on the common system of value added tax as regards the period of application of the value added tax arrangements applicable to radio and television broadcasting services and certain electronically supplied services [2006] OJ L 384, pp. 92–93.
31. COM (2000) 349 final, Proposal for a Council Directive amending Directive 77/388/EEC as regards the value added tax arrangements applicable to certain services supplied by electronic means, CNS 2000/0148.
32. European Commission 'http://ec.europa.eu/taxation_customs/taxation/vat/how_vat_works/e-services/index_en.htm' (last update 4 Feb. 2015) accessed 5 Mar. 2015.

Apart from e-traders ignoring the EU VAT rules,[33] the E-commerce Directive has created scope for VAT optimization in business-to-(EU)consumer transactions. E-traders have had the possibility to choose (for those not yet established) or to modify (by way of relocation for all others) their place of establishment for VAT purposes in order to benefit from the competitive advantage that a low VAT rate would bring.[34] The Commission acknowledged that this form of establishment/forum-shopping created a new field of competition between Member States:[35]

> in practice suppliers...chose that Member State for registration with the lowest tax rate applicable to the respective service to be supplied. In this respect, a new field of tax competition between the Member States...arises.[36]

Tax forum-shopping was supported by the fact that in the electronic commerce context, the place of establishment of the seller is not considered per se as a criterion for the client, as no travel is needed to obtain the delivery. Another force at play was the Court of Justice of the European Union (hereinafter the 'CJEU' or the 'Court') which had made clear that businesses were allowed to take economic decisions influenced by tax factors so that the decision to establish in a particular Member State for its low VAT rate became officially legal.[37] Moreover, the relative uncertainty around the required features to determine the place of establishment of the e-trader (and therefore the place of taxation of the electronic services supplied to non-taxable clients) also supported tax-forum shopping. In that respect, guidelines had already been provided by the CJEU, but their practical application to the case of an e-trader appeared not as straightforward: the Court relied on the presence of a structure with a sufficient degree of permanence, in terms of human and technical resources, to supply the services in

33. This phenomenon should not be underestimated. R. Heinen noted in 2014 that non-EU e-traders hardly adopted the '*voluntary compliance*' attitude that is required further to the lack of means of monitoring, and therefore of enforceability, of the implementation of European VAT legislation by non-EU e-traders. R. Heinen (2014): 'Le régime de TVA applicable au commerce électronique', Le Code Fiscal of March 2014 at 26–27.
34. Before 2012 the VAT rate in Madeira rose from 13% to 15% then 16% and eventually 22% (Law 55-A/2010 dated 31 Dec. 2011 and no. 14-A/2012 of 30 Mar. 2012). It was before the increase, the lowest VAT rate together with Luxembourg. See European Commission 'VAT rates applied in the member and accession states of the European Community' DOC 2402/2003 EN; See also R. Minor, C. Gartner (2012): 'VAT on Electronically Supplied Services to EU Consumers – A Practical Compliance Guide for Cross-Border Suppliers', Spitze Publishing 2012 at 25.
35. European Commission, 'VAT Package: Commission welcomes adoption by ECOFIN Council of new rules on the place of supply of services and a new procedure for VAT refunds', (2008) European Commission Press Releases IP/08/208, http://europa.eu/rapid/press-release_IP-08-208_en.htm?locale=EN (last update 12 Feb. 2015) accessed 28 Mar. 2015; See also A. Sinyor (2002): 'EU VAT on e-commerce: the practical implications', 13 International Tax Review 6 of 2002 at 32 (32–33).
36. M. Massbaum, K. Eicker (2001): 'The Proposal for an EC Council Directive Regarding the VAT Arrangement Applicable to Services Supplied by Electronic Means', 29 Intertax 3 of 2001 at 96 (91–97).
37. CJEU Case C-4/94 BLP *Group plc v. Commissioners of Customs & Excise* [1995] ECR I-00983. See in particular B. Gasparotto (2013): 'TVA: focus sur l'actualité jurisprudentielle communautaire 2010–2013', Kluwer 2013 at 107: 'l'optimisation TVA est autorisée pour améliorer la position concurrentielle de l'assujetti', free translation by the author: 'VAT optimisation is allowed to improve the competitive position of the taxpayer.'

question on an independent basis.[38] Following these guidelines, to conclude that an e-trader has its place of establishment somewhere, it needs offices (which could consist of a domiciliation) and personnel assigned to administrative and business functions (which could be supply services of personnel). It is to be noted that contrary to the OECD approach in the area of corporate income taxation,[39] the Court's case law[40] has been considered as not treating the mere presence of servers or clusters of servers in a Member State as a place of supply of electronic services for VAT purposes.[41] Also to me, it seems that a server is merely a computer that can execute a programmed list of instructions,[42] that its location is not relevant in respect of the guidelines of the CJEU and that, as a consequence, the physical presence of a server does not seem relevant when locating the service when the other functions regarding business and administration are carried out from a given Member State. What is needed, in my view, is the potential for the personnel to operate the server from the said Member State.

Since the new VAT location rules (bundled together as the so-called VAT Package), the VAT taxation of intra-Community commercial transactions is based on the destination principle.[43] [...] Intra-community supplies of services are exempt from VAT in the Member State of origin [...] and VAT is charged in the Member State of destination at the same rate and on the same taxable basis as domestic production. The destination principle ensures the allocation of VAT revenue in conformity with the consumption pattern of VAT as VAT revenue is allocated to the Member State where the final consumption occurs.[44] The VAT regime applicable under the

---

38. See in particular CJEU Case *C-168/84 Gunter Berkholz against Finanzamt Hamburg-Mitte-Altstadt* [1985] ECR 2251 and Case *C-190/95 ARO Lease BV against Inspecteur van de Belastingdienst Grote Ondernemingen Amsterdam* [1997] ECR I-4383.
39. Committee on Fiscal Affairs of the OECD, 'Clarification on the Application of the Permanent Establishment Definition in E-commerce: Changes to the Commentary on Article 5', paragraph 42.2: '*...the server on which the web site is stored and through which it is accessible is a piece of equipment having a physical location and such location may thus constitute a "fixed place of business" of the enterprise that operates that server.*' 22 Dec. 2000.
40. CJEU Case *C-168/84 Berkholz and Case C-190/95 ARO Lease* (n 39).
41. See in particular D.M. Parrilli (2008): 'Grid and Taxation: The Server as Permanent Establishment in International Grids', in J. Altmann and others (eds) (2008): 'Grid Economics and Business Models: 5th International Workshop, GECON 2008', Springer Verlag 2008 at 89–102; See also from the same author 'Tax Treatment of Companies Providing Grid Services: Direct v Indirect Taxation' in M. Lang, P. Melz, et al. (eds) (2009): 'Value Added Tax and Direct Taxation, similarities and differences', IBFD 2009 at 763 (743–769).
42. In support of this view, see the definitions given respectively by A.J. Cockfield and M. Gianni that underline the technical characteristics of services provided by a server: '*A server is a computer networked to the Internet that enables businesses, inter alia, to post websites and to sell goods or services over the Internet*' and '*The server does not think or exercise any business judgment.*' A.J. Cockfield (2000): 'Should We Really Tax Profits From Computer Servers? A Case Study in E-Commerce Taxation', 21 Tax notes Int'l of 2000 at 2407; M. Gianni (2014): 'The OECD'S Flawed and Dated Approach to Computer Servers Creating Permanent Establishments', Vanderbilt J. of Entertainment & Technology L. of 2014 at p. 5.
43. By derogation, before the VAT package, the destination principle was already, and rather often, applying. The rules on the place of supply were hybrid: the principle was the taxation at origin (the place where services were deemed to be supplied was the place of establishment of the person supplying them) but the scope of application of the origin principle so restricted by numerous exceptions applying the destination principle that it eventually became the exception.
44. In the context of international trade, the destination principle is at the heart of the VAT system. It makes VAT, an economically neutral method of taxation and has been accepted as an

E-commerce Directive was not fully permitting such allocation to the extent that B2C sales by EU operators were taxed according to the origin principle. This framework was causing regulatory heterogeneity[45] and businesses relocation. Additionally, as the place where taxation occurs is especially important in the context of B2C supplies (as VAT is not deductible and therefore constitutes an income for the Member State), Member States imposing the lowest VAT rates attracted e-operators and collected the VAT revenue on all e-sales subject to the origin principle, regardless of their place of consumption. The VAT regime of the E-commerce Directive was responsible for very substantial differences in VAT revenue between Member States. As a whole, this [...] situation created deep discontent within the Member States and generated the preconditions required to change the place of taxation for e-services.[46]

3.4 IN SWITZERLAND

Effective 1 January 2015, any electronic service supplied by an EU operator to a non-taxable customer[47] within the EU is subject to VAT where the customer is situated.[48] The full application of the principle of the place of taxation at destination aims at eliminating unevenness of the global level playing field with respect to EU e-traders and to adjust the location of e-trade under the consumption pattern of VAT.

international standard (the General Agreement on [...] Tariffs and Trade 1947 (hereinafter 'GATT') already provided that destination principle could be applied to indirect taxes. World Trade Organization, the successor of GATT, also supports taxation at destination. See B. Terra (1998): 'The Place of Supply in European VAT', Kluwer Law International, 1998 at p. 5.

45. The simultaneous operation of the origin and destination regimes was causing increased administrative costs to the businesses.
46. The repeated references to the matter of the Member States VAT revenues from e-commerce denote the depth of the issue. See notably the press release 2836th of the Council meeting Economic and Financial Affairs Brussels, 4 Dec. 2007 (Presse 270) where it was stated that VAT revenue would need to be transferred from the supplier's Member State to that of the customer; See also the tenth recital of Directive 2008/8/EC that insists on the impact on the budget of Member States of the change of place of taxation and see also the following quote from László Kovács, Commissioner responsible for Taxation and Customs (European Commission Press Releases IP/08/208): '*I am content that the change in the rules on the place of supply of services will ensure a more even playing field for businesses supplying services throughout the Community. This is particularly true of services which can be supplied at a distance where, as a result of current rules, businesses have been locating in countries with lower VAT rates ...*'
47. The changes introduced by the Council implementing regulation (EU) No. 1042/2013 of 7 Oct. 2013 amending implementing regulation (see Appendices II and IV) (EU) No. 282/2011 as regards the place of supply of services do not amend the rules for VAT status determination. As a result, and in accordance with the terms of the Article 9 of the VAT Directive, '*Taxable person shall mean any person who, independently, carries out in any place any economic activity, whatever the purpose or results of that activity*'. In this connection, it should be noted that the VAT registration per se has no impact on the VAT status.
48. Article 5 of Directive 2008/8/CE (effective 1 Jan. 2015 it changes Article 58 of the VAT Directive).

3.4.1 VAT Package

The VAT package provisions relevant to this contribution are in Directive 2008/8/EC and in its implementing regulation (for the text see Appendix III).[49] These provisions relate to the location rules of e-services (from now on, in all circumstances in the Member State of the customer) and to the extension in terms of services and beneficiaries, of the scheme of simplified VAT administration (from now on extended to telecommunication-, radio- and television broadcasting services[50] and to EU e-traders).[51]

Some of these rules entered into force later,[52] but the majority of the rules of the VAT package on the place-of-supply of services[53] came into force in 2010. The location rules of services supplied electronically to non-taxable EU customers were intended to enter into force much earlier (in 2006) (for the text see Appendix III).[54] However, the process of debating draft legislation suspended their entry into force. Now that the rules have been voted and implemented, there is and will be until 2019, a substantial practical limit on them: Member States are entitled to retain part of the VAT revenue collected on EU B2C sales from locally established e-traders.[55] *Ceteris paribus*, the wider application of the re-distribution of VAT revenue between Member States, which the Commission considered unrealistic less than ten years ago,[56] ensures that taxation reflects, for a part now and entirely from 2019, the place where consumption takes place.[57]

For consumers in Europe, the change to the VAT system means that all services supplied electronically are subject to local VAT.

For EU e-traders, whether their supplies are delivered to taxable persons[58] or to non-taxable persons,[59] the place-of-supply is the Member State where the customer is established. As a result of this approximation with the scheme applicable since 2003 to

49. Council implementing regulation (EU) No. 1042/2013 (n 48). See Appendix IV for the relevant provisions of this Regulation.
50. Article 5, 11) of the Directive 2008/8/EC (new Article 359 of the VAT Directive).
51. Article 5, 15) of the Directive 2008/8/EC (new Article 369b of the VAT Directive).
52. The new place of supply of long-term hire of means of transport entered into force on 1 Jan. 2013. Article 4 of the Directive 2008/8/EC (new Article 56, 2 of the VAT directive).
53. The VAT Package changes to the location of services are in Council Directive 2008/8/EC cited above.
54. Amended proposal for a Council Directive amending Directive 77/388/EEC as regards the place of supply of services. COM(2005)334, 2.7.
55. A description of the negotiations is available from R. Heinen (2014): 'Le régime de TVA applicable au commerce électronique', Le Code Fiscal of March 2014 at 52–59.
56. Proposal for a Council directive amending Directive 77/388/EEC with a view to simplifying value added tax obligations, COM(2004)728, 2: '*Developing the kind of major treasury function needed to handle the volume of money flows which would be inherent to a much wider application [of the re-distribution of money received from taxable] would not be a realistic option.*'
57. To allow Member States to manage the transition, the Economic and Financial Affairs Council, also known as the ECOFIN council, reached a political agreement from which part of the VAT revenues from EU e-trade will remain during a period of four years with the Member States of establishment of EU e-traders. In 2015 and 2016, the Member State of establishment of the EU e-trader will retain 30% and in 2017 and 2018, 15% of the VAT collected. See notably the 4 Dec. 2007 2836th Council press release at 27; See also Council Regulation (EU) No. 904/2010 of 7 Oct. 2010 on administrative cooperation and combating fraud in the field of value added tax, Article 46, paragraph 3 and the 10ème recital of the Directive 2008/8/CE.
58. Article 44 of the VAT Directive.
59. New Article 58 of the VAT Directive.

non-EU e-traders, EU e-traders are faced with myriad VAT regimes and rates applicable across the EU. As a matter of fact, the new rules do not alter the person liable for payment of the VAT. This remains the obligation of the customer whenever the reverse-charge mechanism applies, or the supplier, when the customer is a non-taxable person. The change lies in the fact that, when the customer is a non-taxable person, the supplier is now liable for foreign VAT. In addition to the new rules concerning the place-of-supply of services, the Mini One Stop Shop (MOSS) for non-EU e-traders has been extended to cover EU e-traders in order to reduce and ease their [...] fiscal obligations.[60] The objective of this scheme, without which VAT registration would be mandatory in every single Member State as from the first sale there, is to enable e-traders established within the EU not to register for VAT in each Member State where they supply B2C e-services. As from now it is from their Member State of establishment that EU e-traders declare and pay both the local and the foreign VAT which they invoiced.[61]

3.4.2 Outcome versus Intentions

The general application of taxation in the country of destination is in line with the nature and logic of VAT. The new place-of-supply rules ensure that the e-commerce supplier's Member State of establishment is not influenced by the VAT rate applied, thus the influence of the VAT rates is neutral towards consumption patterns. This change constitutes an important step forward [...] in achieving fair competition and therefore, an important step forward in countering base erosion and profit shifting, i.e., in the direction of the OECD BEPS project.

Even if the new rules are beneficial for competition and as regards fairness and [...] distribution of VAT receipts to the appropriate Member State, the fact [...] remains that there still are many problematic issues. The most obvious difficulty is without doubt the necessity to rely on other Member States to collect one's own revenue,[62] but other problems have also been exposed. As a result of the various problems emerging from the practical implementation of the new rules, their application, scheduled for 2006, was delayed [...].[63] Even with these deferments, however, the problems did not disappear.

60. Until 31 Dec. 2014, the simplified registration scheme for VAT was only available to services electronically delivered and to non-EU e-traders. Since 1 Jan. 2015, the scheme is extended to EU e-traders and to broadcasting and telecommunications services. Council regulation (EU) No. 967/2012 of 9 Oct. 2012 amending Implementing Regulation (EU) No. 282/2011 as regards the special schemes for non-established taxable persons supplying telecommunications services, broadcasting services or electronic services to non-taxable persons, [2012] OJ L290/1 (see Appendix VI).
61. Member States redistribute VAT back to the Member [...] State where the customer is established.
62. Romain Heinen addresses this problem very clearly when he questions: '*qui travaille pour qui dans un modèle basé sur la solidarité communautaire?*' R. Heinen (2014): 'Le régime de TVA applicable au commerce électronique', Le Code Fiscal of March 2014 at p. 50. Free translation by the author: '*who works for who in a model based on community solidarity ?*'.
63. R. Heinen (2014): 'Le régime de TVA applicable au commerce électronique', Le Code Fiscal of March 2014 at p. 55.

Further to the publication of the implementing regulation in 2013, the Commission published explanatory notes to clarify the practical application of the new place-of-supply rules so as to provide: '*help in understanding the meaning of certain issues contained in the articles of the Implementing Regulation*'.[64] In particular, the process of determining the place where a non-taxable customer is established remains a fairly delicate issue. The OECD suggested relying on: '*some form of registration-based mechanism for B2C transactions*',[65] but this proposal was not adopted, and, the customer's domicile or habitual place of residence is the proxy for VAT taxation,[66] in the same manner as for electronic services supplied by non-EU e-traders.[67] Because e-traders cannot rely on a physical delivery address when digital products are downloaded or electronically supplied, the place-of-supply is determined on the basis of evidence foreseen by the legislator.[68] In order to tax where consumption takes place, specific rules may apply such as the place of actual take up of services,[69] and in cases where it would be impossible to ascertain the customer's domicile or habitual place of residence, rebuttable presumptions may be used (see also Chapter 4).[70] The scheme refers to a large arsenal of evidence that is somewhat perplexing and has led a number of commentators to question its efficiency:

> expecting from e-suppliers that they proceed to transaction based verifications on the basis of different indicators from different sources depending on the factual circumstances surrounding each e-supply is not reasonable in a digital context, no matter how specific the legislator can be regarding the type of information that should be processed, essentially because it imposes an insurmountable compliance burden on e-suppliers still without ensuring legal certainty, and because it also does often not allow tax administrations to verify that VAT has been correctly assessed at the stage of the audit.[71]

---

64. European Commission 'Explanatory notes on the EU VAT changes to the place of supply of telecommunications, broadcasting and electronic services that enter into force in 2013', published on 3 Apr. 2014 (see Appendix V).
65. OECD (2001): 'Taxation and Electronic Commerce–Implementing the Ottawa Taxation Framework Conditions,' OECD Publishing, 2001 at p. 21.
66. Council implementing regulation (EU) No. 1042/2013 (n 48). Guidelines about B2C supplies have not yet been adopted by the OECD but a project exists and has been subject to public consultation. See Lamensch (2014): 'The Treatment of Digital products and Other E-Services Under VAT', in M. Lang and I. Lejeune (eds.): 'VAT/GST in a Global Digital Economy', to be published (Kluwer).
67. Article 58 of the VAT Directive.
68. Article 1(2)(d)(i) of Council implementing Regulation No. 1042/2013 inserting Article 24 e and f in implementing Regulation No. 282/2011.
69. Article 1(2)(d)(i) of Council implementing Regulation No. 1042/2013 inserting Article 24 a in implementing Regulation No. 282/2011.
70. Article 1(2)(d)(i) of Council implementing Regulation No. 1042/2013 inserting Article 24 a and b in implementing Regulation No. 282/2011. Presumptions can be rebutted on the basis of three items of non-contradictory evidence. See L. Grençon, J. Denton (2014): '2015 VAT changes: the details and the practicalities', 6 ACE of 2014 at 16 to 19.
71. M. Lamensch (2014): 'The Treatment of Digital products and Other E-Services Under VAT', in M. Lang and I. Lejeune (eds.): 'VAT/GST in a Global Digital Economy', to be published (Kluwer).

The OECD has stressed this problem and held a public consultation regarding the place of taxation for B2C supplies of services.[72] The project notably proposes the use of two proxies, aimed at levying VAT on services and intangibles where it can reasonably be assumed that those services or intangibles are used or consumed. The first proxy targets the so-called *on-the-spot supplies* and sets out that the place of taxation is where the final consumer is located when consuming them. The second proxy targets all the other supplies, including electronically delivered services, and sets out that the place of taxation is the jurisdiction of the usual residence of the customer. In that respect, jurisdictions are encouraged to permit suppliers to rely on information collected in the course of their normal business activity such as information collected from the customer within business processes. It can notably be the jurisdiction of the bank account used for payment. The OECD project may not be the complete answer to the difficulties encountered, but it revamps the proxies currently in use, and, brings greater simplicity to the matter. In November 2015, representatives from countries and territories taking part in the third meeting of the OECD Global Forum[73] should ratify the proposed guidelines and, if so, the proxies currently in force may be subject to change.

Another matter is the VAT status of the customer. Under the new place-of-supply rules, the VAT status of the customer as a taxable person, or a non-taxable person, does not impact the place of taxation but it remains important as it determines the person liable to VAT (reverse charge applies only to taxable persons). In this context, the legislator requires that the VAT status of the customer is assumed in the absence of a VAT identification number:

> However, irrespective of information to the contrary, the supplier of telecommunications, broadcasting or electronically supplied services may regard a customer established within the Community as a non-taxable person as long as that customer has not communicated his individual VAT identification number to him.[74]

Under that provision, a supplier who has not been provided with the VAT identification number of a client is authorized to collect VAT, even though there is evidence that self-assessment is mandatory for the said client, therefore that there is evidence of its taxable person status. There is a risk of an element of double taxation as it is easier and less risky for the supplier to apply VAT on their supply (i.e., the scheme intended for non-taxable person), than to treat a client as a taxable person despite the absence of a VAT identification number: the burden of proof being incumbent on him

72. OCDE, 'Discussion Drafts for Public Consultation, International VAT/GST guidelines, guidelines on place of taxation for business-to-consumer supplies of services and intangibles' (2014) 6: '*These developments [that is the growth in international B2C trade in remotely supplied services and intangibles] created challenges for VAT systems, as the application of a proxy based on the supplier's location or the place of performance to determine the place of taxation is unlikely to lead to an appropriate result for such remote supplies.*'
73. The third meeting of the OECD Global Forum on VAT has been planned at the occasion of the second meeting of that same forum in Tokyo on 17–18 Apr. 2014, see 'Statement of Outcomes on the OECD International VAT/GST Guidelines'.
74. Article 1(2)(b) of Council implementing Regulation No. 1042/2013 inserting Article 18(2) in the implementing Regulation No. 282/2011 (n 48).

and therefore potentially, the liability for payment of VAT that would not have been invoiced.[75]

The clients' place and VAT status are not the sole questionable elements. The identification of the supplier is also at the origin of practical difficulties. When services are provided over telecommunications networks, a portal or, a Web interface, the number of actors in the distribution of the services as well as their implication can complicate the supplier's identification.[76] This identification is important to ensure the collection of the VAT, as the supplier is responsible for the VAT on e-supplies to final customers.[77] A wrong assessment by an e-trader of his liability could be disastrous for the preservation of his activity: in the case an e-trader would wrongfully believe to be free from VAT liability, thus not invoicing VAT to his client, he would, nonetheless, remain liable to pay VAT to the Treasury.[78]

In the face of the uncertainty regarding the supplier and thus the VAT liability, it was important [...] to ensure supplier confidence by providing for the long recognized EU principle of legal certainty.[79] The European legislator introduced a rebuttable presumption for the identification of the supplier: the supplier status is assumed for any person who takes part in the supply of electronic services on behalf of the provider of these services.[80] In practical terms this means that in the case of failure to meet the formal requirements specifically foreseen, each intermediary is deemed to have

75. Apart from its inherent defect, it is interesting to view this rule in the context of the Court's decision in Case C-273/11 *Mecsek-Gabona*. According to this decision, the zero-rating of an intra-Community delivery cannot be refused following a removal of the VAT registration number from the register with retroactive effect and, within the anti-fraud context, it is justified to apply a requirement of good faith. The comparison between that case law and the place-of-supply rule shows that in one situation the correct application of the VAT mechanism is preserved but that in the other it is not: whether the registration number can or cannot undermine the right to the correct VAT treatment. Furthermore, in one case good faith is given great importance and in the other, it is kicked into the long grass. CJEU Case C-273/11 *Mecsek-Gabona Kft v. Nemzeti Adó- és Vámhivatal Dél-dunántúli Regionális Adó Főigazgatósága,* [2012] ECR 547.
76. European Commission 'Explanatory notes' cited above.
77. New Article 58 of the VAT Directive applicable as from 1 Jan. 2015.
78. Article 193 of the VAT Directive.
79. According to settled CJEU case law, '*Community legislation must be certain and its application foreseeable by those subject to it*'. CJEU Case C-325/85, *Ireland v. Commission of the European Communities* [1987] ECR 5041 paragraph 18; See also CJEU Case C-325/91 *French Republic v. Commission of the European Communities* [1993] ECR I-3283 paragraph 26; Case C-30/89 Commission of the *European Communities v. French Republic* [1990] ECR I-691 paragraph 23; Case C-257/86 *Commission of the European Communities v. Italian Republic* [1988] ECR 3249 paragraph 12; Case C-370/07 *Commission of the European Communities v. Council of the European Union* [2009] ECR I-8917 paragraph 39. Before the CJEU, as [...] far back as the eighteenth century, Adam Smith wrote that the uncertainty in tax matters was not acceptable and that the tax rule had to be clear, precise, and intelligible. Adam Smith (1776), 'An Inquiry Into the Nature and Causes of the Wealth of Nations', book V, Ch. II, Part II: '*The time of payment, the manner of payment, the quantity to be paid, ought all to be clear and plain to the contributor, and to every other person.*'
80. Article 28 of the VAT Directive envisages the general legal situation upon which the presumption applicable to e-services is based. The presumption is found in Article 1(c) of Council implementing Regulation No. 1042/2013 inserting Article 9a in the implementing Regulation No. 282/2011 (n 48). The legal provision and its aims are explained in European Commission '*Explanatory notes*' at 3.4.1 and also in the contribution of S. Claessens, T. Corbette (2014):

supplied the e-services.[81] It should be pointed out that this presumption and its implementation are not in line with the simplification of the reporting requirements foreseen in the VAT package.

In addition to questions about the customers, the suppliers and the person liable for the VAT, the additional query that arises relates to the monitoring and control of transactions: e-traders established outside the EU could be reluctant to invoice EU VAT. In that context, the enforcement measures at the disposal of the EU are poorly adapted and, as a consequence, could, in the near future, be faced with a major 'exodus' of e-businesses. Switzerland has been identified as the country that is most likely to welcome EU e-immigrants. These immigrants would be bordering the EU and benefit from the efficient infrastructure and the qualified labour force of the country. Moreover, Switzerland does not impose VAT on the supply of electronic services outside of its borders therefore ensuring taxation neutrality for established e-traders.[82]

3.5 A LITTLE FURTHER ON, PAST THE FUTURE

In 2011, the communication from the Commission on the future of VAT prioritized the smooth introduction of the MOSS.[83] The Commission has created the means to meet its target: the system has been implemented progressively (the implementation has first been limited to certain services electronically delivered and to certain beneficiaries) and over a period of sixteen years.[84] The implementation has been supported by the publication of guidelines,[85] explanatory notes[86] and with seminars and workshops.[87]

'Intermediary delivery and third party billing: Implications for the operation of VAT systems around the world', conference 'The Future of VAT in a Digital Global Economy' Vienna, 24–26 Sep. 2014 (to be published).

81. The standard of proof for rebuttal to take place are listed in Article 1(c) of Council implementing Regulation No. 1042/2013 inserting Article 9a in the implementing Regulation No. 282/2011 (n 48).
82. Article 8 paragraph 1 Federal Act on Value Added Tax of 12 Jan. 2009 (SR 641.20) (CH).
83. See COM(2011) 851 final 'Communication from the Commission to the European Parliament, the Council and the European Economic and Social Committee on the future of VAT, Towards a simpler, more robust and efficient VAT system tailored to the single market', point 5.1.1.
84. Since July 2003 (i.e., since the E-Commerce VAT Directive, a one-stop scheme has developed and it will continue improving until 2019 (i.e., when the re-distribution of VAT revenue between Member States will be terminated). Most writing refer to the MOSS as if it had started in 2008 with the VAT package, neither wrong nor quite true, this vision forgets the experience acquired as from 2003 through the scheme for non-EU e-traders involved in B2C activities in the EU. In that respect, the Commission claimed in 2003 to intend to monitor the workings of this scheme because it had potential for a broader application in the intra-community context. See COM(2003) 822 final, Proposal for a Council Directive amending Directive 77/388/EEC as regards the place of supply of services.
85. European Commission, 'Guide to the VAT mini One Stop Shop' (2013) and 'Information for businesses signing up for the Mini One-Stop Shop – Additional guidelines – auditing under the MOSS'.
86. European Commission 'Explanatory notes', cited above.
87. Seminars and workshops have been held on the following locations and dates: Malta November 2008, Malmö June 2011, Luxembourg March 2012, Cyprus May 2013, and, the Netherlands November 2013. See 'Report from the Commission to the Council on Article 6 of Council Directive 2008/8/EC', COM(2014)380 final.

This approach has enabled the Member States, their e-traders and the rest of the world, to prepare for the new scheme.[88]

The Commission has remained true to its original intent to implement a one-stop-shop, and, now with the full trust that the MOSS will be a success,[89] the Commission envisages a broadening of the concept:

> The natural 'next step', and one that was envisaged in the Communication on the Future of VAT, is to introduce a broader One Stop Shop for all EU B2C supplies of goods and services. The current requirement for suppliers (above applicable thresholds) to register and account in each Member State to which it makes B2C supplies is a clear obstacle to cross border trade. Furthermore a broader One-Stop-Shop is a crucial instrument to facilitate access to the single market.... The Commission services consider that the development of the broader One Stop Shop should proceed as a priority.[90]

Apart from the fact that the MOSS is likely to have a positive effect on the motivation of businesses to comply with their VAT obligations and thus on the amount of VAT revenue collected, one may wonder what other reasons the Commission may have to be so dedicated to generalizing the MOSS. In that respect, it seems appropriate to look at the extent of the changes brought about by the MOSS and to understand how these may help shape the future of VAT.

An important change brought about by the MOSS is that the 'revenue rule', mos majorum of all, which states that one country cannot collect the tax revenue for another country, is facing extinction in Europe.[91] The mechanism of the MOSS under which EU taxable operators pay the VAT collected in one Member State to the treasury of another Member State, is an important factor in this decay. The principle that the place of taxation also determines the country where tax returns must be filed and VAT must be paid is also abandoned. This creates a mutual dependence between Member States as regards the collection of VAT and thus a mutual responsibility for each other's VAT revenue. A close cooperation is expected as a result of this mutual dependency, which should increase the intake of VAT revenue and which should, in the future, also allow the extension of MOSS to online distance sales of goods, supplies involving

88. For more details about these measures see, R. de la Feria (2014): 'Finance Act 2014 notes: section 103: VAT: special schemes; section 104: VAT: place of belonging; section 105: VAT: place of supply orders: disapplication of transitional provision; section 106: VAT: supply of services through agents; section 107: VAT: refunds to health service bodies; section 108: VAT: prompt payment discounts', British Tax Review 4 of 2014 at 431 (428–433). See also the report from the Commission to the Council on Article 6 of Council Directive 2008/8/EC, COM(2014)380 final.
89. The relatively low number of MOSS registrations in the first two months of functioning of the scheme does not appear alarming to D. Raponi who underlined that the scheme is at its very beginning. See J. Stanley-Smith (2015): 'MOSS registration figures lower than expected', International Tax Review of 4 Mar. 2015.
90. 'Working Paper on VAT issues – Follow up to the 2nd meeting of the Commission Expert Group on Taxation of the digital economy', Digit/007/2014, 31 Jan. 2014; see also COM(2011) 851 final, point 5.1.1 (n 84).
91. In relation to the 'revenue rule', the principle and its limitations, see Ph. Baker (1999): 'Transnational Enforcement of Tax Liabilities', British Tax Law Review of 1999 at 313–318; see also R. de la Feria (2014): 'Finance Act 2014 notes...', British Tax Review 4 of 2014.

installation or assembly, sales at exhibitions, fairs or markets, work on immovable property, etc.[92]

Beyond the technical level, Member States which now cooperate closely with one another through the VAT information exchange system (the so-called VIES) and, to a lesser extent, through requests for mutual assistance, should logically, thanks to the experience gained with the collection and re-distribution system of the MOSS, get over their discomfort and cooperate more easily, also on other issues.

Such a close cooperation between Member States could enable multilateral and simultaneous audits, which in turn should enable a more efficient intra-Community combating of VAT fraud. For the Commission this is an important objective in view of the sheer size of the VAT revenue gap (see Chapter 5), and of the fact that any decrease in the level of VAT fraud automatically means increased income for the Member States as well as the EU.[93] In addition, one could also hope that this mutual dependence will be the first step towards the application of qualified majority voting in the taxation field, so fervently supported by the Commission, in particular for practical issues that could facilitate the assessment and collection of VAT on cross border trade.[94] This voting system could help modernize and simplify the VAT legislation, including by means of streamlining VAT exemptions and derogations which result from the horse-trading attached to the unanimity rule and which, in most cases, infringe the very principles on which the VAT system is based.

As stated by Rita de la Feria, there is everything to gain with the MOSS and nothing to lose, '*no pressure then*'.[95]

92. Expert group on taxation of the digital economy, 'Working Paper on VAT issues – Follow up to the 1st meeting of the Commission Expert Group on Taxation of the digital economy' Digit/005/2014, 14–15 Jan. 2014, paragraph 3; See also COM(2004) 728 final 'Proposal for a Council Directive amending Directive 77/388/EEC with a view to simplifying value added tax obligations', part 2.
93. The budget of the European Union is financed at 99% from the communities' own resources (VAT is part of the communities' own resources).
94. The Commission has repeatedly demonstrated its support to qualified majority voting, see examples in F. Bolkestein (2003): 'Fiscalité européenne: la Convention fait fausse route', Le Monde of 12 Jun. 2003 Horizons-Débats at 16.
95. R. de la Feria (2014): 'Finance Act 2014 notes', British Tax Review 4 of 2014 at 433.

CHAPTER 4

Tax Assessment in a Digital Context: A Critical Analysis of the 2015 EU Rules

Marie Lamensch[*]

4.1 INTRODUCTION

A little revolution took place on 1 January 2015 for EU suppliers of electronically supplied services. Until that date, they were charging and collecting VAT at origin on all their supplies to non-taxable persons residing in the EU ('intra-EU B2C supplies').[1] Since 1 January 2015, they have to charge and collect VAT on these supplies at destination,[2] as was already the case on their supplies to taxable persons established in the EU ('intra-EU B2B supplies'),[3] and on their supplies to taxable and non-taxable

* Prof. Dr Marie Lamensch teaches VAT law at the Catholic University of Louvain (UCL) and International and European Taxation at the Institute for European Studies of the Vrije Universiteit Brussel (IES-VUB), where she also works as a postdoctoral research fellow. Her PhD thesis entitled: 'European Value-added Tax in the Digital Era: A Critical Analysis and Proposals for Reform' (and on which this contribution is based) will be published as Volume 36 in the Doctoral series of the IBFD.

1. In accordance with Article 45 of Council Directive 2006/112/EC of 28 Nov. 2006 on the common system of value-added-tax, O.J. 11 Dec. 2006 L347/1 (hereinafter: 'the VAT Directive'), which provides that: '*The place of supply of services to a non-taxable person shall be the place where the supplier has established his business. However, if those services are provided from a fixed establishment of the supplier located in a place other than the place where he has established his business, the place of supply of those services shall be the place where that fixed establishment is located. In the absence of such place of establishment or fixed establishment, the place of supply of services shall be the place where the supplier has his permanent address or usually resides*'.
2. In accordance with Article 58 c) of the VAT Directive as amended by Article 5 of Council Directive 2008/8 (applicable as of 1 Jan. 2015). This provision will read as follows: '*The place of supply of the following services to a non- taxable person shall be the place where that person is established, has his permanent address or usually resides: (…) (c) electronically supplied services, in particular those referred to in Annex II. Where the supplier of a service and the customer communicate via electronic mail, that shall not of itself mean that the service supplied is an electronically supplied service.*'
3. In accordance with Article 44 of the VAT Directive, which provides that: '*The place of supply of services to a taxable person acting as such shall be the place where that person has established his*

persons established/residing outside of the EU ('outbound B2B and B2C supplies').[4] Taxation at destination is the jurisdiction rule that also already applied since 2003 to non-EU suppliers of electronically supplied services on their supplies to taxable and non-taxable persons established/residing in the EU ('inbound B2B and B2C supplies').[5]

Taxing all electronically supplied services at destination is the only way to avoid distortions of consumption choices and establishment decisions.[6] The change of jurisdiction rule is therefore a positive development.[7] The flip side of the coin, however, is that implementing and enforcing a destination based consumption tax on electronically supplied services raises substantial practical difficulties from a tax

business. However, if those services are provided to a fixed establishment of the taxable person located in a place other than the place where he has established his business, the place of supply of those services shall be the place where that fixed establishment is located. In the absence of such place of establishment or fixed establishment, the place of supply of services shall be the place where the taxable person who receives such services has his permanent address or usually resides.'

4. Outbound B2B and B2C supplies are also already taxed at destination, thus outside the EU (Article 59k VAT Directive). Hence, they are not subject to EU VAT.
5. In accordance with Article 58 of the VAT Directive, which provides that: '*The place of supply of electronically supplied services, in particular those referred to in Annex II, when supplied to non-taxable persons who are established in a Member State, or who have their permanent address or usually reside in a Member State, by a taxable person who has established his business outside the Community or has a fixed establishment there from which the service is supplied, or who, in the absence of such a place of business or fixed establishment, has his permanent address or usually resides outside the Community, shall be the place where the non-taxable person is established, or where he has his permanent address or usually resides. Where the supplier of a service and the customer communicate via electronic mail, that shall not of itself mean that the service supplied is an electronically supplied service.*'
6. Because the same tax rules and thus the same tax burden applies to all supplies in destination-based taxes, irrespective of origin. On the contrary, in the absence of harmonization, origin based taxes cause revenue shifts in favour of net exporters and risk distorting competition and trade, because consumers prefer to buy from, and suppliers prefer to establish in, low VAT jurisdictions, in particular in the case of electronically supplied services which are made irrespective of 'location' and without transport costs.
7. And is in line with international recommendations. See OECD 2014 International VAT/GST guidelines on neutrality (available at http://www.oecd.org/ctp/consumption/international-vat-gst-guidelines.pdf), p. 7. Historically, the objective of the European Commission was to set up an origin based VAT in the interest of Internal Market without frontiers, but no agreement could be reached in the Council between the Member States because of tax rate diversity and revenue allocation concerns. That is why the 1993 transitional arrangements broadly provide for a destination based taxation of intra-EU B2B (and outbound) supplies of services, and for an origin based taxation of intra-EU B2C (and inbound) supplies of services (except for new means of transport and distance sales). When e-commerce started developing, however, it rapidly became clear that the application of the origin principle to intra-EU B2C supplies in that sector was untenable, because EU suppliers had to charge VAT on their supplies to EU consumers whereas their non-EU competitors were not obliged to do so (and EU and third country suppliers could supply cheaper from a low VAT Member State). Unsurprisingly therefore, Council Directive 2002/38 which introduced specific provisions for electronically supplied services in the VAT Directive (O.J. 15 May 2002, L 128/41) provided for the application of the destination principle to all supplies of electronically supplied services, to the exception of intra-EU B2C supplies. There were indeed political reasons why Member States could agree to switch to the destination principle for these supplies only from January 2015 onwards (essentially because Luxembourg was extremely reluctant to loose its status as e-hub for Europe, thanks to its low VAT rate (likewise for telecommunications services), and since Council decisions on taxation require unanimity it could insist on a long transitional period. The switch to a destination based taxation for intra-EU B2C electronically supplied services as of 2015 is one of the main reasons why Luxembourg will soon increase its VAT rate from 15% to 17%).

assessment and compliance perspective. In general terms, a destination based consumption tax indeed implies that suppliers must gather status and location information on their customers before each transaction is completed, because this information will determine the amount of tax to be charged and collected. As a matter of fact, in the case of intra-EU and inbound B2B supplies, suppliers need to ascertain that the supply is effectively made to a business customer established in another jurisdiction before proceeding to a zero-rated supply (on which the supplier incurs no VAT liability and the business customer is liable to VAT under the reverse charge system while being entitled to an input VAT credit and refund).[8] And in the case of inbound and intra-EU B2C supplies, they must know the location of the customer so as to correctly assess and collect the tax due. While these compliance obligations are already burdensome for suppliers of conventional services,[9] they prove particularly challenging in the case of electronically supplied services, because of the scarcity of reliable information concerning customers and because of the very short time frame in which the transactions, and related tax assessment, is expected to take place.

Against this background, this contribution seeks to summarize and comment the rules concerning customer identification and location for VAT assessment purposes in the context of electronically supplied services.

4.2 IDENTIFYING AND LOCATING CUSTOMERS OF ELECTRONICALLY SUPPLIED SERVICES: A SUMMARY AND CRITICAL ANALYSIS OF THE CURRENT RULES

4.2.1 General

Effective since 1 July 2011, Council Regulation 282/2011 (see Appendix III)[10] seeks to provide guidance on the question of customer identification and location in the case of supplies of services taxable at destination (all of them, not only electronically supplied services). Accordingly, it is applicable to intra-EU B2C supplies only since the 1 January 2015. On that same date, Council Regulation1042/213 (see Appendix IV)[11] entered into

8. In accordance with Article 194 of the VAT Directive, which provides that '*1. Where the taxable supply of goods or services is carried out by a taxable person who is not established in the Member State in which the VAT is due, Member States may provide that the person liable for payment of VAT is the person to whom the goods or services are supplied.* (...)'. The OECD 2014 International VAT/GST guidelines on the place of taxation of B2B supplies of services and intangibles (available at http://www.oecd.org/ctp/consumption/international-vat-gst-guidelines.pdf) pt. 3.45 confirms that: '*the tax administration of the supplier may therefore require the supplier to produce evidence that the customer is a business and that this business is located in another jurisdiction.*'.
9. See I. Lejeune, E. Cortvriend and D. Accorsi (2011): 'Implementing Measures Relating to EU Place-of-Supply Rules: Are Business Issues Solved and Certainty Provided?' 22 International VAT Monitor 3 of 2011 at 144.
10. Council Regulation 282/2011 of 15 Mar. 2011 laying down implementing measures for Directive 2006/112/EC on the common system of value-added-tax, O.J. 23 Mar. 2011, L 77/1.
11. Council Directive 2013/43/EU of 22 Jul. 2013 amending Directive 2006/112/EC on the common system of value-added-tax, as regards an optional and temporary application of the reverse charge mechanism in relation to supplies of certain goods and services susceptible to fraud, OJ L 201, 26.7.2013, p. 4–6.

effect. This Regulation substantially amends Council Regulation 282/2011. The amendments concern both EU and non-EU suppliers in respect of their B2C and (to a lesser extent to) B2B supplies (See Appendices III and IV for the relevant provisions of these Regulations). The European Commission has released very detailed explanatory notes for these new implementing provisions that are, however, not binding on Member States, some of whom have already expressed their disagreement with the interpretations proposed by the European Commission.[12] Based on Council Regulations 282/2011 and 1042/2013 (and the explanatory notes, keeping in mind their non-binding and controversial nature), the rules concerning customers' identification and location for VAT assessment purposes in the case of electronically supplied services can be summarized as follows.

4.2.2 Customer Identification

In the case of outbound B2B supplies to third countries, suppliers of electronically supplied services are expected, under Article 18(3) of Council Regulation 282/2011, to obtain a certificate issued by the customer's competent tax authorities as confirmation that the customer is engaged in economic activities.[13] In the absence of such a certificate, they should obtain a VAT number or a similar number that is attributed to the customer by the country of establishment and that is used to identify businesses. Alternatively, they should rely on: '*any other proof which demonstrates that the customer is a taxable person and if the supplier carries out a reasonable level of verification of the accuracy of the information provided by the customer, by normal commercial security measures such as those relating to identity or payment checks*'.[14] No amendment of this provision is foreseen under Council Regulation 1042/2013.

In our view, these verification requirements are very difficult, if not impossible, to implement in a digital context as may be illustrated by some basic questions. First, on what basis does the EU legislator assume that third countries are at all prepared to issue such certificates (in particular in the absence of international mutual assistance agreements), and if so, what information should be contained in these certificates and in what language should they be drawn up? Second, the notion of a VAT number or a similar number may not even exist in certain third countries and even if it does and the number can be obtained, how can it possibly be verified by the supplier that the number actually corresponds to a specific taxpayer. Third, the requirement that '*any*

12. European Commission (2014): Explanatory Notes for Council Regulation 1042/2013, available at http://ec.europa.eu/taxation_customs/resources/documents/taxation/vat/how_vat_works/telecom/explanatory_notes_2015_en.pdf (hereinafter 'European Commission explanatory notes') (see Appendix V).
13. Article 18(3)a) provides that: '*3. Unless he has information to the contrary, the supplier may regard a customer established outside the Community as a taxable person: (a) if he obtains from the customer a certificate issued by the customer's competent tax authorities as confirmation that the customer is engaged in economic activities in order to enable him to obtain a refund of VAT under Council Directive 86/560/EEC of 17 November 1986 on the harmonization of the laws of the Member States relating to turnover taxes – Arrangements for the refund of value added tax to taxable persons not established in Community territory (2).*'
14. Article 18(3)b) of Council Regulation 282/2011.

other proof be considered casts doubt on the extent of suppliers' verification obligations (does it refer to any other proof that the supplier 'has' or that he should 'look for'?), and also seems unrealistic in view of the context in which supplies of electronically supplied services are taking place. In that respect, such extensive verification obligations are actually quite surprising in view of the fact that 'electronically supplied services' are defined under the VAT Directive as 'automated' in their delivery and content and made with 'minimal human intervention'.[15] It indeed seems a contradiction, on the one hand, to define 'electronically supplied services' as automated and made with minimal human intervention but, on the other hand, to require transaction based and clearly 'human' processed verifications for tax assessment purposes.

This having been said, the scope of application of Article 18(3) is actually quite limited, because outbound supplies to third countries are generally not subject to EU VAT. Accordingly, once the supplier has determined that a client is established or resides outside of the EU, he can proceed to a VAT free supply, without further need for status verifications (as illustrated below, however, the question of customer location is not so easy to settle).

In cases of intra-EU and inbound B2B supplies in which the business customer does not communicate a VAT number, Article 18(2) of Council regulation 282/2011 allows, as a general rule, suppliers to deny him status as a taxable person '*unless (the supplier) has information to the contrary*'. Since 1 January 2015, suppliers of electronically supplied services '*may*' deny taxable status to an EU customer who has not communicated a VAT number, without having to consider '*information to the contrary*'.[16] This amendment was no doubt meant to provide relief to suppliers. In practice, however, the risk of losing the customers to which a supplier would deny taxable status should not be underestimated, because a taxable person who is refused the benefit of the reverse charge system would not be able to eventually deduct any VAT charged to him. In that respect, the explanatory notes for Council Regulation 1042/2013 actually confirm that a customer initially treated as a non-taxable person should not be able to eventually recover his input VAT. The notes, however, add that he should be given the possibility, within a reasonable time,[17] to rectify the situation with the supplier, who would need to make the necessary adjustments, which may imply refunding any VAT previously charged.[18] This clarification is, in our view, not satisfactory, however, first,

15. Article 7(1) of Council Regulation 282/2011 indeed provides that: '*Electronically supplied services' as referred to in Directive 2006/112/EC shall include services which are delivered over the Internet or an electronic network and the nature of which renders their supply essentially automated and involving minimal human intervention, and impossible to ensure in the absence of information technology.*'
16. With effect as of 1 Jan. 2015, Council Directive 1042/2013 adds the following second subparagraph: '*However, irrespective of information to the contrary, the supplier of (...) electronic services may regard a customer established within the Community as a non-taxable person as long as that customer has not communicated his individual VAT identification number to the supplier.*' The explanatory notes confirm that the provision is optional for suppliers, as long as the customer has not communicated his VAT number. European Commission explanatory notes p. 48.
17. European Commission explanatory notes p. 50.
18. European Commission explanatory notes p. 50. The notes highlight that only the circumstances existing at the time of the taxable event are relevant. It is thus only when the customer qualified as a taxable person at the moment of the taxable event but was not able to provide a VAT

because the possibility of a late adjustment may not be entirely convincing for a customer who still might be tempted to look for another supplier who would immediately treat him as a taxable person and, second, because numerous adjustment demands would again substantially increase the compliance burden and costs for suppliers of electronically supplied services.

Finally, the explanatory notes provide that even when a customer communicates a VAT number that has been successfully verified and there is no information suggesting that the customer is not a taxable person, the supplier may still, in case of doubt, decide that the communication of the VAT number is not sufficient.[19] Not only does this clarification mean that taxable persons are not certain they can purchase electronically supplied services and be treated as taxable persons in these transactions, but also that the Member States may consider that in some cases even a verified VAT number is not enough, which increases the legal uncertainty surrounding customer identification from a suppliers' perspective, even though identification verifications are to be carried out in the context of transactions taking place in an automated fashion, with minimal human intervention.

In the case of intra-EU and inbound B2B supplies, even if the business customer does communicate a VAT number, this information is not always verifiable because of the limits of the VIES. For example, the current VIES only allows for the uploading of VAT numbers attributed to suppliers who are themselves engaged in intra-EU supplies, so that a supplier who only supplies domestically (but who buys his input cross-border) will not be able to prove that he has a valid VAT number through the VIES system. This is not a minor issue in view of the fact that the OECD recently reported that businesses rely more on the Internet for purchasing than for selling (e.g., in 2010, on average, 35 % of all businesses with ten or more persons employed used the Internet for purchasing, and only 18 % for selling goods and services).[20]

Another delicate situation occurs when the VIES confirms the validity of a VAT number but does not display the corresponding name and address. In that case, the question arises whether and how suppliers are expected to verify that the VAT number corresponds to the name and address given by the customer, as required by Article 18(1) of Council Regulation 282/2011?[21] Also, how are they expected to verify whether a customer is perhaps using a VAT number and matching name and address that do not belong to him at all? Moreover, in a sector in which transactions are concluded 365 days per year, and 24 hours a day, any temporary unavailability of the VIES is also most

number at that time that a rectification is possible, and not when the customer was not yet a taxable person at the time of the taxable event but becomes one shortly after.

19. European Commission explanatory notes p. 50.
20. OECD (2012): 'Internet Economy Outlook 2012 highlights', OECD Publishing, http://www.oecd.org/sti/ieconomy/internet-economy-outlook-2012-highlights.pdf p. 4.
21. European Commission website, FAQ on the VIES, Question no. 15: '*Is it possible to have the name and/or the address linked to a VAT number?*' Answer: '*Certain Member States permit the display of the name and address of the taxable person where the VAT number is currently valid. If no name/address is displayed, this means that the relevant Member State does not permit the display of this data. Customers have the right to get confirmation from their own tax administration if a VAT identification number is associated with a name and/or address.*'

problematic.[22] In short, whenever the VIES cannot be relied on for whatever reason, we do not see how suppliers can verify EU VAT numbers on a real time basis.

More fundamentally, transaction based verification requirements seem unrealistic for supplies of electronically supplied services, and again surprising in view of the fact that these supplies are defined under the VAT Directive as 'automated' in their delivery and content and made with 'minimal human intervention'.[23]

4.2.3 Customer Location

4.2.3.1 The General Rules of Council Regulation 282/2011

As regards customer location,[24] in the case of intra-EU B2B supplies to customers located in a single jurisdiction, suppliers must identify the place of establishment or usual residence of their customers.[25] For that purpose, they must rely on information received from those customers (self-identification), but should then verify that information by: '*normal commercial security measures such as those relating to identity or payment checks*'.[26] Possible limitations to the availability and reliability of VAT numbers for identification purposes were already discussed above, and the same conclusions can be drawn regarding the location information that a customer's VAT number can provide. Other identity information could possibly be drawn from the billing address provided by the customer, but this type of data can, in our view, not be considered as a reliable indicator in the context of electronically supplied services, because the customer does not need the supplier to know where he resides, and giving

22. European Commission website, FAQ on the VIES, Question no. 14: What do I have to do if the web site does not run? Answer: '*The Commission's web site is a real-time system which checks the validity of VAT identification numbers against the databases maintained by Member States. In other words, when you check a number, it is the database of that Member State that is being checked. Some parts of the system may be unavailable at certain times due to the necessity to back-up the Member States' databases. This is a known problem, and the Commission is working with Member States to ensure that the length of time that their databases are down for updating is kept to a minimum.*'
23. As provided by Article 7(1) of Council Regulation 282/2011 (cited above).
24. As noted above, the question of customer location is key in the case of outbound supplies because both outbound B2B and B2C supplies are untaxed. It is also important in the case of inbound (and as of 2015 also intra-EU) B2C supplies because the location of the customer determines under which rules the supplier must assess tax (e.g., which tax rate applies, taking into account local reduced rates and exemptions) and to which jurisdiction VAT must be remitted through the one-stop-scheme (see next section). Finally, the location of the customer is also important in the case of intra-EU and inbound B2B supplies, because only cross-border supplies to EU business customers can be reverse charged.
25. That is, the place of taxation under Article 44 of the VAT Directive.
26. Article 20 of Council Regulation 282/2011 provides that: '*Where a supply of services carried out for a taxable person, or a non-taxable legal person deemed to be a taxable person, falls within the scope of Article 44 of Directive 2006/112/EC, and where that taxable person is established in a single country, or, in the absence of a place of establishment of a business or a fixed establishment, has his permanent address and usually resides in a single country, that supply of services shall be taxable in that country. The supplier shall establish that place based on information from the customer, and verify that information by normal commercial security measures such as those relating to identity or payment checks. The information may include the VAT identification number attributed by the Member State where the customer is established.*'

a wrong billing address with the objective to obtain a lower VAT rate will have no consequences for him. Finally, suppliers do not always have access to payment details (e.g., when the transaction passes through intermediaries such as *Paypal*) or when the customer uses 'e-cash', in which case his payments are totally anonymous.[27]

In more complicated (but quite common) situations of intra-EU B2B supplies to customers located in several countries, verification obligations are even more challenging. When the supply is made to a fixed establishment of the customer located in another jurisdiction that is receiving the service and using it for its own needs, the supply is indeed deemed to take place there.[28] Beyond the question of the costs associated with these verifications, legal certainty is not ensured because the concept of fixed establishment itself (which is defined as: '*any establishment other than the place where the taxable person has established his business characterized by a certain degree of permanence and suitable structure in terms of human and technical resources to enable it to receive and use the services supplied to it for its own needs or to provide the services which it supplies, respectively*'),[29] may be interpreted differently by each Member State (it being understood that this issue is not specific to electronically supplied services).[30]

More fundamentally, the question also remains open how suppliers of electronically supplied services are at all able to determine whether a fixed establishment has: '*a sufficient degree of permanence and a suitable structure in terms of human and technical resources to receive and use the service*', or whether it acquires a given supply for its own need or is acquiring (or paying) the supply for mere organizational reasons within the company, and therefore whether it should effectively benefit from a zero-rated supply under reverse charging. For example, a provider of electronically supplied services providing market reports or statistics should be able to determine whether the fixed establishment acquiring one of his products is able to, and is effectively going to, use it for its own needs, and is not simply acting as paymaster among the several entities of the company. Council Regulation 282/2011 clarifies that in order to determine that a customer's fixed establishment is going to use a supply, suppliers are expected to consider the '*nature and use*' of the supply provided.[31] Where the nature and use of the supply provided do not allow identifying the fixed establishment to which the service is provided, suppliers are expected to:

27. E-cash is currently still in its infancy but is likely to develop in the coming years.
28. Article 21 of Council Regulation 282/2011 provides that: '*Where a supply of services to a taxable person, or a non-taxable legal person deemed to be a taxable person, falls within the scope of Article 44 of Directive 2006/112/EC, and the taxable person is established in more than one country, that supply shall be taxable in the country where that taxable person has established his business. However, where the service is provided to a fixed establishment of the taxable person located in a place other than that where the customer has established his business, that supply shall be taxable at the place of the fixed establishment receiving that service and using it for its own needs. Where the taxable person does not have a place of establishment of a business or a fixed establishment, the supply shall be taxable at his permanent address or usual residence.*'
29. Article 11 of Council Regulation 282/2011.
30. I. Lejeune, E. Cortvriend and D. Accorsi (2011): 'Implementing Measures Relating to EU Place-of-Supply Rules: Are Business Issues Solved and Certainty Provided?', 22 International VAT Monitor 3 at 147.
31. Article 22 paragraph 1 of Council Regulation 282/2011.

> pay particular attention to whether the contract, the order form and the VAT identification number attributed by the Member State of the customer and communicated to him by the customer identify the fixed establishment as the customer of the service and whether the fixed establishment is the entity paying for the service.[32]

Finally, in cases in which the customer's fixed establishment to which the supply is made cannot be determined in accordance with these elements, or in cases in which supplies are made under: '*a contract covering one or more services used in an unidentifiable and non-quantifiable manner*', suppliers may legitimately consider that the supply has been provided at the place where the customer has established his business.[33] In a digital context, these respective verifications and case by case assessments may, in our view, be very difficult to comply with, because electronically supplied services are 'automated' supplies, made with 'minimal human intervention' under the VAT Directive. Council Regulation 1042/2013 does not address the issue.

An even more delicate scenario concerns the location of the customer in the case of inbound and intra-EU B2C supplies,[34] for which self-identification verified by suppliers is also the rule.[35] In the absence of 'official' information available for non-taxable persons (such as a VAT number), verifications must be made on the basis of: '*normal commercial security measures such as those relating to identity or payment checks*'.[36] Fact is, however, that suppliers again do not always have access to payment details (e.g., when the transaction passes through intermediaries such as *Paypal* or if the customer uses e-cash), and it remains unclear to us what the EU legislator means by 'identity checks' that could be performed by the supplier of electronically supplied services to non-taxable persons, be it from a legal, commercial or timing perspective (once again taking into account that the category 'electronically supplied services' only covers supplies that are 'automated', made with 'minimal human intervention').[37]

Additional verifications are furthermore needed when the consumer is established in more than one country or has his permanent address in one country and his usual residence in another (multiple location customer). In that case, the supplier must determine the: '*place that best ensures taxation at the place of actual consumption*'.[38]

---

32. Article 22 paragraph 2 of Council Regulation 282/2011.
33. Article 22 paragraph 3 of Council Regulation 282/2011.
34. Concerning status, as discussed above, a supplier may consider that a client is a non-taxable person when he has not been communicated a VAT registration number or '*any other proofs*' or has '*information to the contrary*'. As concluded above, this provision is not readily implementable with legal certainty and in a timely fashion. It may furthermore involve delicate 'commercial' decisions from the side of the supplier.
35. In accordance with Article 23(1) of Council Regulation 282/2011.
36. Article 23(2) of Council Regulation 282/2011.
37. Would 'identity check' relate to the customer's Internet Protocol (IP) address? As will be discussed below, IP addresses are not reliable as proxies. In addition, in Case C-70/10 *Scarlet/SABAM* the CJEU decided that IP addresses are personal data because they allow those users to be precisely identified (paragraph 51). The European Commission also took the view that IP addresses are personal data in its recent proposals to reform the EU data protection framework. European Commission (2012a): 'Data protection reform: Frequently asked questions' MEMO/12/403.
38. Article 24(2) of Council Regulation 282/2011 before its amendment by Council Regulation 1042/2013.

Council Regulation 1042/2013 clarifies this concept by introducing a hierarchy. For non-taxable legal persons central administration comes first, unless there is evidence that the service is used at a fixed establishment. For non-taxable natural persons, the place of residence comes first, unless there is evidence that the service is used at the permanent address.

Quite unfortunately, Council Regulation 1042/2013 does not give any guidance either on how to determine where these places are effectively located, or on how to determine that consumption occurs at a fixed establishment or at a permanent address (i.e., the lowest ranked proxy). For example, a provider of electronically supplied services may not in all reasonableness be expected to be able to determine whether a consumer will listen to the music or watch the movies he has downloaded, at his principal or secondary residence. Nor may he be expected to be able to determine whether a private customer *is* a multiple or single location customer, hence whether the tax should be assessed in accordance with the rules applicable in the country of residence or establishment of the customer or whether further investigation should be performed to determine the place that: '*best ensures taxation at the place of actual consumption*'. In practice, how are suppliers supposed to settle that question? Should they ask their customers to describe their specific situation as part of the self-identification procedure? Should they explain to their customers the different places of supply that apply depending on the situation of the customer? Are suppliers responsible to make sure that a customer understands the rules? And in cases in which a customer declares having a second residence or an establishment other than his principal establishment where the service will be used, how can suppliers verify that information? More fundamentally again, it is regrettable that transaction based verification obligations are imposed on suppliers of electronically supplied services because they seem incompatible with the nature of their offer. For B2C supplies in particular, a related element that should not be underestimated is the average sales price and profit margin of electronically supplied services and the high number of daily transactions ('low value high volume'). Many electronically supplied services are indeed cheap (e.g., a few cents or a couple of euros for a song) and the number of daily cross-border transactions is much higher than in conventional commerce. This means that imposing transaction-based verifications may risk causing costs equal to or even exceeding the benefit of most transactions.

Finally, when a Member State makes use of the 'use and enjoyment' clause,[39] EU suppliers are required to consider that supplies made within their territory or outside the EU should, respectively, be taxed outside the EU or within their territory if this is

39. Article 59a of the VAT Directive provides that: '*In order to prevent double taxation, non-taxation or distortion of competition, Member States may, with regard to services the place of supply of which is governed by Articles 44, 45, 56 and 59: (a) consider the place of supply of any or all of those services, if situated within their territory, as being situated outside the Community if the effective use and enjoyment of the services takes place outside the Community; (b) consider the place of supply of any or all of those services, if situated outside the Community, as being situated within their territory if the effective use and enjoyment of the services takes place within their territory. However, this provision shall not apply to the electronically supplied services where those services are rendered to non- taxable persons not established within the Community.*'

where the supplies are effectively 'used and enjoyed'.[40] We do not see how this clause could apply in a digital context. As a matter of fact, in the absence of any contacts between the parties and the high speed of transactions, we don't see how suppliers could determine whether an electronically supplied service was effectively used and enjoyed at the place where it was supplied. This is particularly the case because of the way 'electronically supplied services' are defined under the VAT Directive (see above). How could suppliers of such products be able to assess the actual place of consumption of these fully 'automated' supplies? Neither the VAT Directive nor Council Regulation 282/2011 offers any implementation criteria. Accordingly, this clause should, in our view, be suppressed, also because it seeks to localize effective consumption, which is at odds with the general reliance on proxies for defining the place-of-supply for VAT purposes.

4.2.3.2 The Specific Rules of Council Regulation 1042/2013

4.2.3.2.1. General

Effective since 1 January 2015, Council Regulation 1042/2013 provides for a series of presumptions that should apply when it proves: '*extremely difficult, if not practically impossible, for the supplier to know where the customer is actually established, has his permanent address or usually resides*'.[41] It remains unclear whether to '*know*' in this case actually means '*to verify*' customer location on the basis of the rules described above, but we assume that it is indeed only when these verifications have remained unfruitful that suppliers should rely on the presumptions. The questions may, however, be raised whether suppliers are aware of the fact that they cannot directly rely on the presumptions but should first try to apply the normal rules, and whether they will have to demonstrate to the tax administration that their efforts have remained unfruitful to justify the use of the presumptions at the stage of the audit. Last but not least, the question may also be raised whether the presumptions are an improvement, i.e., whether they effectively facilitate suppliers' task and increase legal certainty.

4.2.3.2.2. The Presumptions

A first presumption (the '*wi-fi hotspot and internet café presumption*')[42] is applicable in cases of intra-EU and inbound B2B, B2C and use and enjoyment supplies that are delivered at a certain location at which the recipient is physically present (such as a wi-fi hotspot, an Internet café, a restaurant or a hotel lobby).[43] These supplies are

40. Article 59a) of the VAT Directive as amended by Council Directive 2008/8 (applicable as of 1 Jan. 2015).
41. European Commission explanatory notes p. 55.
42. Article 24a paragraphs 1 and 2 of Council Regulation 1042/2013.
43. A 'wi-fi hotspot' is a wireless access point providing Internet access to mobile devices such as laptop or smartphone, typically available in public locations such as public parks, university campuses, but also in restaurants and hotel lobbies. The question is then what do 'Restaurants

taxable at that location, on the presumption that the supply is effectively used and enjoyed there (first paragraph of the '*wi-fi hotspot and internet café presumption*').[44] This presumption thus seeks to tax electronically supplied services at the place where the customer is effectively located when he uses them (except for supplies made on board a means of transport, which are taxed in the country of departure under the second paragraph of the '*wi-fi hotspot and internet café presumption*').[45]

Importantly, the explanatory notes clarify that this presumption is only applicable for supplies '*rendered by the supplier at his location*' (e.g., the supply of access to the Internet at a wi-fi hotspot), thus excluding '*over the top*' or 'subsequent' supplies (e.g., the supplies which are subsequently purchased by the customer through the Internet access provided at a wi-fi hotspot).[46] The '*wi-fi hotspot and internet café presumption*' thus seems to mostly concern telecommunication and broadcasting services,[47] although in rare cases it could also concern electronically supplied services, for example, when a supplier offers '*gaming relying on localized servers in cafés or kiosks*' (example provided in the explanatory notes).[48] Such cases are admittedly extremely rare because it is only when gaming is effectively '*delivered*' to the customer '*over the Internet or an electronic network*',[49] and not when the customer pays to play from a machine with a software program pre-installed in the machine and without Internet connection, that the presumption applies. The list of 'places' provided for under Article 24a paragraph 1 is only illustrative ('*such as*').

---

and hotel lobbies' cover. This wording perhaps allows distinguishing between restaurants and hotels' wi-fi hotspots allowing customers to access the Internet via their own devices, and cases in which a computer is made available to customers in a restaurant or a hotel for accessing the Internet (no clarification of this wording in the explanatory notes).

44. Article 24a of Council Regulation 282/2011 as amended by Council Regulation 1042/2013 provides: '*1. Where a supplier of (...) electronic services provides those services at a location such as a telephone box, a telephone kiosk, a wi-fi hotspot, an internet café, a restaurant or a hotel lobby where the physical presence of the recipient of the service at that location is needed for the service to be rendered to him by that supplier, the presumption shall be that, for the application of Articles 44, 58 and 59a of Directive 2006/112/EC, the customer is established, has his permanent address or usually resides at the place of that location and the service is effectively used and enjoyed there. 2. If the location referred to in paragraph 1 of this Article is on board a ship, aircraft or train carrying out a passenger transport operation within the Community pursuant to Articles 37 and 57 of Directive 2006/112/EC, the country of the location shall be the country of departure of the passenger transport operation.*' This presumption applies to B2B (Article 44 VAT Directive) and B2C supplies (Article 58 VAT Directive) and to situations where the use and enjoyment clause is applicable (Article 59a VAT Directive).
45. Article 24a paragraph 2 further provides that in case these places are located on board a ship, plane or train during a passenger transport operation within the Community, the supply is presumed to be made (i.e., taxation must take place) in the country of departure of the passenger transport operation. This provision only concerns transport operations within the Community without any stopover outside of the Community, and the point of departure is determined by the entire journey of the means of transport (within the Community) and not by the journey completed by each passenger (in line with Articles 37 and 57 of the VAT Directive concerning the supply of goods and services on board ships, aircraft or trains).
46. European Commission explanatory notes p. 56.
47. Article 6a(g) of Council Regulation 282/2011.
48. European Commission explanatory notes p. 56.
49. Article 7(1) of Council Regulation 282/2011 (definition of electronically supplied services).

A second presumption (the '*fixed land line presumption*') concerns intra-EU and inbound B2C supplies of electronically supplied services made to a customer through his fixed landline. These supplies are taxable at the place of installation of the fixed landline.[50] According to the explanatory notes, this corresponds to '*the place where the services will be used*' and '*the presumption is that the customer belongs there*'.[51] But the explanatory notes add that this '*fixed land line presumption*' in fact should only apply when there is '*a link between the fixed land line and the customer*', which in practice means that it should only apply to residential landlines, and not to landlines used for running a business.[52] The explanatory notes further clarify that '*fixed main line*' should cover '*copper wire*', '*fiber optic cable*', '*broadband cable*', '*other type of cable used to transmit data to premises*' and '*satellite*'.[53] The term 'fixed land line' thus allows for both wired and wireless (wi-fi) connections to the Internet (a wi-fi landline based access to the Internet being different than the wi-fi hotspot discussed above).

A third presumption (the '*mobile network presumption*') concerns intra-EU and inbound B2C supplies of electronically supplied services made through mobile networks. These supplies are taxable in the country identified by the mobile country code of the SIM card used when receiving those services.[54] The explanatory notes clarify that this should only apply to those supplies received (and charged) through the SIM card (e.g., when the supply is delivered by SMS), and thus to supplies of digitized products and services via a traditional telecommunication network, in which case the customer will typically be charged the basic rate for the telecom service (the SMS) and a surcharge to pay for the electronically supplied service.[55] The '*mobile network presumption*' also covers cases in which the customer pays with a prepaid SIM card (in which case the cost of the electronically supplied service is deducted from the customer's credit on the prepaid card).[56] This presumption thus seems to concern supplies that are not made via the Internet but via a traditional telecommunication network, although its actual scope of application may not be entirely clear as will be discussed below.

A fourth presumption ('*the decoder presumption*') concerns intra-EU and inbound B2C supplies of electronically services supplied by making use of a decoder (or viewing card). These supplies are taxable at the place where the decoder is located (or

50. Article 24b(a) of Council Regulation 282/2011 as amended by Council Regulation 1042/2013 provides: '*(...) where telecommunications, broadcasting or electronically supplied services are supplied to a non-taxable person:(a) through his fixed landline, it shall be presumed that the customer is established, has his permanent address or usually resides at the place of installation of the fixed landline*'.
51. European Commission explanatory notes p. 58.
52. European Commission explanatory notes p. 58.
53. European Commission explanatory notes p. 13.
54. Article 24b(b) of Council Regulation 282/2011 as amended by Council Regulation 1042/2013 provides: '*(...) where telecommunications, broadcasting or electronically supplied services are supplied to a non-taxable person: (b) through mobile networks, it shall be presumed that the place where the customer is established, has his permanent address or usually resides is the country identified by the mobile country code of the SIM card used when receiving those services*'.
55. European Commission explanatory notes p. 59.
56. European Commission explanatory notes p. 59.

to which the viewing card is sent).[57] This presumption only applies when the device is sold with the installation to use it and when the viewing card is sent to the customer, and thus applies to supplies of content and services through a traditional broadcasting network. If a fixed landline is used together with a decoder or a viewing card, the fixed landline presumption applies.[58] This type of supply that is delivered through traditional broadcasting networks and not via the Internet will not be further analysed in this contribution.[59]

A fifth presumption (the '*other circumstances presumption*') is applicable in cases of intra-EU and inbound B2C supplies of electronically supplied services made in other circumstances. These supplies are taxable at the place identified by the supplier on the basis of two items of non-contradictory evidence[60] that are taken from a non-exhaustive list, such as:

> (a) the billing address of the customer; (b) the internet Protocol (IP) address of the device used by the customer or any method of geolocation; (c) bank details such as the location of the bank account used for payment or the billing address of the customer held by that bank; (d) the Mobile Country Code (MCC) of the International Mobile Subscriber Identity (IMSI) stored on the Subscriber Identity Module (SIM) card used by the customer; (e) the location of the customer's fixed landline through which the service is supplied to him; (f) other commercially relevant information.[61]

The supplier decides which two items he considers most reliable and the tax administration may only challenge his choice in case there are indications of misuse or abuse by the supplier.[62] The explanatory notes hold that this method would allow for sufficient flexibility because the supplier can use '*any commercially relevant information*', and that it will be appropriate to embrace any future services and technologies.

A sixth presumption (the '*hotel presumption*') concerns electronically supplied intra-EU and inbound B2C and B2B services that are supplied together with accommodation (in the hotel sector or similar). These supplies are deemed to be supplied at this

57. Article 24b(c) of Council Regulation 282/2011 as amended by Council Regulation 1042/2013, provides: '*(...) where telecommunications, broadcasting or electronically supplied services are supplied to a non-taxable person: (c) for which the use of a decoder or similar device or a viewing card is needed and a fixed landline is not used, it shall be presumed that the customer is established, has his permanent address or usually resides at the place where that decoder or similar device is located, or if that place is not known, at the place to which the viewing card is sent with a view to being used there (...)*'.
58. European Commission explanatory notes p. 59.
59. In this case the supplier will not be confronted with the same difficulties as suppliers of electronically supplied services to assess the tax because the parties already 'know' each other in the context of a broader broadcasting contractual relationship.
60. Article 24b(d) of Council Regulation 282/2011 as amended by Council Regulation 1042/2013 provides: '*(...) where telecommunications, broadcasting or electronically supplied services are supplied to a non-taxable person: (d) under circumstances other than those referred to in Article 24a and in points (a), (b) and (c) of this Article, it shall be presumed that the customer is established, has his permanent address or usually resides at the place identified as such by the supplier on the basis of two items of non-contradictory evidence as listed in Article 24f of this Regulation*'.
61. Article 24b(f) of Council Regulation 282/2011 as amended by Council Regulation 1042/2013.
62. European Commission explanatory notes p. 60.

location,[63] but in the same way as the '*wi-fi hotspot and internet café presumption*', this '*hotel presumption*' does not cover over the top supplies.[64]

Finally, a seventh presumption (the '*abuse presumption*') applies in case of 'abuse'. For these supplies, three pieces of non-contradictory evidence from the list referred to above may be used by the supplier and the tax administration to rebut some or all of the above presumptions[65] (but a *de minimis* rule applies to the '*wi-fi hotspot and internet café presumption*' for which suppliers should not be expected to make further verifications in view of the occasional nature and traditionally low value of the supplies made at such specific locations).[66]

4.2.3.2.3. Analysis

A general remark concerns the legality of these presumptions. Not only does it seem rather odd to use a Regulation to implement another Regulation, while in effect implementing a Directive, but the question also arises what the legal status of the presumptions is whenever the implementing regulation changes the rules provided for in the VAT Directive.[67] Another source of concern is that, and surprisingly perhaps, when tested as to their relevance (for implementing the proxy of the residence/establishment of the non-taxable customer and in general), their reliability (for being

63. New Article 31c of Council Regulation 282/2011 as amended by Council Regulation 1042/2013, provides: '*For the purpose of determining the place of supply of telecommunications, broadcasting or electronically supplied services provided by a taxable person acting in his own name together with accommodation in the hotel sector or in sectors with a similar function, such as holiday camps or sites developed for use as camping sites, those services shall be regarded as being supplied at those locations.*'
64. European Commission explanatory notes p. 74.
65. Article 24d of Council Regulation 282/2011 as amended by Council Regulation 1042/2013 provides: '*1. Where a supplier supplies a service listed in Article 58 of Directive 2006/112/EC, he may rebut a presumption referred to in Article 24a or in point (a), (b) or (c) of Article 24b of this Regulation on the basis of three items of non-contradictory evidence indicating that the customer is established, has his permanent address or usually resides elsewhere. 2. A tax authority may rebut presumptions that have been made under Article 24a, 24b or 24c where there are indications of misuse or abuse by the supplier.*'
66. This is in line with Recital 10 of the Preamble to Council Regulation 1042/2013, which provides: '*In certain cases where the service is occasional, habitually involves small amounts and requires the physical presence of the customer, such as the supply of telecommunications, broadcasting or electronically supplied services at a wi-fi hotspot or an internet café, or habitually does not give rise to payment receipts or other evidence of the service provided, as is the case with telephone boxes, the provision and control of evidence with respect to the place of establishment of the customer or his permanent address or usual residence would impose a disproportionate burden, or could pose problems of data protection.*' As indicated above, this provision is of little practical value for electronically supplied services because it does not cover the supplies delivered to customers *through* these locations.
67. The Treaty on the Functioning of the European Union ('TFEU') makes a distinction between legislative acts, delegated acts and implementing acts in Articles 289, 290 and 291 and suggests a hierarchy between these three types of acts. The TFEU was first published in the O.J. of 17 Dec. 2007 (C 306) and entered into force on 1 Dec. 2009, following the ratification of the Treaty of Lisbon. A Consolidated version of the TFEU is available at http://register.consilium.europa.eu/doc/srv?l = EN&t = PDF&gc = true&sc = false&f = ST%206655%202008%20REV%207.

accurate and fraud proof) and the feasibility of their implementation (for being easily determinable, and allowing for a reasonable compliance burden and legal certainty for the supplier), some of these presumptions unfortunately prove as burdensome and difficult to implement as the normal rules.

First, the *'wi-fi hot spot and internet café presumption'* concerns supplies made 'at' a specific place (while the other presumptions concern supplies made 'through' a specific means). According to the explanatory notes, it mostly concerns telecommunication and broadcasting services (e.g., the supply of access to the Internet, also when these 'places' are located on board a means of transport), and notably excludes 'over the top' or subsequent supplies.[68] Since the explanatory notes are not legally binding, the question may be raised whether this is a correct interpretation of Council Regulation 1042/2013 and one that will be endorsed by the national tax administrations and would be confirmed by the CJEU, in particular in view of the fact that the summarizing chart in the explanatory notes surprisingly uses the same preposition *'via'* to refer to the services supplied *'at'* a wi-fi hotspot and those supplied *'through'* a fixed main line or a mobile connection.[69]

If the *'wi-fi hotspot and internet café presumption'* does not apply to 'over the top' supplies (i.e., if the use of the preposition 'at' in the wording of this presumption as opposed to 'through' in the wording of the other presumptions should indeed be interpreted as excluding 'over the top supplies' from its scope of application, which, in our view, is probably a correct interpretation of the text of the Regulation), it has a very narrow scope of application, and it will be easy and straightforward to apply to electronically supplied services, because suppliers will simply have to account for VAT in accordance with their local rules (in case of wi-fi hotspot and Internet access supplies, paragraph 1 of the presumption) or in accordance with the rules applicable in the jurisdiction of departure (in case of supplies on board a means of transport, paragraph 2 of the presumption). In the latter case, tax assessment may however be slightly more complex when the journey makes a stopover outside of the EU, because there will be two points of departure in the EU (i.e., the first point of departure and the point of re-entry) and therefore potentially two different places of supply for the same service, depending on the section of the transport operation in which the supply takes place.[70] In these cases, the February 2014 draft of the explanatory notes holds that it is the first paragraph of the *'wi-fi hotspot and internet café presumption'* that should apply (which, according to the European Commission, leads to taxation at *'the physical location of the boat at the moment a service is provided'*) or the various presumptions under 24b (e.g., when the customer uses his SIM card to purchase online, see below *'mobile network presumption'*).[71]

Even if the implementation of the *'wi-fi hotspot and internet cafe'* presumption as interpreted narrowly (i.e., not including 'over the top supplies') is thus rather

68. Article 6a(g) of Council Regulation 282/2011.
69. European Commission explanatory notes p. 61.
70. European Commission explanatory notes p. 57.
71. European Commission explanatory notes pp. 57 and 58.

straightforward, the deemed location of the supply will not always correspond to the place of residence/establishment of the customer (in the case of hotel lobbies or during intra-EU transport operations, it may even be assumed that it hardly ever will). Accordingly, the '*wi-fi hotspot and internet cafe*' presumption is not fully relevant to implement the proxy of the place of residence/establishment of the customer but rather tends to be a real consumption test compare the use and enjoyment clause (Article 59a VAT Directive). In contrast with our conclusion above that the use and enjoyment clause is currently difficult, if not impossible to implement, a real consumption test can be implemented in the cases covered by the '*wi-fi hotspot and internet cafe*' presumption as interpreted narrowly, and in these cases a deviation from the traditional proxy of the place of residence/establishment of the customer seems indeed relevant. It must be noted, however, that the supply is not made on a remote basis because the customer needs to be present at the location of the supplier, which, exceptionally for an 'electronically supplied service', makes it easy for the supplier to determine where the supply was enjoyed (in all other cases, the use and enjoyment clause remains difficult to implement in a digital context). Moreover, the '*wi-fi hotspot and internet cafe*' presumption is the only one to make direct reference to the use and enjoyment clause, and in the scenarios covered by this presumption, the result of both rules will be the same so that there is no potential conflict between them. In contrast, conflict may arise in relation to the other presumptions and there, the explanatory notes hold that when the use and enjoyment clause applies, it prevails.[72]

If the '*wi-fi hotspot and internet café presumption*' includes 'over the top' supplies (i.e., if the national tax administrations and the CJEU do not endorse the interpretation made by the European Commission in the explanatory notes), it seems difficult if not impossible to implement. As a matter of fact, we do not see how suppliers would be able to determine that a customer is effectively acceding the Internet from such places. Furthermore, in the cases in which these places are located on board a means of transport, it seems unrealistic to expect from suppliers that they determine where the transport operation started, or whether the transport operation is effectively an intra-EU journey (stopovers outside of the EU giving rise to the application of different rules as indicated above). The deemed location of the supply will, moreover, again not always correspond to the place of residence/establishment of the customer, and in this case it is possible that the supply is not used or enjoyed at the location where it is purchased (e.g., a customer downloading a movie through a wi-fi hotspot located in an airport and watching it after flying to another country), so that the presumption would not always be economically relevant.

Second, the '*fixed land line presumption*' should, according to the explanatory notes, only apply when the customer uses a residential (and not a business) landline,[73]

72. New Article 31c of Council Regulation 282/2011 provides that: '*For the purpose of determining the place of supply of telecommunications, broadcasting or electronically supplied services provided by a taxable person acting in his own name together with accommodation in the hotel sector or in sectors with a similar function, such as holiday camps or sites developed for use as camping sites, those services shall be regarded as being supplied at those locations.*'
73. European Commission explanatory notes p. 58.

which means that, in order to decide how to assess the tax, suppliers of electronically supplied services must, as of 2015, determine whether their customers are using a fixed landline, and if so whether it is a *residential* or a *business* landline. In our view, while the interpretation offered in the explanatory notes for the '*wi-fi hotspot and internet café*' presumption seems like a sound interpretation of the different prepositions used in the text of Council Regulation 1042/2013 (i.e., 'at' versus 'through'), there is not, in this case, any indication in the Regulation that the presumption should be interpreted as only applying to 'residential' landlines. Accordingly, and since the explanatory notes are not binding, the national tax administrations and the CJEU could reject it.

If the narrow interpretation offered in the explanatory notes were endorsed by the national tax administrations and the CJEU (i.e., if the fixed landline presumption should indeed only apply when the customer uses a residential landline, which we do not think is a correct interpretation of the text of the Regulation),[74] and since the location of a residential fixed landline used by a customer corresponds in most cases to his place of residence (i.e., except when he is travelling and has access to a residential landline connection abroad), it would constitute a relevant criterion for implementing that proxy. The problem, however, is that neither Council Regulation 1042/2013 (unsurprisingly because it does not make the distinction between 'residential' and 'business' landlines as indicated above), nor the explanatory notes do clarify how suppliers of electronically supplied services are supposed to determine that the customer is purchasing through a residential fixed landline connection. In practice, however, it seems to us that suppliers of electronically supplied services neither have the right nor the means to access the details of a fixed landline subscription. Moreover, even if such information would be available, it seems to us that this presumption (interpreted as only applicable in the cases in which a fixed landline is used) would actually impose more burdensome transaction based verification obligations, without giving suppliers any certainty that they have taken the right tax decision. As a matter of fact, in this case suppliers would have to assess, on a case-by-case basis, whether the details of the fixed landline subscription that is used to make a purchase are likely to correspond to a taxable or to a non-taxable person, which seems an impossible task (what is in the name of an Internet subscription? In any language? Including different alphabets? And how relevant is the distinction made between residential and business landline in case of non-taxable legal entities?).

If the distinction between 'residential' and 'business' landline were not endorsed by the national tax administrations and the CJEU,[75] the deemed location of the supply would again in the great majority of the cases correspond to the residence/

74. The exclusion of 'non-residential' landlines would, for example, allow excluding the over the top supplies made from an Internet café (not falling under the wi-fi hotspot and Internet café presumption).
75. And, for example, when a customer uses Internet access in an Internet café to purchase online (i.e., an 'over the top' supply as defined in the wi-fi hotspot and Internet café presumption), this purchase would be caught by the fixed landline presumption and be taxed in the jurisdiction where the Internet café is located.

establishment of the customer (i.e., in all cases except when the customer is travelling).[76] The question remains, however, how suppliers are expected to determine where the fixed landline used by the customer is located in view of the fact that, as noted above, they do not have access to the details of that landline subscription (not to determine whether it is 'residential' or not, and not to locate it either).[77] Accordingly, this presumption is very difficult if not impossible to implement, unless the supplier has access to details concerning the fixed landline.[78]

Third, the *'mobile network presumption'* locates the customer in the country identified by the mobile country code of his SIM card.[79] The explanatory notes again give a narrow interpretation of this presumption and hold that it only applies when the customer uses his SIM card to receive the supply, in which case he will normally be charged for the telecom service and for the electronically supplied service (even when the customer uses a prepaid SIM card).[80] This presumption would therefore not apply to supplies delivered to a smartphone via a wi-fi connection to the Internet and charged to a credit card (in which case the *'fixed land line'* presumption applies). It should, according to the European Commission, not apply either when the customer uses his smartphone to connect to the Internet via a 4G connection, for example. In our view, however, this narrow scope of application of the *'mobile network presumption'* does not clearly follow from the wording of the Article (which broadly refers to 'mobile network' and therefore could also cover 'mobile Internet networks'), and would have been difficult to grasp for suppliers of electronically supplied services in the absence of the European Commission explanatory notes. This is not a reassuring thought in view of the fact that the explanatory notes are not binding on Member States and that some of them may therefore interpret that provision in a much broader way, i.e., as providing that whenever a customer uses a 'mobile Internet' connection to purchase online, the supplier should be able to identify his SIM country code. This interpretation could actually be appealing for national tax administrations, because it would allow them to claim VAT on all purchases made by 'their' residents (the place of residence being *the*

76. The distinction between residential and non-residential landlines would actually allow increasing relevance because a customer using a fixed landline while travelling abroad will often use non-residential landlines (e.g., at the hotel or Internet café). Such distinction may, however, in our view, not be made on the basis of the text of the Regulation.
77. The question of how to locate the fixed landline is also an open question when the fixed landline presumption is interpreted restrictively as only applying to 'residential' fixed landline. We did not address it in the previous paragraph because the impossibility to make the distinction between residential and non-residential fixed landline already renders the presumption unworkable in our view.
78. In view of the impossibility for suppliers to determine that a customer is using a residential landline, it is irrelevant to discuss the possibility to conceal or falsify that information (which is not available to suppliers anyway).
79. *'For the application of Article 58 of Directive 2006/112/EC* (B2C), *where (...) electronically supplied services are supplied to a non-taxable person: (b) through mobile networks, it shall be presumed that the place where the customer is established, has his permanent address or usually resides is the country identified by the mobile country code of the SIM card used when receiving those services.'*
80. In this case, the cost of the electronically supplied service is not charged by the telecommunication company on the telephone bill but is deducted from the customer's credit on the prepaid card. European Commission explanatory notes pp. 41 and 59.

proxy that the implementing regulations should seek to implement), even when they are travelling abroad.

In the limited cases covered by the interpretation of the European Commission in the explanatory notes, the provision seems easy to implement but actually concerns supplies that fall outside the scope of the research because not delivered via the Internet.

In contrast, if Member States interpret the *'mobile network presumption'* as covering all supplies made to a customer through his smartphone (including supplies for which the customer does not communicate telephone numbers to receive the supply but which he downloads directly from the Internet using a mobile Internet connection which, as noted above, is an interpretation that seems appealing for the tax administrations and is in our view possible on the basis of the text of the Regulation), then suppliers would in our view not be in the position to determine, first, that a customer has used his smartphone to access the Internet (in the same way as they cannot, in our, view determine that the customer has used a fixed line connection or has passed through a wi-fi hotspot) and, second, to identify the SIM country code of the smartphone used to access the Internet. Such a broad interpretation would, therefore be most problematic for suppliers of electronically supplied services.

The *'mobile network presumption'* is probably relevant because the SIM card country code generally corresponds to the country of residence of the customer. Exceptionally, however, territories of Union Member States share the same telephone country code (e.g., the Canary Islands and Spain), but may be outside the scope of EU VAT (e.g., the Canary Islands),[81] so that an provider of electronically supplied services would (wrongfully) charge ES VAT on a supply to a customer located in the Canary Islands when applying this presumption (which is in that case thus based on a non-relevant criterion).

The *'mobile network presumption'* is quite reliable because it is difficult for customers to mask or modify a SIM country code. In theory, a customer can use a SIM card related to a 'foreign' telephone number, which would thus give a non-relevant indication to the supplier, but, at the moment, this scenario is quite unrealistic (and in any case would remain extremely marginal) in view of the roaming costs (the presumption is therefore relatively fraud proof). However, as of July 2014 (and therefore from the entry into effect of the presumption in January 2015), it will be possible to enter into an agreement with a foreign 'Alternative Roaming Provider' for use throughout the EU,[82] so that, from that moment on, a SIM card country code will be less relevant and less reliable.

Fourth, the *'other circumstances presumption'* requires the supplier to identify the place of taxation on the basis of two pieces of non-contradictory evidence, such as the

81. Mount Athos; the Canary Islands; the French overseas departments; the Åland Islands; the Channel Islands; the Island of Heligoland; the territory of Büsingen; Ceuta; Melilla; Livigno; Campione d'Italia; the Italian waters of Lake Lugano.
82. The right to contract with a provider of international roaming services ('Alternative Roaming provider') is open as of 1 Jul. 2014 in accordance with Regulation 531/2012 of the European Parliament and the Council of 13 Jun. 2012 on roaming on public mobile communications networks within the Union (O.J. 30 June 2012, L 172, p. 10).

billing address, the Internet Protocol (IP) address, bank details, the Mobile Country Code (MCC) of the International Mobile Subscriber Identity (IMSI) stored on the Subscriber Identity Module (SIM) card used by the customer, the location of the customer's fixed landline, and other commercially relevant information.[83] Council Regulation 1042/2013 does not set any hierarchy between these proposed indicators and the list is not exhaustive ('*in particular*').[84]

A first question that arises is whether a supplier may use these proposed indicators also in the context of the other presumptions discussed above (unlikely),[85] and if not what other indicators suppliers of electronically supplied services should use according to the EU legislator for the implementation of those presumptions.

The second question is what the '*circumstances other*' than those identified in the previous presumptions, really are? According to the interim explanatory notes this presumption '*should apply only if it is not possible for a specific presumption to be used*'[86] i.e., only if the supplier does not have and could not have collected information or evidence which should have triggered one of the other presumptions (including when two delivery channels could have been used and the supplier cannot determine which one was used).[87] This residual category therefore does not apply to supplies delivered though a fixed main line (cabled and wireless; only residential according to the explanatory notes but the distinction does not bind the national tax administrations), through a mobile network when a SIM card is used for the purchase (or under a broader interpretation of Article 24b(b) when a supply is made via mobile Internet network), but it would apply to over the top supplies delivered to the customer using a wi-fi hotspot and to purchases made using a mobile Internet connection to access the Internet (assuming these are not covered by the previous presumptions). In our view, however, suppliers will in many cases not be in the position to apply the specific presumptions, so that we foresee a more extensive use of this '*other circumstances*' presumption.

A third question concerns the relevance, reliability and practical nature of the indicators from which the supplier may choose the two most reliable with only the tax administration (and not the customer) being able to challenge his choice in case there are indications of misuse or abuse. The explanatory notes hold that this method would allow for sufficient flexibility because the supplier can use '*any commercially relevant*

83. '*For the application of Article 58 of Directive 2006/112/EC* (B2C), *where (...) electronically supplied services are supplied to a non-taxable person: (d) under circumstances other than those referred to in Article 24a and in points (a), (b) and (c) of this Article, it shall be presumed that the customer is established, has his permanent address or usually resides at the place identified as such by the supplier on the basis of two items of non-contradictory evidence as listed in Article 24f of this Regulation.*'
84. As confirmed in the European Commission explanatory notes pp. 68 and 69.
85. The wording: '*in circumstances other than those referred to in Article 24a and in points (a), (b) and (c) of this Article*' indeed in our view excludes their use for implementing the presumptions under Article 24a and 24b (a) to (c).
86. The same comment as above applies in case the supply is charged directly to the customer's telephone bill.
87. See also European Commission explanatory notes pp. 60 and 61 that clarify that in case of doubt whether the specific presumptions under 24a or 24b(a) to (c) or the general presumption under 24b(d) should apply, the former should always prevail.

information', and that it will be appropriate to embrace any future services and technologies.[88] In our view, however, the use of these indicators is not without problems and they may be inappropriate in a digital environment:

- *Billing address*: Although relevant (as it usually corresponds to residence) and easily available (on demand), a billing address can, in our view, not be considered as a reliable indicator in the context of electronically delivered supplies, because the customer does not need the supplier to know where he resides and giving a wrong billing address with the objective to obtain a lower VAT rate will have no consequences for him.[89]
- *IP address*:[90] The IP address (or more precisely the translation of an IP address into a geographical location based on information stored by the provider of the geolocation service) is a criterion that we are naturally inclined to think of in a digital environment and it can be easily identified by suppliers by means of IP trackers, and thus seems easy to implement, but there are a number of difficulties. A first question is whether it is acceptable to require from all suppliers of electronically supplied services that they invest in IP trackers in the framework of their VAT compliance obligations. In particular if tax administrations do not accept any IP tracker but impose the use of 'certified' devices to ensure a maximum level of reliability, their acquisition in all taxing jurisdictions may constitute a non-negligible cost for the supplier.

  A second question is whether the use of IP trackers to locate customers and the storage of this information for several years complies with the EU data protection Directive,[91] which applies in view of the CJEU's decision in C-360/10 *Scarlet/SABAM,* that IP addresses are personal data because they allow users to be precisely identified.[92] It seems questionable for the VAT Regulation to suggest that suppliers use these data for tax assessment purposes (and keep them on file for years) and that Member States should amend data protection legislation for that purpose.[93] The explanatory notes highlight that

88. European Commission explanatory notes p. 60.
89. The billing addresses held by the telecommunication or broadcasting companies providing electronically supplied services to their customers is more relevant, in the context of a broader contractual relationship.
90. Since we believe that the wording: '*in circumstances other than those referred to in Article 24a and in points (a), (b) and (c) of this Article*' excludes the use of the indicators listed under this provision for implementing the presumptions under Article 24a and 24b(a) to (c), the customer's IP address is therefore not an indicator that suppliers are expected to rely on in order to locate a customer's fixed landline.
91. Directive 95/46/EC of the European Parliament and of the Council of 24 Oct. 1995 on the protection of individuals with regard to the processing of personal data and on the free movement of such data, O.J. 23 Nov. 1995, L 281, p. 31.
92. In its recent proposals to reform the EU data protection framework the European Commission also explicitly held that IP addresses are personal data (see European Commission (2012a): 'Data protection reform: Frequently asked questions' MEMO/12/403.
93. Recital 17 of the Regulation provides: '*For the purposes of this Regulation, it may be appropriate for Member States to adopt legislative measures limiting certain rights and obligations laid down by Directive 95/46/EC of the European Parliament and of the Council (in order to safeguard an important economic or financial interest of a Member State or of the European Union, including*

the characteristics and purpose of such processing should be specified and explicitly provided for in national law,[94] which begs the question how we can be sure that businesses collect and use IP address exclusively for tax purposes (and not for marketing purposes).

Third, an IP address is not always a relevant criterion to implement the proxy of the customer's place of residence/establishment. It is for instance not relevant when the customer is purchasing from an airport or a hotel lobby hotspot (e.g., a French customer downloads a movie from an IT airport hot spot before flying back home). In that case, taxation on the basis of the IP address would result in a disputable allocation of the taxing rights (e.g., the French customer downloads a movie from a French supplier but needs to pay IT VAT on that purchase). But an IP address may be more relevant when it indicates that the customer is in a restaurant, a public park or a university campus, for example.

Fourth, there are several arguments to conclude that IP addresses do not constitute a reliable indicator. In fact, collecting accurate data is not an easy task and geolocation service suppliers tend to overestimate accuracy (some even claim over 99% accuracy!).[95] False results may also occur when the customer connects through a major Internet Service Provider.[96] An IP address may indeed *identify a unique computer, but not when a network of computers connects to the Internet via a single Internet connection.*[97] Furthermore, geolocation is prone to fraud. Customers of electronically supplied services can easily mask their actual IP address and display a fake IP address to show the tracker that he is located in another jurisdiction.[98] Accordingly, if a non-EU IP address combined with (an easily falsifiable) billing address would allow customers to obtain tax-free supplies, fraud can be expected.[99] In conclusion, IP addresses are in our view a rather weak indicator for customer location purposes.

---

monetary, budgetary and taxation matters, where such measures are necessary and proportionate in view of the risk of tax fraud and tax evasion in Member States, and in view of the need to ensure the correct collection of VAT covered by this Regulation'.

94. European Commission explanatory notes p. 73.
95. Svantesson (2008): 'How Does the Accuracy of Geo-location Technologies Affect the Law?', 2 Masaryk University Journal of Law and Technology, 1 of 2008 at 11–21, making reference to a claim by 'Digital Element' regarding their product 'NetAcuity' (at 14).
96. Such as America on Line (AOL).
97. For example, the IP address of a computer located in the Belgian branch of a hotel may indicate an NL address because the computer in question is acceding the Internet through a regional connection used by all the hotels of the group located in a given territory (e.g., the BENELUX).
98. For example, The Cloak, Anonymous; HideMyAss, Easy Security Web Proxy, HotSurfLive Web Proxy, New Anonymous Web Proxy, Nu3ga Myspace Proxy.
99. A customer acquiring a digital product could also be acquiring it for someone else in order to make him benefit from the low VAT rate applicable in the jurisdiction where he buys the product (and the case is more likely to happen than in conventional commerce), at least for those that can be transferred (e.g., a musical score). Accordingly, if the further transfer of the acquired data is not made impossible by the suppler, the system could be abused, without the supplier being able to find out. Admittedly however, such kind of risk again remains rather marginal.

- *Bank location and customer's billing address as held by the bank:* In many cases the location of the customer's bank may well reflect his place of residence/establishment which would make it a rather relevant criterion. Such information may, moreover, not be easily falsified by the customer (reliable). One problem, however, is that customers may have different banks in different locations, and even if this does not concern the majority of customers of electronically supplied services, this is an element that should perhaps not be underestimated in our age of free capital movements and online banking. Another difficulty is that the relevant payment details are not always available to suppliers (in particular not when the customer uses intermediaries such as *Paypal*). As to *'the billing address of the customer held by that bank'*, we wonder how the EU legislator expects that information to be channelled (in an automated and instantaneous way in the context of a supply of electronically supplied services) to any supplier who would make the request.
- *SIM country code*: If the supplier is able to identify the SIM country code of the customer, it is surprising that the '*mobile network*' presumption did not apply (as this presumption and the indicators listed here are only relevant when the previous (specific) presumptions do not apply). The fact that SIM country codes can be used as indicia in the context of this presumption probably means that the European Commission's narrow interpretation of the scope of application of the '*mobile network presumption*' is the correct one (although, as noted, it does not clearly appear from the wording of the provision). In the case where a supply is made on a smartphone via a mobile Internet connection and not paid via the SIM card, the supplier would therefore be invited to use the customer SIM card country code as indicator. As indicated above, however, we doubt that suppliers are able to obtain that information. This indicator is thus either useless (if the '*mobile network presumption*' must be interpreted broadly) or hardly implementable (if the '*mobile network presumption*' must indeed be interpreted narrowly).
- *Fixed landline*: The reliance on the customer's '*fixed landline through which the service is supplied to him*' in the context of this presumption is also quite surprising. As a matter of fact, it seems to us that if the supplier is able to determine that the customer is purchasing through a fixed landline, the '*fixed landline presumption*' should apply and not the 'other circumstances' presumption. Perhaps this covers cases in which the supplier could not use the fixed landline presumption because the customer used a 'business type of fixed land line' (if the distinction made between residential and non-residential fixed landline made by the European Commission is correct, keeping in mind that nothing in the text of the Regulation suggests that this distinction should be made).
- '*Other commercially relevant information*': the early draft of the explanatory notes gave several examples including '*local language website*' and '*consumer trading history*'. Irrespective of the relevance of these criteria, requiring from suppliers of electronically supplied services that they collect such information

(different type of information in each case) and analyse it on a transaction basis is, in our view, inappropriate in the context of supplies that are defined under the VAT Directive as fully automated and involving minimal human intervention, and that are in practice taking place every second, 24/7. The explanatory notes add to that list of examples '*unique payment systems*' (i.e., payment systems that are proper to one jurisdiction in particular), self-identification, gift cards and '*documentation of third party payment service suppliers*'.[100] Regarding the latter, we noted above that banking details collected by payment intermediaries are usually not shared with suppliers, so that this indicator is difficult, if not impossible to implement (we also wonder why it is again listed here under '*other commercially relevant information*'). Concerning self-identification, the explanatory notes clarify that it could not be used together with a billing address, because the two pieces of evidence would be merely 'duplicating' each other,[101] and we would indeed argue that self-identification is as non-reliable as a billing address in the context of an electronically supplied service. Finally, requiring from suppliers that they proceed to different types of verification on a case-by-case basis, in case a unique payment system or a gift card would be used does, again not fit with the reality of electronically supplied services.

The '*abuse presumption*', finally, provides that the '*fixed land line*' and '*mobile network*', presumptions may be rebutted by the supplier (paragraph 1 of the presumption) or the tax administration (paragraph 2 of the presumption) on the basis of three pieces of non-contradictory evidence[102] taken from the above list of indicators (i.e., billing address, IP, bank details, SIM country code, fixed land line and any other commercial information). The explanatory notes recall that whenever the supplier is able to identify where his supply is going to be used and enjoyed, the use and enjoyment clause prevails.[103]

It seems unrealistic in the case of electronically supplied services to expect from suppliers that they collect and analyse various indicators depending on the factual circumstances of each supply in order to potentially rebut a presumption (which itself is difficult, if not impossible to implement). The question may also be raised whether leaving such a margin of manoeuvre is at all appropriate. According to the explanatory notes, the supplier is indeed '*not obliged to rebut a presumption. Even though there can*

100. European Commission explanatory notes p. 69.
101. European Commission explanatory notes p. 71.
102. Article 24d reads as follows: '*1. Where a supplier supplies a service listed in Article 58 of Directive 2006/112/EC* (B2C), *he may rebut a presumption referred to in Article 24a or in point (a), (b) or (c) of Article 24b of this Regulation on the basis of three items of non-contradictory evidence indicating that the customer is established, has his permanent address or usually resides elsewhere. 2. A tax authority may rebut presumptions that have been made under Article 24a, 24b or 24c where there are indications of misuse or abuse by the supplier.*'
103. Provided this place is located outside the Community while the place-of-supply rule that should in principle apply would result in taxation within the territory of the supplier, or is located within their territory while the place-of-supply rule that should in principle apply would result in taxation outside of the Community.

be evidence to the contrary, the supplier may for determining the location of the customer decide to rely on the presumption and disregard evidence to the contrary'.[104] For example, let us assume that a supplier of downloadable movies established in BE determines that a customer is making a purchase through a residential fixed landline located in the NL (provided he can do it), which triggers the presumption of taxation in the NL (high tax), he may (even if the IP address indicates that the customer is effectively located in the NL at the time of the purchase) prefer to rebut that presumption to have the supply taxed in LU (low tax), on the basis of the fact that the customer pays with an LU credit card (provided the supplier had access to that information), has provided an LU billing address (no matter how relevant that information is in a digital context), and is browsing on the German page of the supplier's website (no matter again how relevant that information is to determine a place of residence). In this case, it may be relevant to tax the transaction in Luxembourg (e.g., a Luxembourgish lawyer making a private purchase from his office computer having a Dutch IP address because part of a Dutch office network), or not. It seems to us that the choice should not be left to the supplier, in particular as it could be reassessed in the context of audit, and if the tax administration can gather sufficient evidence to counter the indicators relied on by the supplier.[105]

The second paragraph of the '*abuse presumption*' provides that the tax administration may rebut a presumption if there are indications of fraud or abuse by the supplier. This includes cases in which: '*a supplier adopts a practice that would see the place of supply incorrectly determined in relation to a proportion of his customers that is not negligible, even if this may not necessarily result in a clear advantage for the supplier or his customer*'. The explanatory notes clarify that only '*deliberate actions or negligence*' on the part of the supplier are targeted.[106] In view of the fact that online suppliers will seek to automate the assessment procedure, however, leaving no room for case-by-case arbitrages in spite of the new requirements imposed by the EU legislator, and in view of the fact that the abuse presumption may also apply in the cases in which the incorrect assessment did not result in a tax advantage for the supplier or his customers, the question remains how the concept of good faith will be interpreted by the tax administrations.

The explanatory notes further clarify, quite unrealistically in our view, that the: '*applicability of each presumption has to be assessed by the supplier on the basis of available information (i.e. any information a supplier has or should have)*',[107] and that suppliers are expected to take account of the reliability of the information used and that they should be able to justify why the information sounded relevant to them,[108] taking into consideration the particularity of the type of supply they make. The explanatory notes even clarify that, in case of contradictory evidence and when two pieces of

104. European Commission explanatory notes p. 65.
105. In the same way as under the current rules, tax administrations are indeed not in a better position to determine the location of a customer of electronically supplied services, in particular *a posteriori*.
106. European Commission explanatory notes p. 65.
107. European Commission explanatory notes p. 56.
108. European Commission explanatory notes February 2014 p. 69.

non-contradictory evidence are not readily available, the supplier '*should continue to seek further*'.[109]

4.2.3.2.4. *Intermediate Conclusion and Final Remarks*

The main conclusion that we draw from the analysis of the rules related to customer identification and location in the case of electronically supplied services (and more generally of the approach adopted by the EU legislator) is that the '*automated*' character of these supplies and the requirement that they be made '*with minimal human intervention*' seems to be in contradiction with the requirement that suppliers of these services proceed to transaction based verifications. This is more so in view of the fact that these verifications differ depending on the factual circumstances of the supply.[110]

A further complicating factor is that the explanatory notes are not binding on Member States, and that there is no formal path to address disputes between the Member States possibly leading to double taxation.[111]

A final remark is that the VAT Directive, Council Regulation 282/2011 and Council Regulation 1042/2013 all remain silent on the way suppliers must store the information on which they have based their assessment, as well as the format and the period during which this information must be retained. This question therefore falls under the competence of Member States, each potentially having different standards and expectations (and also potentially applying different privacy rules to these data).

4.3 CONCLUSIONS

Taxing electronically supplied services at destination is appropriate from an economic neutrality perspective but raises substantial practical difficulties. In particular, it is challenging for their suppliers to identify and locate customers on a transaction basis for the purpose of charging them a correct amount of VAT.[112] While all electronically supplied services except intra-EU B2C supplies have been taxed at destination in the EU since July 2003, the EU legislator only tackled the question of customer identification and location for the first time in 2011 when it adopted implementing provisions for all supplies of services. Amending provisions for these implementing rules have entered into force in 2015 (when EU suppliers also became obliged to assess and collect VAT at destination on their supplies to EU customers), which this time specifically concern

109. European Commission explanatory notes February 2014 p. 72.
110. The explanatory notes consider that when a supplier has a regular relationship with a customer, location information should not be controlled on a transaction basis, but that '*a pro-active verification should take place on a regular basis*'. European Commission explanatory notes 71.
111. It should be noted that the European Commission has already (unsuccessfully) tried to establish a procedure in cases of double (non-)taxation in 2007.
112. It being understood that the absence of readily implementable assessment rules also affects the collection of the tax, because a prerequisite in tax collection, before addressing the technical question of how to organize it, is to know 'what to collect' and 'where to remit' it.

electronically supplied services. Unfortunately, the amendments concerning the question of customer identification are of little interest, as they do not really help suppliers. As to the amendments concerned with the question of customer location, their analysis shows that far from settling the difficulties encountered by suppliers under the general rules, they seem even more difficult and burdensome to implement as compared to the general rules.

At the moment, it remains quite unclear how tax administrations will appraise suppliers' efforts in correctly assessing the VAT due on their supplies under the new rules. Understanding the difficulties which suppliers face in this respect may result in a certain tolerance towards them (keeping in mind that enforcing the new rules may also prove difficult for the tax administration in the absence of relevant data). Still, legal certainty and neutrality would be preferable for suppliers of electronically supplied services, as would reasonable and achievable compliance obligations. In fact, it seems to us that requiring suppliers to assess and collect VAT should only be considered legitimate if they have the effective means to ensure at a reasonable cost that they assess and collect the tax in a correct way. A radical change of approach would, in our view, be necessary to reach that objective.

CHAPTER 5
VAT Fraud and the Digital Economy within the European Union: Risks and Opportunities

Edoardo Traversa & Emanuele Ceci[*]

5.1 INTRODUCTION

Since the adoption of VAT, EU and Members States' policy-makers and administrations have been confronted with fraud and avoidance (abuse), often on a (very) large scale. Despite all the efforts made in order to improve the fight against this phenomenon, VAT fraud numbers remain worrying. According to the latest VAT Gap study, published by the Commission in 2014, EUR 177 billion in VAT revenues were lost due to non-compliance or non-collection of VAT in 2012.[1] VAT fraud not only negatively affects the financial interests of the Member States, but it also constitutes a serious issue for business, because VAT malpractices distort the normal conditions of fair competition in which compliant businesses operate.[2]

The transformation of business models through information and communication technologies paves the way for new forms of VAT fraud, particularly in an EU cross-border context. This is in part due to the inadequacy of the design of the present VAT system. As the Commission pointed out, the common system is not entirely '*well-fitted for today's society*'[3] and '*inconsistent with the idea of a Single*

---

* Edoardo Traversa is Professor of Tax Law at the Université Catholique de Louvain and at the Katholieke Universiteit Leuven and 'avocat' Of Counsel at Liedekerke in Brussels. Emanuele Ceci is Assistant at the Université Catholique de Louvain and 'avocat' in Brussels.

1. European Commission (2014): 'Taxation: Study confirms billions lost in VAT Gap', 23 October 2014, http://europa.eu/rapid/press-release_IP-14-1187_en.htm; European Commission (2013): '2012 Update Report to the Study to quantify and analyse the VAT Gap in the EU-27 Member States', TAXUD/2013/DE/321, p. 7, ec.europa.eu.
2. European Commission (2011): 'Questions and Answers: Value Added Tax (VAT)', 6 Dec. 2011, p. 7, http://europa.eu/rapid/press-release_MEMO-11-874_en.htm?locale = en.
3. *Ibid.*, p. 2.

Market'.[4] Adopted more than forty years ago, it also suffers from the institutional rigidity of the unanimity rule and barely takes into account recent developments, in particular the digitalization of the economy.

Digital commerce follows its own specific pattern, and one could wonder how traditional tax rules '*would interact with the new technologies that enabled global electronic commerce*'.[5] Action 1 of the OECD BEPS Report is related to the tax challenges of the digital economy and recognizes that the present tax rules, also in the area of income taxation, are not adapted to the new business environment.[6] Even if this situation does not necessarily imply that specific VAT regimes have to be set up for digital transactions,[7] it certainly forces all concerned to rethink the manner in which VAT rules are applied and in which the fight against VAT fraud is conducted.

5.2 THE FIGHT AGAINST FRAUD AS A FOCAL POINT OF EU DIGITAL VAT POLICY

Tackling VAT fraud has always been a main concern for EU Members States, especially since the implementation of the so-called transitional VAT system, which has been considered as particularly exposed to VAT fraud schemes.[8] Despite the existence of a common harmonized EU system, VAT fraud remains primarily an issue for the Member States, since it affects their ability to raise revenue and hence their capacity to fund public policies or to alleviate the burden caused by other forms of taxation.[9] As a

4. CFE (2009): 'Opinion Statement of the CFE Fiscal Committee on the European Commission's Proposal for a Directive and Action Plan to Better Combat VAT Fraud', Paper submitted by the Confédération Fiscale Européenne to the European Institutions in February 2009, European Taxation of May 2009 at p. 284.
5. A. Cockfield, W. Hellerstein, R. Millar, C. Warzeggers (2013): 'Taxing Global Digital Commerce', Kluwer Law International, 2013 at 3 and 4. See also J. Li (2003): 'International Taxation in the Age of Electronic Commerce: A Comparative Study', Canadian Tax Foundation, 2003 at 1–28.
6. N. Gaoua (2014): 'Taxation of the Digital Economy: French Reflections', 54 European Taxation 1 Jan. 2014 at 10.
7. The Expert Group on Taxation of the Digital Economy shares the same opinion and considers that '*it is not necessary to create a special tax regime for digital economy because the goal is achievable just adapting the existing rules …*'. See P. Centore and M. T. Sutich (2014): 'Taxation and Digital Economy: Europe is Ready', 42 Intertax 12 of 2014 at 785. See also B. Westberg (2014): 'Taxation of the Digital Economy: An EU Perspective', 54 European Taxation 12 of Dec. 2014 at 541.
8. The development of carrousel fraud is the perfect example of that situation. See among others A. Cockfield, W. Hellerstein, R. Millar, C. Warzeggers (2013): 'Taxing Global Digital Commerce', Kluwer Law International, 2013 at 278 and 279; C. Amand and K. Boucquez (2011): 'A New Defence for Victims of EU Missing-Trader Fraud?', 22 International VAT Monitor of July/August 2011 at 234.

   Some authors even believe that the only way to eradicate VAT fraud will be to '*fundamentally change the current VAT system*'. See M. Griffioen, L. van der Hel (2014): 'New European Approach to Combat VAT Fraud?', 42 Intertax 5 of 2014 at 298.
9. Many EU Member States have recently increased VAT rates in order to lower, or at least to avoid rising, direct taxes, in particular on labour. See European Commission (2014): 'Taxation trends in the European Union', 2014 at 25–27, http://ec.europa.eu (ISSN 1831-8789).

consequence, the right for EU Member States to adopt specific measures to fight fraud is recognized by the EU VAT directive.[10]

Due to the threat it represents to the credibility of EU tax harmonization, fraud has also become a major priority for the EU institutions. The European Commission published several documents on the topic. In December 2008, in the context of the 'Anti-Fraud Strategy' started in 2006,[11] the Commission presented a short-term action plan with a certain number of measures such as the creation of Eurofisc and the improvement of the exchange of information between Member States.[12] The Commission adopted a revised Anti-Fraud Strategy (CAFS) in 2011 with the objective:

> to improve prevention, detection and the conditions for investigations of fraud and to achieve adequate reparation and deterrence, with proportionate and dissuasive sanctions, and respecting the due process, especially by introducing anti-fraud strategies at Commission Service level respecting and clarifying the different responsibilities of the various stakeholders.[13]

According to MS tax administrations, it is essential to opt for a preventive approach instead of just reacting to the development of fraudulent schemes.[14] Since then, many priority actions established in the 2011 CAFS have been implemented.[15]

This Strategy also vowed a longer term reflection on ways in which to fight VAT fraud,[16] which resulted in the 2012 Action Plan to strengthen the fight against tax fraud and tax evasion.[17] The European Commission has been very active on the legislative side, by issuing proposals, most of which have been adopted by the Council. Notable legislative changes are the adoption of Council Regulation (EC) no. 1798/2003 of

10. See Directive 2006/112/EC of 28 November 2006 on the common system of value added tax. The preamble mentions some references in that respect (see points 27, 42, 55 and 59), as well as some specific parties (see Title XII, Chapter 4, section 4; Title XIII, Cha. 2, section 1).
11. Communication from the Commission to the Council, the European Parliament and the European Economic and Social Committee concerning the need to develop a coordinated strategy to improve the fight against fiscal fraud, 31 May 2006, COM (2006) 254 final, http://eur-lex.europa.eu. The main goal of this Communication was to enhance the need to provide a clear anti-fraud Strategy and to present some means to explore. This Communication represents for some authors '*the first of the EU's tangible initiatives on countering fiscal fraud*'. See P. Kavelaars (2013): 'EU and OECD: Fighting against Tax Avoidance', 41 Intertax 10 of 2013 at 507.
12. Communication from the Commission to the Council, the European Parliament, the European Economic and Social Committee on a coordinated strategy to improve the fight against VAT fraud in the European Union, 1 Dec. 2008, COM (2008) 807 final, http://eur-lex.europa.eu.
13. Commission Staff Working Document (2014): 'Implementation of the Commission Anti-Fraud Strategy (CAFS)', Brussels SWD(2014) 248 final of 17 Jul. 2014 at http://eur-lex.europa.eu, p. 5.
14. See M. Griffioen, L. van der Hel (2014): 'New European Approach to Combat VAT Fraud?', 42 Intertax 5 of 2014 at 300 and 301.
15. For more information, see Commission Staff Working Document (2014): 'Implementation of the Commission Anti-Fraud Strategy (CAFS)', Brussels SWD (2014) 248 final of 17 Jul. 2014 at http://eur-lex.europa.eu.
16. European Commission (2011): 'Questions and Answers: Value Added Tax (VAT)', of 6 Dec. 2011 at p. 7, http://europa.eu/rapid/press-release_MEMO-11-874_en.htm?locale = en.
17. Communication from the Commission to the European Parliament and the Council, An Action Plan to strengthen the fight against tax fraud and tax evasion, 6 Dec. 2012, COM(2012) 722 final, http://eur-lex.europa.eu. See also P. Kavelaars (2013): 'EU and OECD: Fighting against Tax Avoidance', 41 Intertax 10 of 2013 at 508–510.

7 October 2003 on administrative cooperation in the field of value added tax,[18] recast by Regulation 904/2010 of 7 October 2010,[19] and, more recently, two directives establishing a Quick Reaction Mechanism against VAT fraud and an optional application of the VAT reverse charge mechanism in relation to supplies of certain goods and services susceptible to fraud.[20] Those instruments mainly aim at better organizing the cooperation between MS tax administrations, by providing clear and binding rules that improve the quality and timing of exchange of information (better procedures, form requirements, better timing to provide the information ...), facilitate cross-border VAT investigations and allow the quick adoption of specific anti-fraud measures.

Besides these specific measures, the Commission also considers that better fraud prevention should include a thorough revision of the EU VAT system. In its 2010 Green Paper on the future of VAT,[21] the Commission considered that a reform towards '*a comprehensive VAT system that can adapt to changes in the economic and technological environment and is solid enough to resist attacks of fraud* (...)' could play a crucial role in the implementation of the Europe 2020 strategy and the return to growth within the EU. This viewpoint was confirmed in the 2011 Commission Communication on the future of VAT,[22] and, more recently, in a 2014 EU VAT expert group opinion on the definitive VAT system[23] and a 2014 Commission working document on the implementation of the definitive VAT regime for intra-EU trade,[24] in which the Commission again pointed out that the present system is '*out of step with the new economic, digital and international environment*'. Those documents clearly state that resistance to fraud has to be one of the guidelines for any future reform of the EU VAT system, along with simplicity and legal certainty, neutrality and proportionality,

18. This Regulation repealed the former Council Regulation (EEC) no. 218/92 of 27 Jan. 1992 on administrative cooperation in the field of indirect taxation, which was not fit for purpose anymore considering the evolution of the internal market. See also Commission implementing Regulation (EC) no. 1925/2004 of 29 Oct. 2004.
19. For more information, See Report from the Commission to the Council and the European Parliament on the application of Council Regulation (EU) No. 904/2010 concerning administrative cooperation and combating fraud in the field of value added tax, 12 Feb. 2014, COM (2014) 71 final, http://eur-lex.europa.eu.
20. Directive 2013/42/EU of 22 Jul. 2013, amending Directive 2006/112/EC on the common system of value added tax, as regards a Quick Reaction Mechanism against VAT fraud, O.J., L 201/1, 26 Jul. 2013 and Directive 2013/43/EU of 22 Jul. 2013, amending Directive 2006/112/EC on the common system of value added tax, as regards an optional and temporary application of the reverse charge mechanism in relation to supplies of certain goods and services susceptible to fraud,, O.J., L 201/4, 26 Jul. 2013. See also the Council Directive 2010/23/EU of 16 March 2010 amending Directive 2006/112/EC on the common system of value added tax, as regards an optional and temporary application of the reverse charge mechanism in relation to supplies of certain services susceptible to fraud, O.J., L 72, 20 Mar. 2010, p. 1.
21. See Green Paper on the future of VAT. Towards a simpler, more robust and efficient VAT system, 1 Dec.r 2010, http://ec.europa.eu. See also H. Kogels (2011): 'The European Commission's Green Paper on VAT', 22 International VAT Monitor of 2011 at 141–143.
22. Communication from the Commission to the European Parliament, the Council and the European Economic and Social Committee on the future of VAT, Brussels, 6 Dec. 2011, http://ec.europa.eu.
23. Opinion of the VAT Expert Group on the Definitive VAT Regime, 12 Jun. 2014, p. 2, http://ec.europa.eu.
24. Commission Staff Working Document on the implementation of the definitive VAT regime for intra-EU trade, 29 Oct. 2014, http://ec.europa.eu.

efficiency and cooperation between Member States. The fight against fraud is therefore not only seen as an important objective in itself, it is also one of the main drivers of EU VAT harmonization as a whole.

There seems to be a consensus among experts, EU institutions and Member States that the current VAT system is not sufficiently equipped to prevent fraudulent behaviour and that it needs to be adapted with simple rules and efficient tools. There are, however, divergences on how to achieve this objective because Member States tend to be reluctant towards solutions that imply a further harmonization of the VAT taxable base and rates, and they fear the budgetary consequences of any modification of the current system, especially as regards location rules. Sometimes, Member States even seem to be reluctant to develop a broader administrative cooperation between them. Moreover, some anti-fraud measures are quite effective in ensuring the collection of tax by the tax administration on a case-by-case basis, but do not offer structural solutions to eradicate (or at least decrease) the development of tax fraud schemes.[25]

The growing importance of the digital economy reinforces the inevitable need for a discussion on the necessary evolution of the VAT system. E-commerce is indeed quite different from the classic way of doing business, mainly because of the intangible nature of electronic products or services and the fact that business transactions are carried out in a way that makes '*distance and time differences virtually meaningless*'.[26] Moreover, digital commerce very often, if not always, has a cross-border dimension, which inevitably raises issues linked to the boundaries of the tax sovereignty of the States and the limits to international administrative cooperation in the field of taxation.[27]

Therefore, the primary question to be asked in order to efficiently prevent VAT fraud is how the present VAT rules could be applied to digital transactions. Several well-known reports have recently been published on this issue: the report of the Commission expert group on taxation of the digital economy,[28] the OECD International VAT/GST Guidelines, in particular on the location of taxable supplies[29] and the OECD Report on Addressing the Tax Challenges of the Digital economy in the framework of the BEPS Action Plan.[30] These reports build on the experience gained by the OECD and

25. See C. Amand and K. Boucquez (2011): 'A New Defence for Victims of EU Missing-Trader Fraud?', 22 International VAT Monitor of July/August 2011 at 237 and 238.
26. J. Li (2003): 'International Taxation in the Age of Electronic Commerce: A Comparative Study', Canadian Tax Foundation, 2003 at pp. 1–28.
27. See among others A. Cockfield, W. Hellerstein, R. Millar, C. Warzeggers (2013): 'Taxing Global Digital Commerce', Kluwer Law International, 2013 at 552; S. Basu (2007): 'Global Perspectives on E-Commerce Taxation Law', Ashgate Publishing, 2007; R. L. Doernberg and L. Hinnekens (1999): 'Electronic Commerce and International Taxation', Kluwer Law International, 1999; L. Hinnekens (1998): 'The Challenges of Applying VAT and Income Tax Territoriality Concepts and Rules to International Electronic Commerce', 26 Intertax of 1998 at 52–70.
28. European Commission, Report of the Expert Group on Taxation of the digital economy, 28 May 2014, pp. 31–40, http://ec.europa.eu.
29. International VAT/GST Guidelines, April 2014, http://www.oecd.org; International VAT/GST Guidelines on place of taxation for business-to-consumer supplies of services and intangibles, Discussion Draft for Public consultation, 18 Dec. 2014–20 Feb. 2015, http://www.oecd.org.
30. OECD, BEPS Action 1: Address the tax challenges of the digital economy, 16 Sep. 2014. See also the Discussion Draft released on 24 Mar. 2014.

the EU and their respective Member States since the 1990s in addressing the issues raised by e-commerce and by the digitalization of the economy.[31] In this respect, it is worth recalling the principles laid down in the Ottawa Taxation Framework which at the time were considered applicable to both traditional and e-commerce,[32] and still are:[33]

- *Neutrality*: Taxation should seek to be neutral and equitable between forms of electronic commerce and between conventional and electronic forms of commerce. Business decisions should be motivated by economic rather than tax considerations. Taxpayers in similar situations carrying out similar transactions should be subject to similar levels of taxation.
- *Efficiency*: Compliance costs for taxpayers and administrative costs for the tax authorities should be minimized as far as possible.
- *Certainty and Simplicity*: The tax rules should be clear and simple to understand so that taxpayers can anticipate the tax consequences in advance of a transaction, including knowing when, where and how the tax is to be accounted.
- *Effectiveness and Fairness*: Taxation should produce the right amount of tax at the right time. The potential for tax evasion and avoidance should be minimized while keeping counteracting measures proportionate to the risks involved.
- *Flexibility*: The systems for taxation should be flexible and dynamic to ensure that they keep pace with technological and commercial developments.

However, those general principles have to be reconciled with the diversity of the issues to be addressed when trying to apply VAT rules to digital commerce,[34] such as the qualification of the concept of '*transactions in the digital economy*', the identification of the recipient and the location and effective taxation of the transactions. The

31. See OECD (1998): 'Ottawa Ministerial Conference on Electronic Commerce' and OECD Committee on Fiscal Affairs (1998): 'Electronic Commerce: Taxation Framework Conditions'; Commission of the European Community, 'E-Commerce and Indirect Taxation', Communication to the Council of Ministers, the European Parliament and to the Economic and Social Committee, COM (98) 374; Commission of the European Community 'VAT on E-Commerce – Why the Rule Need To Be Changed, The Key', Taxation and Customs Union DG of the Commission, October, 2000. For a comment, see A. Cockfield, W. Hellerstein, R. Millar, C. Warzeggers (2013): 'Taxing Global Digital Commerce', Kluwer Law International 2013 at 193–233.
32. See P. Rendahl (2009): 'Cross-Border Consumption Taxation of Digital Supplies', IBFD Amsterdam, Doctoral Series, 2009, Vol. 18 at 68.
33. See OECD Committee on Fiscal Affairs (1998):'Electronic Commerce: Taxation Framework Conditions', 1998; OECD (2001): 'Taxation and Electronic Commerce – Implementing the Ottawa taxation framework conditions', 2001 at p. 10, www.oecd.org. For more details, see P. Rendahl (2009): 'Cross-Border Consumption Taxation of Digital Supplies', Amsterdam, IBFD, Doctoral Series, 2009, Vol. 18 at 67–122.
34. See P. Rendahl (2009): 'Cross-Border Consumption Taxation of Digital Supplies', Amsterdam, IBFD, Doctoral Series, 2009, Vol. 18 at 123; pp. 179–326; A. Bal (2014): 'The Myth of Taxing Cloud Computing under EU VAT', 25 International VAT Monitor of November/December 2014 at 343–349.

design of these rules, and their implementation, will undeniably have an impact on the extent of VAT fraud and on the choice of the tools to combat it.

5.3 IDENTIFYING AND LOCATING DIGITAL SUPPLIES IN ORDER TO MINIMIZE VAT FRAUD: THE DESTINATION PRINCIPLE AS A PANACEA?

The best way to limit VAT fraud is preventing it, by the adoption of rules that are not easily circumvented. Within the EU single market, and more generally from a cross-border perspective, fraud-proof location rules are key to the implementation of a robust VAT system. It is therefore necessary to discuss whether the idea according to which VAT should be collected at destination, if implemented thoroughly and coherently, could be one (if not the) solution to make the EU common system more robust as regards the taxation of digital supplies.

5.3.1 An Internationally Recognized and Implemented Principle

There seems to be a growing international consensus on the fact that VAT on digital supplies[35] should be collected according to the destination principle,[36] i.e., in the country where the consumer is established. The use of the destination principle was also recommended by the Ottawa Taxation Framework conditions.[37] An origin-based taxation distorts consumption decisions in favour of suppliers located in jurisdictions applying a low rate of VAT and creates an incentive for VAT suppliers to get established, even fraudulently, in such jurisdictions.[38] This is even more true for digital supplies, and it was confirmed in the report of the EU Commission Expert Group on Taxation of the Digital Economy, that the destination principle should ensure economic efficiency and neutrality.[39] The OECD International VAT/GST Guidelines also recognize that '*VAT neutrality in international trade is generally achieved through the*

35. P. Rendahl (2009): 'Cross-Border Consumption Taxation of Digital Supplies', IBFD Amsterdam, Doctoral Series, 2009, Vol. 18 at p. 123; p. 181.
36. See among others, A. Cockfield, W. Hellerstein, R. Millar, C. Warzeggers (2013): 'Taxing Global Digital Commerce', Kluwer Law International, 2013 at 200; P. Rendahl (2009): 'Cross-Border Consumption Taxation of Digital Supplies', Amsterdam IBFD, Doctoral Series, 2009, Vol. 18 at 275 and 276; M. Lamensch (2012): 'Are reverse charging and the one-stop-scheme efficient ways to collect VAT on digital supplies?', 1 WJOVL 1 of 2012 at 1; P. Centore and M. T. Sutich (2014): 'Taxation and Digital Economy: Europe is Ready', 42 Intertax 12 of 2014 at 785 and 786; B. Westberg (2014): 'Taxation of the Digital Economy: An EU Perspective', 54 European Taxation of December 2014 at 542 and 543.
37. A. Cockfield, W. Hellerstein, R. Millar, C. Warzeggers (2013): 'Taxing Global Digital Commerce', Kluwer Law International, 2013 at 200.
38. See M. Lamensch (2014): 'The Treatment of "Digital products" and other "E-Services" under VAT', p. 3, in M. Lang and I. Lejeune (eds): 'VAT/GST in a Global Digital Economy', to be published (Kluwer); P. Centore and M. T. Sutich (2014): 'Taxation and Digital Economy: Europe is Ready', 42 Intertax 12 of 2014 at 786.
39. Report of the Commission Expert Group on Taxation of the digital economy, 28 May 2014, p. 31 http://ec.europa.eu.

implementation of the "destination principle"',[40] facilitating the ultimate objective of VAT, which is to tax final consumption. Therefore, '*internationally traded services and intangibles should be taxed according to the rules of the jurisdiction of consumption*'. This solution should also be positive in terms of 'distributional equity', as every Member State will collect VAT on supplies effectively consumed on its territory '*sharing the cost of taxation amongst individuals*'.[41]

The traditional proxies used for implementing the destination principle are the customer's principal place of business for B2B supplies, and the customer's place of residence for B2C supplies. This is in line with the recently implemented EU VAT rules for supplies of telecommunications, broadcasting, and electronically supplied services to a final consumer which locate the place of supply in the country of the customer.[42]

Alternative proxies, such as the place of actual performance, could also be applied in specific situations.[43] However, unlike most non-digital transactions, the place of establishment of the supplier or the place of performance should not be taken as a general proxy. According to OECD International VAT/GST Guidelines: '*(...) the application of a proxy based on the supplier's location or place of performance to determine the place of taxation is unlikely to lead to an appropriate result* [...]'.[44] This 'place of supplier' criterion is indeed usually not relevant to determine the place of consumption of e-services or e-products, as they '*can be supplied remotely to customers who may be located anywhere in the world when consuming* [the service or product concerned]'.[45] Moreover, this criterion most likely increases the risk of fraud or avoidance, because taxable persons could be tempted to fictitiously locate their place of business in a low- or no-tax jurisdiction. Therefore, locating VAT taxable transactions at the customer's location, appears to be the best option, also considering the fact that it is likely that the customer will effectively use and enjoy the service or product in the country where he or she resides.

5.3.2 Obstacles to Implementing the Destination Principle in a Borderless Economy

The OECD International VAT/GST Guidelines however underlined that the application of the destination principle is more difficult in the case of e-commerce, because

40. International VAT/GST Guidelines, April 2014, http://www.oecd.org; International VAT/GST Guidelines on place of taxation for business-to-consumer supplies of services and intangibles, Discussion Draft for Public consultation, 18 Dec. 2014–20 Feb. 2015, http://www.oecd.org, p. 3.
41. P. P. Centore and M. T. Sutich (2014): 'Taxation and Digital Economy: Europe is Ready', 42 Intertax 12 of 2014 at 786.
42. Directive 2006/112/EC, Article 44 (for B2B) and Article 58, applicable as for 1 Jan.2015 (for B2C).
43. See International VAT/GST Guidelines, April 2014, http://www.oecd.org; International VAT/GST Guidelines on place of taxation for business-to-consumer supplies of services and intangibles, Discussion Draft for Public consultation, 18 Dec. 2014–20 Feb. 2015, http://www.oecd.org.
44. International VAT/GST Guidelines on place of taxation for business-to-consumer supplies of services and intangibles, Discussion Draft for Public consultation, 18 Dec. 2014–20 Feb. 2015, p. 6 http://www.oecd.org.
45. *Ibid.*

electronically supplied products and services cannot be subject to border controls in the same way as goods.[46] This situation can also lead to some issues regarding VAT fraud, because it will be more difficult to track the e-transactions and therefore to ensure the correct application of the VAT rules and the assessment and collection of the VAT due. This phenomenon is reinforced by tax planning strategies developed by multinational companies in order to channel the supply of digital services through favourable tax jurisdictions. Paraphrasing Edward Kleinbard, digitalization, together with globalization, may contribute to create 'stateless transactions'.[47]

5.3.2.1 Excessive Compliance Costs for Tax Administrations and Taxable Persons

Even if this choice of locating the supply in the country of the recipient stems from the application of general VAT principles, its application to e-commerce is not self-evident, as some authors already pointed out.[48] It requires the correct determination of the VAT status of the customers and their location.[49] However, in standard e-commerce transactions, the parties involved do not meet and have a minimal level of interaction, and suppliers often deal with anonymous customers (who may, for example, use a pseudo or route their transaction through an unidentifiable or borrowed IP address).[50] Moreover, e-supplies take place at any time of the day and activities often involve a high volume of transactions with relatively small margins. The high volume of e-supplies also means that customers may be located in a potentially high number of Member States. Business to consumer situations are even more problematic because there is usually no established relationship between the parties.

Therefore, identifying and locating taxable and non-taxable persons is far from being an easy task for both tax administrations and suppliers, because digitalization makes it difficult '*to obtain reliable information on [the] e-customers in the short time frame in which the transaction will be completed and in which tax assessment must thus be performed*'.[51]

Tax administrations could be faced with difficulties when they try to establish whether a taxable transaction has taken place within their jurisdiction, let alone when they try to effectively assess and collect the corresponding VAT. However, due to the

46. International VAT/GST Guidelines on place of taxation for business-to-consumer supplies of services and intangibles, Discussion Draft for Public consultation, 18 Dec. 2014–20 Feb. 2015, p. 3, http://www.oecd.org.
47. E. Kleinbard (2011): 'Stateless Income', 11 Florida Tax Review of 2011 at 699.
48. M. Lamensch (2014): 'The Treatment of "Digital products" and other "E-Services" under VAT' at 4 and 5 (to be published); A. Bal (2014): 'The Myth of Taxing Cloud Computing under EU VAT', 25 International VAT Monitor of November/December 2014 at 343–349.
49. M. Lamensch (2012): 'Are reverse charging and the one-stop-scheme efficient ways to collect VAT on digital supplies?', 1 WJOVL 1 of 2012 at 4.
50. M. Lamensch (2014): 'The Treatment of "Digital products" and other "E-Services" under VAT', at 4 and 5, in M. Lang and I. Lejeune (eds): 'VAT/GST in a Global Digital Economy', to be published (Kluwer).
51. M. Lamensch (2014): 'The Treatment of "Digital products" and other "E-Services" under VAT', at 4, in M. Lang and I. Lejeune (eds): 'VAT/GST in a Global Digital Economy', to be published (Kluwer).

fact that VAT is collected by economic operators (usually the suppliers), it is on them that the primary burden falls to identify their customer and to apply the correct VAT treatment.

As the case law of the European Court of Justice on the application of the exemption of intra-community supply of goods has shown,[52] it is sometimes difficult for the supplier to clearly determine his/her customer's location for non-digital transactions. It could prove to be a mission impossible for digital supplies, considering their above-mentioned particularities. This situation creates legal uncertainty for the e-suppliers, and more generally for all the parties involved in digital transactions. It also represents an important issue regarding the fight against VAT fraud.

5.3.2.2 Excessive Burden of Proof for Suppliers

Heavy compliance requirements may represent an excessive burden of proof for suppliers.[53] Since the destination principle requires that taxation takes place at the customer's location, the supplier needs to ascertain the status and location of his customers, which is problematic as mentioned above. Furthermore, in the absence of a reverse charge mechanism, which is usually the case for supplies to non-taxable persons, the supplier will have to assess the VAT due in accordance with the rules that apply in the jurisdiction of consumption, for each single transaction.

These compliance obligations could be so burdensome that e-suppliers could even prefer to take the risk of being convicted of fraud instead of implementing the necessary internal processes to ensure compliance. Due to those compliance difficulties, e-suppliers could contemplate fraud as a sort of second-best solution and voluntarily decide to take the risk not to apply the cumbersome requirements laid down by the applicable legislation.[54] For some authors, e-suppliers could for instance decide to just charge VAT based on the indication by the customer of its VAT number (if any) and its location,[55] without any certainty of the veracity of this information. According to ECJ case law, a party involved in a transaction has to take every reasonable step to avoid a participation in a tax fraud scheme.[56] The ECJ also regularly refers to the well-known 'knowledge test', under which Member States are

52. See CJEU Case C-409/04 *Teleos of 27 September 2007*; CJEU Case C-146/05 *Collée of 27 September 2007*; CJEU Case *Twoh of 27 September 2007*, C-184/05.
53. P. Rendahl (2009): 'Cross-Border Consumption Taxation of Digital Supplies', Amsterdam IBFD, Doctoral Series, 2009, Vol. 18 at 179.
54. See M. Lamensch (2014): 'The Treatment of "Digital products" and other "E-Services" under VAT', at 4, in M. Lang and I. Lejeune (eds): 'VAT/GST in a Global Digital Economy', to be published (Kluwer).
55. A. Bal (2014): 'The Myth of Taxing Cloud Computing under EU VAT', 25 International VAT Monitor of November/December 2014 at 347.
56. See among others CJEU Case C-409/04 *Teleos of 27 September 2007*. For more information, see among others E. Traversa (2014): 'Prevention of Evasion, Avoidance and Abuse in EU VAT Law', in M. Lang, P. Pistone, J. Schuch, C. Staringer, D. Raponi (eds) (2014): 'ECJ – Recent Developments in Value Added Tax: The Evolution of European VAT Jurisprudence and its Role in the EU Common VAT System', Viena, Linde Verlag, at 48–53.

allowed, or even obliged, to sanction a VAT taxable person if it is established that he or she knew or should have known that he or she was involved in VAT fraud.[57] But how could a supplier be certain that he is or will not be involved in VAT fraud when dealing with e-commerce if he has no legal certainty regarding the identification and location of his customers and thus the applicable VAT regime? It will put him in a critical position.

From the perspective of correctly carrying out e-commerce transactions and of fighting VAT fraud, it is therefore crucial for all parties concerned to dispose of clear and effective criteria which will allow the correct identification of the key elements of every e-transaction. These elements will have to take into account '*the automation and the dematerialization of the activity*'.[58]

5.3.3 The Limits of the Proposed Solutions

Unfortunately, the solutions proposed to better implement the destination principle in the area of digital transactions do not appear satisfactory, especially in the light of their concrete implementation.

5.3.3.1 The Presumptions regarding the Place of Supply of E-Services in Regulation 1042/2013/EU

At the European level, Regulation 1042/2013/EU of 7 October 2013 amended Implementing Regulation 282/2011/EU as regards the place of supply of services of telecommunications, broadcasting and electronic services. Explanatory Notes have also been published on 4 April 2014,[59] with the objective to provide more information regarding the new rules and to '*solve any doubt that could arise from the wording of legislative acts*'.[60] These documents (see Appendices III, IV and V) provide some rebuttable presumptions that can be used by the supplier in order to determine how to correctly apply VAT rules.[61]

Concerning the determination of the status of the recipient, Regulation 282/2011/EU provides that the supplier may regard a customer as a VAT taxable person

57. See among others E. Traversa *supra* at 50–53; M. Alvarez Suso (2014): 'The boundaries of Abusive Practices: the Grey Zone', in M. Lang, P. Pistone, J. Schuch, C. Staringer, D. Raponi (eds) (2014): 'ECJ – Recent Developments in Value Added Tax: The Evolution of European VAT Jurisprudence and its Role in the EU Common VAT System', Viena, Linde Verlag, at 64; C. Amand and K. Boucquez (2011): 'A New Defence for Victims of EU Missing-Trader Fraud?', 22 International VAT Monitor of July/August 2011 at 235.
58. P. Centore and M. T. Sutich (2014): 'Taxation and Digital Economy: Europe is Ready', 42 Intertax 12 of 2014 at 786.
59. Explanatory notes on the EU VAT changes to the place of supply of telecommunications, broadcasting and electronic services that enter into force in 2015, 3 Apr. 2014, http://eur-lex.europa.eu (see Appendix V).
60. P. Centore and M. T. Sutich (2014): 'Taxation and Digital Economy: Europe is Ready', 42 Intertax 12 of 2014 at 786.
61. See A. Bal (2015): 'Taxing Virtual Currency: Challenges and Solutions', 43 Intertax 5 of 2015 at 387.

'where the customer has communicated his individual VAT identification number to him, and the supplier obtains confirmation of the validity of that identification number and of the associated name and address [...]'.[62] If the customer does not have a VAT number yet, the presumption is applicable if the latter demonstrates that he is in the process of registering and if the supplier *'carries out a reasonable level of verification of the accuracy of the information provided by the customer, by normal commercial security measures such as those relating to identity or payment checks'.*[63]

This solution is however not optimal. As mentioned, electronic business involves minimum contacts and it will thus be difficult for the supplier to obtain this information from his e-client, especially once that the transaction has taken place.[64] The EU presumptions also imply that a party (the supplier) depends on the reliability of the information submitted by the client, although liability for VAT rests on him.[65] Finally, the compliance burden imposed on the supplier in terms of the '*reasonable level of verification*' when the client is in the process of obtaining a VAT number, is unclear and does not provide the required legal certainty. The Regulation tries to solve some of the issues regarding the application of VAT rules by indicating that if the recipient does not provide any VAT number, the supplier may consider the recipient as a non-taxable person '*irrespective of information to the contrary*',[66] but this is not satisfactory, because it could lead to a wrong application of VAT location rules and possibly to double taxation.

Regulation 282/2011/EU also provides some rebuttable presumptions regarding the determination of the location of the customer (Article 24a-c), to assist suppliers in that respect.[67] For instance, the recipient can be presumed to be established: at the place of installation of his fixed landline, based on the country code of his SIM card, but also '*on the basis of two items of non-contradictory evidence as listed in Article 24f* [...]'. These items include: the billing address of the customer; the bank details (location of the bank account or billing address held by the bank); '*other commercially relevant information*', and, as indicated by the Explanatory Notes, this is a non-exhaustive list.[68]

These presumptions can be rebutted[69] by the supplier '*on the basis of three items of non-contradictory evidence indicating that the customer is established, has his*

62. Article 18, 1, a) of the Implementing Regulation 282/2011/EU of 15 Mar. 2011.
63. Article 18, 1, b) of the Implementing Regulation 282/2011/EU of 15 Mar. 2011.
64. A. Bal (2014): 'The Myth of Taxing Cloud Computing under EU VAT', 25 International VAT Monitor of November/December 2014 at 345; A. Bal (2015): 'Taxing Virtual Currency: Challenges and Solutions', 43 Intertax 5 of 2015 at 388.
65. A. Bal (2014): 'The Myth of Taxing Cloud Computing under EU VAT', 25 International VAT Monitor of November/December 2014 at 345; See A. Bal (2015): 'Taxing Virtual Currency: Challenges and Solutions', 43 Intertax 5 of 2015 at 387 and 388.
66. New Article 18, 2 of the Implementing Regulation 282/2011/EU of 15 Mar. 2011.
67. For more explanations, see A. Bal (2014): 'The Myth of Taxing Cloud Computing under EU VAT', 25 International VAT Monitor of November/December 2014 at 346.
68. Explanatory notes on the EU VAT changes to the place of supply of telecommunications, broadcasting and electronic services that enter into force in 2015, 3 Apr. 2014, at 53, http://eur-lex.europa.eu.
69. See A. Bal (2014): 'The Myth of Taxing Cloud Computing under EU VAT', 25 International VAT Monitor of November/December 2014 at 346.

permanent address or usually resides elsewhere',[70] and by the tax authorities '*where there are indications of misuse or abuse by the supplier*'.[71]

Once again, although interesting, these clarifications offer no legal certainty to the e-supplier who remains dependent on his clients' bona fide cooperation, because in many cases the information will not be accessible otherwise. Moreover, the absence of a clear compliance procedure is also problematic. The perfect example is the listing of: '*items of non-contradictory evidence*'. First of all, no hierarchy is foreseen. What should the supplier therefore do in case of equality between contradictory and non-contradictory evidence? The Regulation stays silent. The Explanatory Notes, which should bring some clarification, mention that: '*It will be for the supplier to decide which two items of non-contradictory evidence he considers most reliable in determining the place where his customer belongs*'.[72] In terms of legal certainty and reliability, this is clearly not satisfactory.

Second, some items are redundant (for instance, if the Mobile Country Code is available, the presumption based on the SIM card country code should be applied) or can be easily falsified (for instance, the IP address).

Finally, some elements are unclear. What is, for instance, covered by the term: '*other commercially relevant information*'? The Explanatory Notes give some examples: the use by the client of a specific payment mechanism from a Member State; the client's trading history; a gift card point of sale; country-locked gift cards; documentation of third-party payment to service providers; customer self-certification.[73] Again, some elements might be difficult to track, and some of them look too specific to be applicable to common e-situations. Moreover, the compliance burden on the supplier remains important: the Explanatory Notes indeed mention that: '*the supplier should also be able to justify why this information is relevant to him*'[74] and that: '*a pro-active verification should take place on a regular basis*'.[75]

Some interesting proposals where thus made, but these remain insufficient to provide all the essential guarantees needed to reach an optimal level of legal certainty, to ensure a correct application of VAT rules and to minimize risks of fraud.[76]

70. New Article 24d, 1 of the Implementing Regulation 282/2011/EU of 15 Mar. 2011.
71. New Article 24d, 2 of the Implementing Regulation 282/2011/EU of 15 Mar. 2011.
72. Explanatory notes on the EU VAT changes to the place of supply of telecommunications, broadcasting and electronic services that enter into force in 2015, 3 Apr. 2014, at 60, http://eur-lex.europa.eu.
73. Explanatory notes on the EU VAT changes to the place of supply of telecommunications, broadcasting and electronic services that enter into force in 2015, 3 Apr. 2014, at 69 and 70, http://eur-lex.europa.eu.
74. Explanatory notes on the EU VAT changes to the place of supply of telecommunications, broadcasting and electronic services that enter into force in 2015, 3 Apr. 2014, at 69, http://eur-lex.europa.eu.
75. Explanatory notes on the EU VAT changes to the place of supply of telecommunications, broadcasting and electronic services that enter into force in 2015, 3 Apr. 2014, at 71, http://eur-lex.europa.eu.
76. It also seems that the vision of how e-commerce is taking place stays blurred. A perfect example is provided by the Explanatory Notes: when they analysed how the supplier should verify information on the recipient, they mentioned that 'in many cases, the customer will have a regular relationship with the supplier'. This is far from the reality of the digital economy, where we already mentioned the limits of interaction between parties. The options offered to deal with

5.3.3.2 *The OECD Guidelines*

The OECD has also offered guidance. The OECD International VAT/GST Guidelines (in their April 2014 version)[77] recommended, for instance, to allow the supplier to ascertain the identity and location of his customers and to proceed to verifications on a transaction basis, based on information available among others in the business agreement concluded by the parties. However, the same remarks, as those made above on the EU proposals, can be made. In the digital economy, it could be extremely difficult to follow this 'transaction by transaction' compliance procedure. Moreover, the suggestion to look at the business agreement cannot be seen as a reasonable solution because e-commerce is usually a 'one shot transaction' (especially in a B2C context) that takes place in the absence of a business agreement between the parties concerned, and the OECD International VAT/GST Guidelines stay silent on the way to act in the absence of an existing business relationship and a detailed business agreement.[78] This solution could be optimal neither regarding the fight against VAT fraud.

As in the case of the EU, the OECD International VAT/GST Guidelines also suggest to refer to the VAT registration number as a way of identification of e-customers. This solution might be interesting, also from a VAT fraud perspective, if it were possible to quickly verify the official VAT registration numbers on a real time basis and with an accurate result. However, the way in which the actual system works does not permit to achieve the desired result: there is indeed no worldwide VAT registration numbers database. It could be argued that this is not totally true: indeed, at the EU level, the VIES system in principle allows verifying the validity of a VAT number issued by any Member State. However, this system is not totally reliable and not always up-to-date. This situation might evolve, as mentioned by the European Commission in a report published on 12 February 2014 regarding administrative cooperation and fight against VAT fraud.[79] The Commission recalled that '*the provisions relating to the VIES database were amended in order to increase the amount and quality of information stored and exchanged*'. A large number of Member States is satisfied with this evolution, which increases the rapidity of the updates and therefore implies a better exchange of information. The situation is however not totally optimal: the European Commission indeed underlined that, despite the amendments, '*there are still discrepancies and retroactive corrections continue to be made to VIES data*'. This

e-commerce would remain insufficient if the perception of what this sector represents stays incorrect. See Explanatory notes on the EU VAT changes to the place of supply of telecommunications, broadcasting and electronic services that enter into force in 2015, 3 Apr. 2014, at 71, http://eur-lex.europa.eu.

77. International VAT/GST Guidelines, April 2014, http://www.oecd.org.
78. M. Lamensch (2014): 'The Treatment of "Digital products" and other "E-Services" under VAT', at 5, in M. Lang and I. Lejeune (eds): 'VAT/GST in a Global Digital Economy', to be published (Kluwer).
79. Report from the Commission to the Council and the European Parliament on the application of Council Regulation (EU) No. 904/2010 concerning administrative cooperation and combating fraud in the field of value added tax, pp. 8 et 9, http://ec.europa.eu.

could still remain an issue in terms of reliability of the VIES database. Therefore the Commission recommended that '*all Member States introduce measures to keep the VIES database up-to-date*'. This should lead to a reliable and updated VIES system, which will be positive in terms of determining essential elements of e-transactions.[80]

The most recent version of the OECD International VAT/GST Guidelines, i.e., the Discussion Draft Guidelines, offers interesting insights regarding 'identification' solutions.[81] These Draft Guidelines seek to complement the first chapters of the existing Guidelines focusing on B2C supplies, among others to correctly determine the place of taxation for B2C supplies of services and intangibles in accordance with the destination principle. The Draft Guidelines were opened to public comments, which were centralized in a report published on 25 February 2015.[82]

The Draft Guidelines start by encouraging jurisdictions to provide '*clear practical guidance on how suppliers could establish the status of their customer (business or non-business)*'.[83] However, this recommendation is at the moment only made for jurisdictions that implement specific approaches for determining the place of taxation and/or provide for different collection mechanisms. This limitation has no sense considering the abovementioned issues related to the determination of the status of e-customers. This was clearly underlined in the public comments Report, which pleads for advising the jurisdictions to provide practical guidance on how suppliers can establish the status of their customers in all circumstances.[84]

The Draft Guidelines continue by recommending:

> a requirement for suppliers to provide a customer's VAT registration number or tax identification number, or other such indicia (e.g., information available in commercial registers) to establish their customer's status. Where a supplier, acting in good faith and having made reasonable efforts, is not able to obtain the appropriate documentation to establish the status of its customer, this could lead to a presumption that this is a non-business customer and that therefore the rules for business-to-consumer supplies apply. To facilitate suppliers' identification and verification of their customers' status, jurisdictions are encouraged to consider implementing an easy-to-use process that would allow suppliers to verify the validity of their customers' VAT registration or tax identification numbers.[85]

80. C. Amand and K. Boucquez (2011): 'A New Defence for Victims of EU Missing-Trader Fraud?', 22 International VAT Monitor of July/August 2011 at 239 and 240.
81. International VAT/GST Guidelines on place of taxation for business-to-consumer supplies of services and intangibles, Discussion Draft for Public consultation, 18 Dec. 2014–20 Feb. 2015, http://www.oecd.org.
82. Comments received on public discussion drafts – International VAT/GST Guidelines on place of taxation for business-to-consumer supplies of services and intangibles, 25 Feb. 2015, http://www.oecd.org.
83. International VAT/GST Guidelines on place of taxation for business-to-consumer supplies of services and intangibles, Discussion Draft for Public consultation, 18 Dec. 2014–20 Feb. 2015, p. 4, http://www.oecd.org.
84. Comments received on public discussion drafts – International VAT/GST Guidelines on place of taxation for business-to-consumer supplies of services and intangibles, 25 Feb. 2015, at 212, http://www.oecd.org.
85. International VAT/GST Guidelines on place of taxation for business-to-consumer supplies of services and intangibles, Discussion Draft for Public consultation, 18 Dec. 2014–20 Feb. 2015, at 4 and 5, http://www.oecd.org.

This recommendation encourages solutions in order to clearly identify the status of the customers, using existing data.[86] It also takes into account the fact that the supplier should face a reasonable burden when determining the status of his customer. Finally, it pleads for having an efficient and reliable system to verify the validity of the VAT number, which is in line with the amendment of the VIES database (compare *supra*). This recommendation could also be more generally used in terms of combating VAT fraud. The determination of the different elements of every e-transaction could be facilitated by using existing data (which should be recorded somewhere – compare *infra*). Moreover, the limitation of the burden of proof should also be considered whenever anti-abuse provisions would apply to non-fraudulent participants in a fraud scheme.

Regarding the '*easy-to-use process*' mentioned in the Draft Guidelines, it is recommended to modify the actual Guidelines:

> to advise the jurisdictions to make a freely available official online tool for real-time verification of the tax status of the customers, where such checks are expected either by the legislation or by the tax practice of the jurisdiction's tax authorities. Especially in the case of the digital economy it is important to have an access to an official tool which enables a real-time verification of the tax status of new customers. E-commerce businesses need to process the transaction immediately and automatically without undue delays. They do not have the luxury of traditional businesses to verify the tax status of their customer manually before deciding whether or not consumption tax should be charged. Any delay increases the risk that the customer will abort the transaction before the sale is made.

This suggestion could be of great help in improving the fight against VAT e-fraud: having an easily accessible online tool which could be used by the VAT parties to check the relevant information will give them some certainty regarding the transaction and each other's status. Obviously, in order to have an efficient tool, it will require from Member States that they ensure the timely updating of this instrument, which might be an issue, as the experience with the VIES system has demonstrated.

The Draft Guidelines also state that due to the specific characteristics of e-commerce (high volume, minimal communication and interaction between parties, ...): '*suppliers might not be able to rely on one single source of information, such as a contract, to reliably determine the place of usual residence of the customer*'.[87] It is therefore recommended that the suppliers are allowed to rely on information that they: '*routinely collect from their customers in the course of their normal business activity, as long as such information provides reasonably reliable evidence of the place of usual residence of their customers*'.[88] In particular, the Draft Guidelines emphasize that

86. The proposed solution of using information available in commercial registers is however not sufficient regarding digital economy, as already pointed out, considering the lack of permanent business connexion between involved parties.
87. International VAT/GST Guidelines on place of taxation for business-to-consumer supplies of services and intangibles, Discussion Draft for Public consultation, 18 Dec. 2014–20 Feb. 2015, at 8, http://www.oecd.org.
88. *Ibid.*

information provided by the customer generally may be considered as important evidence regarding his usual residence. Different examples are mentioned, similar to those provided in the EU implementing Regulation: ordering process, address, bank details, credit card information, IP address, device used to download digital content etc. These are interesting elements, but, as mentioned above, they are clearly not fraud-proof (possible manipulation of some information, dependence on the e-client, ...). Also, as pointed out in the public comments report,[89] this could have a negative impact on the business, since the proposed language used in the Draft Guidelines:

> suggests that suppliers may be required by jurisdictions to obtain additional information supporting the consumer's place of usual residence. This approach is not feasible in the context of high-volume, low-value transactions *[i.e., in e-commerce area]*. The more information a supplier requires a consumer to provide in order to complete a transaction, the more likely it becomes that the consumer will abandon the transaction prior to completion.

It is therefore not in the best interest of the further development of e-activities to provide that a party has to rely on the good will of the other party. Some solutions need to be found in that respect (for instance the use of a third party – compare *infra*).

The draft also encourages an improved international cooperation between Member States, in particular regarding exchange of information and assistance in recovery.[90] It represents the best way to ensure an efficient identification of the parties concerned, the monitoring of the volume of transactions and the proper collection of VAT. Discussion on the options to be favoured is still ongoing: representatives from OECD countries and territories will decide whether to ratify the orientations proposed in the draft guidelines during the third meeting of the OECD Global Forum on VAT that will take place in November 2015.[91]

5.4 FIGHTING VAT FRAUD IN THE AREA OF DIGITAL SUPPLIES: THE NEED FOR COMPREHENSIVE AND INNOVATIVE SOLUTIONS

Despite the clear impact of the above-mentioned issues on the fight against VAT fraud, it is quite surprising that the recent official documents/reports do not contain specific recommendations about how to fight VAT fraud in the digital economy. It is true that Chapter 4 of the OECD Draft Guidelines deals with issues regarding evasion and avoidance. The only goal of this chapter, however, is to describe the main existing

89. Comments received on public discussion drafts – International VAT/GST Guidelines on place of taxation for business-to-consumer supplies of services and intangibles, 25 Feb. 2015, at 182, http://www.oecd.org.
90. International VAT/GST Guidelines on place of taxation for business-to-consumer supplies of services and intangibles, Discussion Draft for Public consultation, 18 Dec. 2014–20 Feb. 2015, at 9 and 10, http://www.oecd.org.
91. The third meeting of the OECD Global Forum on VAT has been planned at the occasion of the second meeting of that same forum in Tokyo on 17–18 Apr. 2014, see 'Statement of Outcomes on the OECD International VAT/GST Guidelines', see http://www.oecd.org/tax/consumption/vat-global-forum.htm.

instruments for exchange of information and mutual assistance that facilitate the fight against VAT fraud (multilateral cooperation, OECD Model Tax Convention etc.). The OECD International VAT/GST Guidelines encourage the use of these existing mechanisms for mutual cooperation, information exchange and mutual assistance, but there is no specific mention of the question whether the existing instruments are fit for the purpose of combating VAT e-fraud.

Considering this situation, the question remains open as to which solutions could be found in order to efficiently combat VAT fraud in e-commerce.

5.4.1 Using Information Technology to Better Trace and Identify VAT Taxable Persons and Transactions

As already mentioned, it will be important for the parties concerned to dispose of clear elements which will allow them to identify the e-transaction and the different parties involved (IP address, ordering process, address, bank details, ...), without being in a 'dependence situation' (see *supra*). It will therefore be important to develop specific e-tools to help collect this information and keep it up to date and at the disposal of e-commerce suppliers. The OECD International VAT/GST Guidelines encourage the use of electronic record keeping systems, which will enable the tax administration: '*to ensure that the tax has been charged and accounted for correctly*'.[92] In that respect, the Guidelines recommend to limit the data to be recorded to what is required to satisfy the jurisdictions and to what could be made available on request within a reasonable delay. The use of electronic identification devices is also an interesting path to follow,[93] as it could provide reliable information, instantaneously. Having the opportunity to access relevant information almost instantly should significantly deter the development of fraudulent schemes.

The involvement of a third party, like financial institutions, in the VAT assessment and collection process also appears promising.[94] These institutions are indeed increasingly required to verify, collect, store and update information concerning their customers. As this information already is or will be available, it could be used also in the fight against VAT fraud. In that respect, the RTvat[95] initiative can be mentioned. It aims at combatting VAT fraud by organizing the collection of VAT at the level of banks. This could have a positive effect as it would remove the VAT collection burden from suppliers.[96]

---

92. International VAT/GST Guidelines on place of taxation for business-to-consumer supplies of services and intangibles, Discussion Draft for Public consultation, 18 Dec. 2014–20 Feb. 2015, at 17, http://www.oecd.org.
93. M. Lamensch (2012): 'Are reverse charging and the one-stop-scheme efficient ways to collect VAT on digital supplies?', 1 WJOVL 1 of 2012 at 17–19.
94. M. Lamensch (2014): 'The Treatment of "Digital products" and other "E-Services" under VAT', at 4, in M. Lang and I. Lejeune (eds): 'VAT/GST in a Global Digital Economy', to be published (Kluwer); M. Lamensch (2012): 'Are reverse charging and the one-stop-scheme efficient ways to collect VAT on digital supplies?', 1 WJOVL 1 of 2012 at 14–17.
95. http://rtvat.net.
96. For more information, see M. Lamensch (2012): 'Are reverse charging and the one-stop-scheme efficient ways to collect VAT on digital supplies?', 1 WJOVL 1 of 2012 at 15 and 16.

5.4.2 Enhancing Administrative Cooperation and Developing Simple Mechanisms for the Assessment and Collection of VAT on Cross-Border Transactions

It will also be crucial to continue developing cooperation and exchange of information between Member States.[97] In a Single, integrated market, the only way to ensure an efficient fraud-proof VAT system is by increasing the efficiency of the cooperation between Member States. This conclusion was recently drawn by the European Commission in its February 2014 report concerning the fight against VAT fraud and the development of administrative cooperation.[98] The aim of the report was to serve as: '*a basis for a permanent and structured dialogue between the Commission, the European Parliament, the Council and the Member States in order to improve the efficiency of administrative cooperation in the field of VAT with the specific objective of fighting VAT fraud more effectively*'. It presented an overview of how the different mechanisms of administrative cooperation have been used by the Member States in fighting VAT fraud.

The conclusion stressed, however, that the current situation is far from being optimal. The European Commission stated that there are numerous unresolved issues mainly due to the behaviour of Member States (lack of replies, delays, etc.).[99] Some initiatives were already taken: for instance, regarding the exchange of information upon request, new e-forms have been drawn up in order to help Member States to quickly handle the treatment of the requests.[100] Moreover, the European Commission is willing to extend administrative cooperation beyond EU borders, by directly negotiating with third countries on behalf of the twenty-eight Member States.[101]

In this context, it will be essential, as recommended in the OECD International VAT/GST Guidelines Discussion Draft, to develop a common standard for the exchange of information that is simple, minimizes the costs for tax administrations and businesses by limiting the amount of data that is exchanged, and which can be implemented in a short timeframe. It will also be crucial to properly improve the use of the feedback mechanism by the Member States. This system should normally lead to a steady improvement in the volume and quality of the information exchanged between the Member States, which the Commission considers unsatisfactory at the moment.[102]

97. M. Griffioen, L. van der Hel (2014): 'New European Approach to Combat VAT Fraud?', 42 Intertax 5 of 2014 at 299.
98. Report from the Commission to the Council and the European Parliament on the application of Council Regulation (EU) No. 904/2010 concerning administrative cooperation and combating fraud in the field of value added tax, 12 Feb. 2014, http://ec.europa.eu.
99. Some authors share the same view. See M. Griffioen, L. van der Hel (2014): 'New European Approach to Combat VAT Fraud?', 42 Intertax 5 of 2014 at 299.
100. Report from the Commission to the Council and the European Parliament on the application of Council Regulation (EU) No. 904/2010 concerning administrative cooperation and combating fraud in the field of value added tax, 12 Feb. 2014, http://ec.europa.eu.
101. Communication from the Commission to the European Parliament and the Council, An Action Plan to strengthen the fight against tax fraud and tax evasion, 6 Dec. 2012, COM(2012) 722 final, at 11.
102. *Ibid.*

Administrative cooperation should also go beyond the mere exchange of information and extend to collaboration in the assessment and collection process. Especially within the EU, Member States' tax administrations should act more as decentralized authorities of one single European tax administration than as independent, water-edged bodies whose responsibilities are limited to the territory of one single Member State.

The compliance burden imposed on the supplier should also be eased by simplification mechanisms. For instance, because the taxable transaction is located in the country of the customer, the correct assessment, collection and remittance of VAT entails (significant) additional costs, generally borne by the supplier, and triggered by the registration in the jurisdictions where the VAT is due. In order to settle that issue, the OECD International VAT/GST Guidelines recommend the implementation of a '*simplified registration and compliance regime*'.[103]

Within the EU, a destination based solution applies since 1 January 2015 to supplies of telecommunications-, broadcasting-, and electronic services to a final consumer, which locates the place of supply in the country of the customer. It has indeed been decided to implement an optional mini One Stop Shop (MOSS). Actually, this represents an extension of an already existing system, the One Stop Shop, which simplifies VAT obligations for non-EU suppliers of electronic services to EU customers. As mentioned by the European Commission,[104] the implementation of the above-mentioned new rule: '*makes it necessary to broaden the current scope of the existing One Stop Shop system*'. This system can be used by digital suppliers to account for their VAT liability online in their Member State of registration rather than obliging them to register in each Member State of consumption. The suppliers may therefore register, declare and pay the VAT due in other Member States: '*via a single web portal in one single Member State, the Member State of identification*'.[105]

The Commission has issued guidelines regarding the concrete functioning of the MOSS.[106] It represents an important progress towards the simplification of all the VAT obligations within the EU, in line with all the above-mentioned proposals made in order to dispose of a better and fraud proof VAT system.

It will be interesting to see how the MOSS will work, also from a VAT fraud perspective. The MOSS could indeed become the proposed, easily accessible, online platform (compare *supra*) that could be used by the VAT parties to quickly dispose of

103. International VAT/GST Guidelines on place of taxation for business-to-consumer supplies of services and intangibles, Discussion Draft for Public consultation, 18 Dec. 2014–20 Feb. 2015, p. 8, http://www.oecd.org.

104. European Commission, 'Taxation: Developing the One Stop Shop for cross border VAT compliance', 13 Jan. 2012, http://europa.eu/rapid/press-release_IP-12-17_en.htm.

105. Report from the Commission to the Council and the European Parliament on the application of Council Regulation (EU) No. 904/2010 concerning administrative cooperation and combating fraud in the field of value added tax, 12 Feb. 2014, at 15, http://ec.europa.eu.

106. These guidelines were issued in October 2013 and June 2014. For more information, see P. Centore and M. T. Sutich (2014): 'Taxation and Digital Economy: Europe is Ready', 42 Intertax 12 of 2014 at 786; M. Lamensch (2012): 'Are reverse charging and the one-stop-scheme efficient ways to collect VAT on digital supplies?', 1 WJOVL 1 of 2012 at 6–9.

all the relevant needed information in order to ensure the correct application of location criteria and therefore the absence of fraudulent behaviour.[107] The success of the MOSS will have an impact beyond the digital economy: indeed, in a 2014 Communication, the European Commission has indicated that this system should be extended to supplies of services and goods other than the e-transactions. Some authors are also in favour of such an extension.[108]

New technologies and new business models create some difficulties for the application of the traditional VAT rules. But this could also be the opportunity to use this new e-environment to rethink the EU common tax system[109] and, among others, to adapt the way in which VAT fraud is fought. Beyond the specific reforms presented in this article (use of electronic devices, online tools, etc.), one could wonder whether an efficient VAT anti-fraud strategy would not necessarily require setting up a common EU digital VAT administration, which would provide for the traditional functions of a tax administration (information, assessment, collection and control) but completely on-line. More than ever, the fragmentation resulting from the existence of twenty-eight different bodies presents many inconveniences and very little, if no, advantages. As the MOSS has shown, digital supplies are the laboratory in which solutions will be elaborated towards a single, unified EU VAT e-administration, which is undoubtedly the most efficient tool against fraud.

Finally, and most importantly from a legal point of view, new anti-fraud rules and mechanisms will have to be designed in accordance with superior norms, in particular human rights.[110] Indeed, the most remarkable developments that have recently occurred in the VAT case law of the European Court of Justice as well as the European Court of Human Rights, concern the application of individual rights and freedoms contained in the Charter of Fundamental Rights of the European Union and in the European Convention of Human Rights and Fundamental Freedoms.[111]

Considering the peculiarities of the matter, one should pay particular attention to the respect of the *ne bis in idem* principle in the area of VAT, not only because of the coexistence in many Member States of administrative and criminal sanctions, but also due to the hybrid nature of the 'sanction' consisting in the refusal to grant the right to deduction in cross-border transactions whenever the supplier has not fully complied either with administrative requirements or with a still rather undetermined duty of

107. P. Centore and M. T. Sutich (2014): 'Taxation and Digital Economy: Europe is Ready', 42 Intertax 12 of 2014 at 787.
108. See B. Westberg (2014): 'Taxation of the Digital Economy: An EU Perspective', 54 European Taxation of December 2014 at 543.
109. J. Li (2003): 'International Taxation in the Age of Electronic Commerce: A Comparative Study', Canadian Tax Foundation, 2003 at p. 2.
110. On human rights and taxation, see P. Pistone, Ph. Baker (2015): 'General report – Subject 2: Practical protection of taxpayers' fundamental rights', IFA Cahiers de droit fiscal international, Volume 100B, Sdu at 21–74: G. Kofler, M. Poiares Maduro, P. Pistone (éd.) (2011): 'Human rights and taxation in Europe and the world', Amsterdam, IBFD Publications, 2011.
111. See on the *ne bis in idem* principle (Article 50 of the Charter), CJEU Case C-617/10 *Akerberg Fransson of 26 February 2013*, as well as ECtHR, 10 February 2009, *Zolotukhin v. Russia* (application No. 14939/03) and 27 November 2014, *Lucky Dev v. Sweden* (application no. 7356/10).

diligence. Moreover, in the digital world, privacy becomes a matter of utmost concern: the constitution of mega-databases containing all sorts of information on taxable persons, taxable transactions and customers would have to be realized in compliance with the data protection standards laid down by international courts.[112]

112. On confidentiality and privacy in tax matters, see E. Kristoffersson, M. Lang, P. Pistone, J. Schuch, C. Staringer, and A. Storck (eds)(2013): 'Tax secrecy and tax transparency: the relevance of confidentiality in tax matters', Peter Lang, Frankfurt, 2013; Ph. Malherbe, E.Traversa (2014): 'Du secret en droit fiscal' in V. Cassiers/ S. Gilson (coord.) (2014): 'L'entreprise et le secret', Larcier, 2014, p. 265–302; E. Traversa and G. D'Angelo (2010): 'Diritto tributario e privacy: un binomio critico' in L. Bolognini, D. Fulco, P. Paganini (eds) (2010) 'Next privacy: Il futuro dei nostri dati nell'era digitale', RCS ETAS of 2010 at 230–249.

CHAPTER 6

The VAT One Stop Shop System: An Efficient Way to Collect VAT on Digital Supplies into the EU Consumer Market?

Ine Lejeune & Sophie Claessens[*]

6.1 INTRODUCTION: VAT COMPLIANCE AND COLLECTION IN A WORLD IN BETA

The Internet, social media and digital transformation in general have produced some serious changes to the business landscape. The size of Business-to-Consumer[1] e-commerce is significant and increasing, accounting for over 5% of GDP in a number of EU countries where access to Internet and per capita income is high.[2] Digital content services facilitated by rapid movements in technology are particularly on the rise. Some of the key performance indicators for e-commerce businesses are *scale* (high volumes), *profitability* (low values), *reach* (remote and mainly cross-border trade) and *speed* (needing real-time compliance solutions).

The increasing digitization of traditional businesses and the spread of purely digitally operating companies pose challenges for the functioning of national and international tax systems, not the least in the field of VAT. Companies incur considerable compliance costs following the practical application of national VAT rules linked

* Ine Lejeune, Advocaat/Avocat/Attorney at the Brussels Bar, Partner Tax Policy, Dispute Resolution and Litigation, Law Square. Sophie Claessens, Senior Manager, Indirect Tax, PwC Belgium.
A special thanks to Julie Boon, student at the University of Antwerp and summer trainee with PwC Belgium, for all her research and support in the drafting of this chapter.

1. Hereinafter referred to as 'B2C'.
2. Boston Consulting Group (2011): 'Turning Local: From Madrid to Moscow, the Internet is going native', September 2011; McKinsey Global Institute (2011): 'Sizing the Internet economy', May 2011; Boston Consulting Group (2012): 'The connected world: The internet economy in the G-20', Mar. 2012; Ecommerce Europe (2014): 'Western Europe B2C E-commerce Report 2014'; Goldman Sachs (2015): 'B2C e-commerce as percentage of global GDP from 2009 to 2018'.

to cross-border e-commerce transactions. By using the destination principle, instead of the origin principle, for B2C digitally supplied service transactions starting from 2015, EU and non-EU business providing digital services and trading in different Member States are concerned about the cost of VAT registration, compliance and audit requirements in multiple countries.

One of the most important tasks and biggest challenges that today's VAT legislation is facing is the design of a simple and fraud-proof taxation system. The recent financial and economic crisis has pushed governments to maximize their tax collection either by introducing a VAT system, which an OECD study sees as the best tax to foster economic growth and provide revenue to countries, or by reforming the existing VAT system to increase its efficiency.[3]

The design of a fraud-proof VAT system does not only bring advantages to governments but is also beneficial for businesses, that are actually the unpaid tax collectors, whom it helps to develop their global activities without being confronted with inconvenient uncertainties and high compliance costs due to unclear VAT rules. Citizens also benefit from a fraud-proof environment as the taxation system would then result, through investments, in better and more sustainable employment, education, infrastructure, etc. The aim should be to deliver a VAT system that is a win-win model for the various stakeholders involved, as illustrated in Figure 6.1.

Figure 6.1 VAT Win-Win Taxation Model[4]

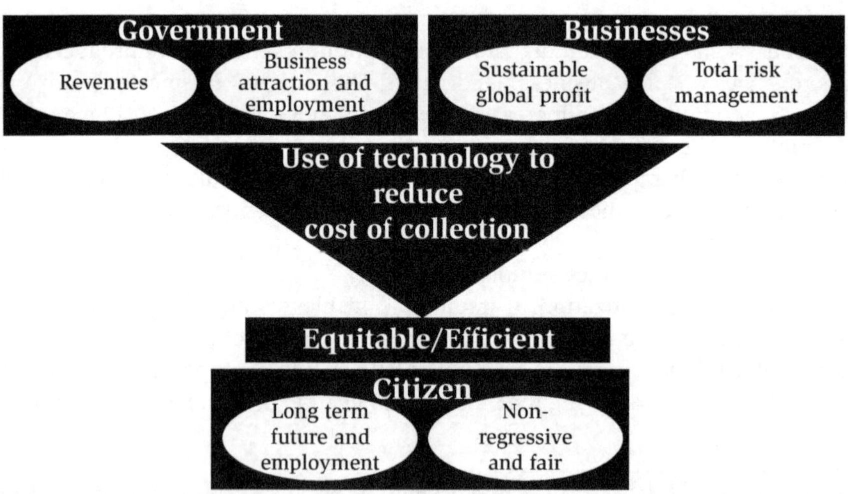

The European Commission also acknowledges that the cost of doing business in the EU is too high and that red tape needs to be reduced, especially when it comes to e-commerce businesses. On 6 May 2015, the European Commission announced its

3. OECD (2010): 'Tax Policy Reform and Economic Growth', OECD Tax Policy Studies, No. 20, OECD Publishing. http://dx.doi.org/10.1787/9789264091085-en.
4. Law Square/PwC (2015).

Digital Single Market Strategy for Europe. The aim is to remove the barriers which currently hinder EU based companies in their attempts to grow and to be (more) competitive compared to the world's internet giants.[5] In the context of VAT, the Commission announced it would make legislative proposals in 2016 to modernize EU VAT for cross-border e-commerce of goods and services and reduce the administrative burden of businesses arising from different VAT regimes.

The VAT related initiatives include extending the single electronic VAT registration and VAT payment mechanism to intra-EU and third country online sales of tangible goods to private customers. This system, also known as the VAT Mini One Stop Shop (MOSS) system,[6] was introduced in 2003 for non-EU businesses supplying e-services[7] to non-business customers (B2C) in the EU and has been extended as of 1 January 2015 to sales of telecoms, broadcasting and electronic services, by both EU and non-EU businesses, into the EU consumer market. The Commission will review the existing system, take stock of the issues with both tax administrations and businesses, and address them in the context of the 2016 proposals.

These ongoing and planned developments raise the question whether the VAT One Stop Shop system is an efficient way to collect VAT on digital supplies in the EU consumer market. This chapter will describe the VAT MOSS system (section 6.2), give an overview of the first six months of application of the VAT MOSS system since the EU 2015 VAT rule changes (section 6.3) and discuss the auditing under the VAT MOSS system (section 6.4). Summary conclusions will be given in section 6.5.

6.2 THE VAT MOSS SYSTEM EXPLAINED

The European Commission recognizes that the cost of doing business in the EU is too high and that the compliance cost needs to be reduced,[8] especially for merchants in e-commerce goods and services wishing to trade cross-border in the EU consumer market.[9]

It is in this very context that the Commission views the new EU 2015 VAT rules for B2C telecoms, broadcasting and electronic services[10] as being so important and a necessary first step 'to create a level playing field' between EU and non-EU digital

5. See European Commission Press Release, 6 May 2015, http://europa.eu/rapid/press-release_IP-15-4919_en.htm; Communication from the Commission to the European Parliament, The Council, the European Economic and Social Committee and the committee of the Regions, COM(2015)192, 6 May 2015, http://ec.europa.eu/priorities/digital-single-market/docs/dsm-communication_en.pdf.
6. Hereinafter referred to as 'VAT MOSS system' or 'VAT MOSS'.
7. The term 'electronic services' or 'e-services' refers to services which are delivered over the internet or an electronic network and the nature of which renders their supply essentially automated and involving minimal human intervention, and impossible to be ensured in the absence of information technology.
8. Commission Communication on the VAT Strategy COM (2003) 614 final dated 20 Oct. 2003; Communication from the Commission on the future of VAT COM (2011) 851 final.
9. Communication from the Commission on A Digital Single Market Strategy for Europe (COM(2015) 192 final of 6 May 2015).
10. New Article 58 of the Recast VAT Directive as applicable as from 1 Jan. 2015.

service providers. One part of that VAT revamp is the introduction of the VAT MOSS system.

6.2.1 What Is the VAT MOSS System?

The VAT MOSS system is a single electronic registration, declaration and payment system for VAT. Since 2003, the VAT MOSS system was already available for non-EU businesses supplying e-services to non-business customers in the EU.[11] As of 1 January 2015, the scope of the VAT MOSS system has been expanded to both EU and non-EU businesses making supplies of telecommunications, broadcasting and e-services to non-business customers.[12] Hence, the system is restricted to specific B2C transactions, i.e., business supplies to final consumers. Business-to-business supplies or other B2C supplies are not in scope of the existing VAT MOSS system.

The VAT MOSS system allows businesses to register for VAT in one Member State (referred to as the 'Member State of identification' or 'MSI'). Once a MSI is selected, all VAT collected on cross-border B2C sales in the EU is declared via a web portal within the MSI and paid to that MSI, on a quarterly basis. In its turn, the MSI distributes the correct VAT to each Member State in which the business recorded cross-border B2C sales ('Member State of consumption' or 'MSC').

Registration for the VAT MOSS system is optional and allows businesses to avoid registering in each Member State in which they are not established and sell to non-business customers (MSC). However, if they wish, businesses can still voluntarily register for VAT in the Member State(s) of consumption.

Finally, the VAT MOSS system is 'all inclusive' meaning that businesses choosing to use it must apply the system in all relevant Member States. It is not an optional system that can be opted for on a Member State by Member State basis.

6.2.2 Who Can Use It? Union versus Non-union VAT MOSS Schemes

All businesses that sell telecoms, broadcasting and e-services for consideration to non-business customers in the EU can use the VAT MOSS system. There is no threshold

11. The introduction of the VAT on Electronic Services (VoES) system was a reflection of the OECD's recommendations following the Ottawa Conference in 1998 and following implementing guidelines in 2000 and 2003, promoting a simplified VAT compliance for B2C transactions (www.oecd.org).
12. The following EU legislation deals with MOSS: Article 369 and 369k Directive 2006/112/EC ('Recast VAT Directive'), as applicable from 1 Jan. 2015; Council Implementing Regulation (EU) No. 967/2012 of 9 Oct. 2012, amending Implementing Regulation (EU) No. 282/2011, provides the detailed rules in relation to the operation of the MOSS scheme; Commission Implementing Regulation (EU) No. 815/2012 of 13 Sep. 2012 laying down detailed rules for the application of Council Regulation (EU) No. 904/2010, as regards special schemes for non-established taxable persons supplying telecommunications, broadcasting or electronic services to non-taxable persons; The EU Commission, in consultation with the Member States, has produced a 'Guide to the VAT Mini One Stop Shop' dated 23 Oct. 2013 and available at: http://ec.europa.eu/taxation_customs/resources/documents/taxation/vat/how_vat_works/telecom/one-stop-shop-guidelines_en.pdf.

limit. Two VAT MOSS schemes are available that operate in a similar way but with some differences.

The *Union scheme* is available for businesses (be it a company or an individual) which have established their business or have some form of fixed establishment in an EU Member State (this covers both EU and non-EU businesses). The business cannot use the VAT MOSS system for supplies made in any Member State in which it has an establishment (business establishment or fixed establishment; see Figure 6.2).[13]

Figure 6.2 The VAT MOSS System: Union Scheme[14]

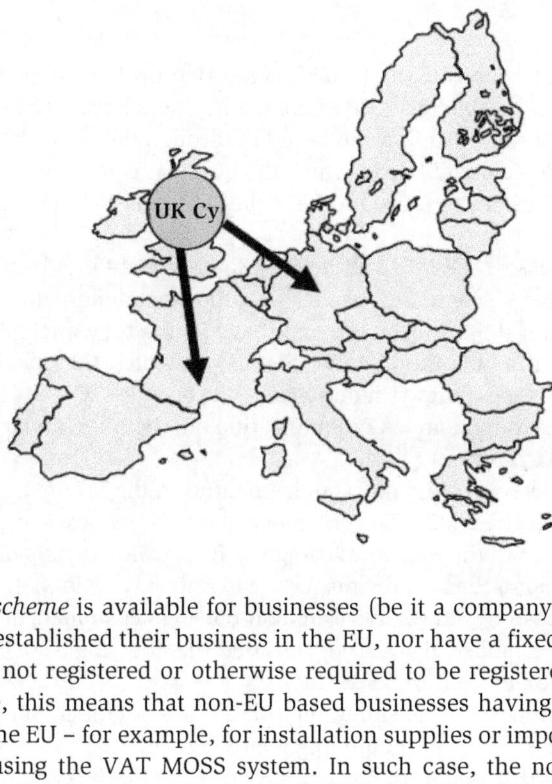

The *non-Union scheme* is available for businesses (be it a company or an individual) which have not established their business in the EU, nor have a fixed establishment in the EU, *and* are not registered or otherwise required to be registered for VAT in the EU.[15] In practice, this means that non-EU based businesses having pre-existing VAT registrations in the EU – for example, for installation supplies or imports of goods – are excluded from using the VAT MOSS system. In such case, the non-EU business is required to register and declare VAT in each Member State in which it has non-business customers to whom the relevant services are supplied (see Figure 6.3).

13. Article 369a Recast VAT Directive, as applicable from 1 Jan. 2015.
14. Source: 'The Mini One Stop Shop', European Commission, DG TAXUD, Patrice Pillet, 2 Jun. 2014, http://www.online-web-presentations.com/HMRC/files/pdf/13.45-14.15-PatricePillet.pdf.
15. Article 358a Recast VAT Directive, as applicable from 1 Jan. 2015.

Figure 6.3 The VAT MOSS System: Non-union Scheme[16]

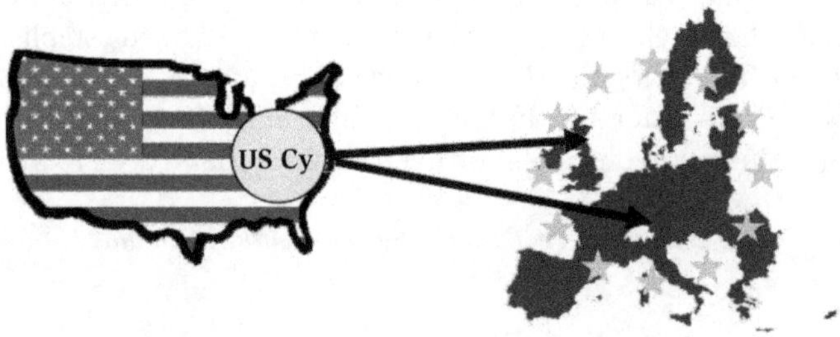

The Member State of establishment ('MSE') is the Member State in which the business of a taxable person is established[17] or where the business has a fixed establishment.[18] The business cannot report supplies in the MSE through the VAT MOSS system.

The MSI is the Member State in which the business is registered for using the EU VAT MOSS, and where it declares and pays the VAT due in the Member State(s) of consumption (MSC).

For EU businesses, the MSI will be the Member State in which the business is established, i.e., where a company has its head office, or an individual has his place of business. However, if the business does not have its main business establishment in the EU, the MSI is (one of) the Member State(s) in which the business has a fixed establishment. In all cases for the Union scheme, the business will be identified for VAT MOSS with the same individual VAT identification number under which it is identified for its domestic VAT returns.

Non-EU businesses having no establishment(s) in the EU are free to choose any EU Member State as their MSI. That Member State will allocate an individual VAT identification number to the business, using the format EUxxxyyyyyz). In both cases (Union and non-Union scheme), the business can only have one MSI, and all supplies of telecoms, broadcasting and e-services to non-business customers in a Member State in which it is not established must be declared via the single MOSS return if the business opts to use the VAT MOSS system.

The Member State of consumption (MSC) is a Member State in which the business makes supplies of telecommunications, broadcasting or e-services to non-business customers (B2C).

It is important to note that the VAT MOSS does not define the VAT liability. Supplies under the VAT MOSS have taken place according to the rates and rules

16. Source: 'The Mini One Stop Shop', European Commission, DG TAXUD, Patrice Pillet, 2 Jun. 2014, http://www.online-web-presentations.com/HMRC/files/pdf/13.45-14.15-PatricePillet.pdf.
17. Article 10 of Council Implementing Regulation (EU) No. 282/2011 (hereinafter 'VAT Implementing Regulation').
18. Article 10 of the VAT Implementing Regulation.

applicable in the MSC, not the MSI nor the Member State of establishment. As such, the rules applicable in the MSC to domestic supplies also apply to supplies under the EU VAT MOSS (see Figure 6.4). They include the rules relating to invoicing, rates, VAT accounting and bad debt relief.

Figure 6.4 VAT MOSS Decision Flowchart[19]

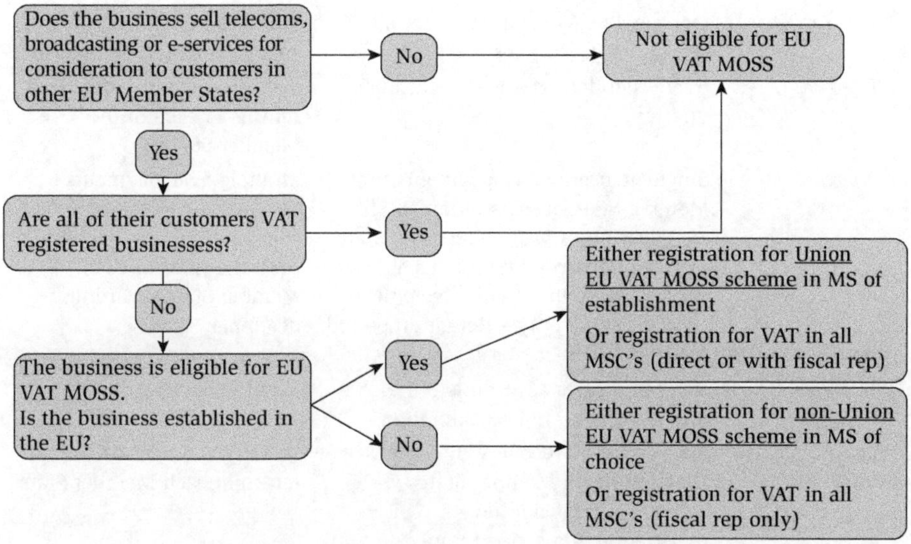

6.2.3 Key Features of the EU VAT MOSS[20]

The new EU 2015 VAT changes result in an increase in compliance obligations for businesses potentially liable to register and account for VAT in each Member State where they have consumers. In order to mitigate the additional cost for businesses, the VAT MOSS has been implemented across the EU from 1 January 2015 onwards. Businesses have the choice between registering individually in each MSC, on the one hand, or through the EU or non-EU MOSS schemes, on the other hand. The below summary (Table 6.1) highlights the main features of the VAT MOSS as compared to individual registrations.

19. PwC (2015).
20. Council Directive 2006/11/EC, Articles 357-369k (as applicable from 1 Jan. 2015); Council Regulation (EU) No. 904/2010 on administrative cooperation and combatting fraud in the field of value added tax (recast); European Commission, DG TAXUD, 'Guide to the VAT mini One Stop Shop', 23 Oct. 2013; European Commission, DG TAXUD, 'Additional guidelines – auditing under the MOSS' (see for text in Appendix VII).

Table 6.1 VAT MOSS versus Individual Registrations

Feature	*MOSS*	*Individual Registrations*
VAT registration	One single VAT registration with limited cost may apply – No registration threshold	Up to twenty-eight VAT registrations with associated administrative and cost burden – Local registration thresholds may apply
VAT ID number	One single VAT ID number for all relevant B2C supplies	Multiple VAT ID numbers in each of the Member States
VAT returns	Single standardized VAT return per quarter	Periodic and/or annual VAT returns in each of the Member States
VAT payments	Single quarterly VAT payments to the Member State of registration (MSI). MSI distributes VAT to Member States of consumption – MSI retains a percentage of the VAT collected (EU MOSS scheme only – Retention period for 2015–2016–2017).[21]	Multiple VAT payments to the Member States of consumption – Required to meet the rules of each Member State regarding deadlines
Output VAT	Rates and rules according to the Member State(s) of consumption	No difference
Input VAT recovery	No input VAT recovery through MOSS VAT return. In Member States where a business does not have a VAT registration, via a claim under Directive 2008/9/EC	Directly via the local VAT return in each Member State
Record retention period	Ten years from the end of the year in which the transaction took place, i.e., up to eleven years	Dependent on local retention rules
Tax audits	Member States of consumption retain the right to carry out controls and audits of a business registered under VAT MOSS – Coordination by MSI in most cases	Local tax audits
Penalties	According to the rules in the Member States of consumption, so up to twenty-eight different penalty systems could be applicable	No difference
Invoicing	Local rates and rules	No difference

21. This '2015 phase out arrangement' (or retention period) results from Council Regulation (EC) No. 143/2008 of 12 Feb. 2008 on administrative cooperation, concerning the inclusion of the 2015 impacted services in the one stop shop scheme. See new Articles 369a and following of the Recast VAT Directive which introduces the MOSS scheme for EU established suppliers of telecom, broadcasting and electronic services and new Article 32 of Regulation (EC) No. 1798/2003 regarding the retention percentages and period, both applicable per 1/1/2015.

6.3 FIRST SIX MONTHS OF THE EU 2015 VAT MOSS GO-LIVE

The VAT MOSS system has been designed to help business deal with the EU 2015 VAT changes, which means that VAT is now payable to the country where the consumer is based, rather than where the supplier is based, as was the case before 2015.[22] In addition to the extensive business consultation during discussion process of the implementing regulations, the European Commission has been driving an intensive communication and consultation campaign in the run-up to the changes, including conferences in the US, Poland, the UK, Belgium and Luxembourg[23] and the Global VAT forum organized by the OECD in Tokyo, Japan.[24] Many Member States have mirrored this approach in their communications with domestic businesses.

6.3.1 VAT MOSS Registration Numbers

With six months into the 2015 VAT Go-Live, the overall consensus is that the place-of-supply changes are working well, but the *number of VAT MOSS registrations* is still lagging behind, especially with smaller businesses.[25] Most large multinationals are reported to be registered, meaning the system is bringing a satisfactory level of revenue.

At the time of drafting this contribution, there were no official figures available yet on the number of MOSS registrations under the EU and non-EU schemes and their distribution over the Member States. Official figures from the EU Commission are expected to be released following the Dublin Fiscalis Seminar on 'Modernizing VAT for cross-border E-Commerce', in September 2015.

In terms of indicative figures,[26] about 10,000 VAT MOSS registrations are reported at the end of Q2 2015, of which approximately 1,000 under the non-EU MOSS scheme and about 9,000 under the EU MOSS scheme. The top three Member States in terms of registrations under the EU MOSS scheme are Germany, the UK and the Netherlands, followed by countries such as Austria, Ireland, the Czech Republic, Poland and Sweden. The top three Member States in terms of registrations under the non-EU MOSS scheme are the UK, Ireland and Germany.

These relatively low registration numbers do not come entirely as a surprise since they may be partly explained by the fact that many of the smaller businesses are selling their electronic content services through digital platforms, such as app marketplaces,[27]

22. New Article 58 of the Recast VAT Directive as applicable from 1 Jan. 2015.
23. See overview of event related to the new 2015 VAT rules on the DG TAXUD dedicated webpage.http://ec.europa.eu/taxation_customs/taxation/vat/how_vat_works/telecom/index_en.htm.
24. See dedicated page http://www.oecd.org/tax/consumption/vat-global-forum.htm.
25. J. Stanley-Smith (2015): 'VAT MOSS losing momentum with smaller businesses but working well for multinationals', International Tax Review of 23 Jul. 2015.
26. Indicative figures shared by Dermot Donegan, Head of VAT Policy at the Irish tax authority (Revenue), during a conference in Dublin on the EU 2015 VAT changes.
27. An app marketplace (or app store) is a type of digital distribution platform for mobile apps. App marketplaces typically take the form of an online store, where users can browse through different app categories, view information about each app (such as reviews or ratings), and

communication service providers,[28] online aggregators,[29] an/or payment facilitators,[30] and not direct through their own websites.

Digital platforms and accounting for VAT
Under the strict operation of the new Article 9a of the VAT Implementing Regulation,[31] digital platforms through which third parties sell e-services are liable to account for VAT on those sales unless each of the following conditions is met: (1) the digital platform and everyone else involved in the supply chain identifies the original content owner[32] in their contractual arrangements; (2) the invoice, bill or sales receipt identifies that content owner and the service supplied; (3) the digital platform does not authorize the charge to the final customer, nor the delivery of the services, nor sets the general terms and conditions of the sale. If digital platform providers do not meet all of these conditions, they must treat the third party e-services sales as if they were their own and declare the appropriate VAT due. Only where all of these conditions are met, the responsibility for accounting for VAT on the B2C supply will go back to the original content owner while the digital platforms are merely providing intermediary services to that person. As a result of this provision, many individuals and micro-businesses selling low-value electronic content, such as ringtones, games, etc., will rely on digital platforms to account for the end-consumer VAT.

6.3.2 VAT MOSS Redistribution of Revenues[33]

In terms of *VAT MOSS revenues*, the figures are more satisfactory and in line with the set targets.

acquire the app (including in-app purchases, if necessary – many apps are offered at no cost). The selected app is offered as an automatic download, after which the app installs. Some well-known examples are iOS App Store, Google Play, Amazon Appstore, Blackberry World, Samsung Galaxy Apps and Windows Store.

28. 'Communications service providers' provide access to networks that can be used to transfer voice and data. They include fixed line and mobile wireless telecommunication networks, cable networks, Internet Service Provider networks and by extension any network enabling access to electronic services.
29. 'Aggregators' are businesses that aggregate content from multiple online sources to sell it on to others.
30. 'Payment facilitators' are businesses that handle the payment transaction and do the final settlement.
31. Council Implementing Regulation (EU) No. 282/2011 of 15 Mar. 2011 laying down implementing measures for Directive 2006/112/EC on the common system of value added tax as amended by Regulation (EU) No. 1042/2013 of 10 Oct. 2013 (hereinafter 'VAT Implementing Regulation'); The new Article 9a was implemented in the VAT Implementing Regulation by Council Implementing Regulation (EU) No. 1042/2013 of 7 Oct. 2013, with effect from 1 Jan. 2015.
32. The notion of 'content owners' covers the businesses that have created the digital content or owns the content rights (electronic publishers). They are often also referred to as 'content providers'. Content providers focus on the content of the services, whereas access providers and other service providers focus on the provision of access to the internet or an electronic network.
33. Under the VAT MOSS system, the MSI collects all the VAT due in the different Member States of consumption, and distributes the collected VAT to the relevant Member States of consumption.

According to Donato Raponi, Head of the VAT unit at the European Union, extrapolating the figures from the first quarter of 2015, currently there can be said to be more or less EUR 3 billion of revenue being redistributed between the Member States.[34]

6.3.3 National Contact Points

Finally, Member States have designated *national contact points*[35] for businesses. These contact points are set up to facilitate the contact with the national administrations on matters relating to the EU 2015 VAT changes and VAT MOSS system.

6.4 AUDITING UNDER MOSS

6.4.1 MOSS Records

A VAT MOSS registered business is required to keep records containing the following information:[36]

- Member State of consumption to which the service is supplied;
- the date of the supply of the service;
- the taxable amount indicating the currency used;
- any subsequent increase or decrease or reduction of the taxable amount;
- the VAT rate applied;
- the amount of VAT payable and the currency used;
- the date and amounts of payments received;
- any payments on account received before the supply of the service;
- where an invoice is issued, the information contained on the invoice;
- the name of the customer (where known);
- the information used to determine the place where the customer is established or has his permanent address or usually resides.

This information must be recorded in such a way that it can be made available by electronic means, without delay, and for each service supplied (i.e., transaction-based record keeping). These MOSS records must be kept for ten years from the end of the year in which the transaction was made,[37] regardless of whether the business has stopped using the scheme or not. In other words, records must be kept for up to eleven years under the VAT MOSS.

34. J. Stanley-Smith (2015): 'VAT MOSS losing momentum with smaller businesses but working well for multinationals', International Tax Review of 23 Jul. 2015.
35. The list of national contact points can be found on the DG TAXUD dedicated 2015 MOSS webpage on http://ec.europa.eu/taxation_customs/resources/documents/taxation/vat/how_vat_works/telecom/list_contact_vat.pdf.
36. Article 63c of Council Regulation (EU) 967/2012.
37. Article 369 and 369k of the Recast VAT Directive.

EU legislation provides that the tax authorities of the MSI may request the MOSS records relating to supplies made in all relevant Member States and that the tax authorities of the MSC may request the MOSS records but only as far as they relate to supplies made in that particular Member State.

6.4.2 Audit Code of Practice

In June 2014, the European Commission and the vast majority of Member States agreed additional guidelines on auditing under the MOSS, an audit code of practice aiming to minimize the risk of imposing unreasonable burdens on businesses.[38] The additional guidelines include information on how to contact businesses as part of an audit and how to request information from traders as part of an audit.

These guidelines – which are not binding on the Member States – include for each guideline a list of those countries that have agreed to implement them. Interestingly, but also worrying for the businesses wishing to comply with the 2015 rules under the VAT MOSS system, Germany, France and Italy, for example, have not yet agreed to any of the recommended guidelines in relation to the auditing under MOSS.

For contacting businesses, the guidelines provide that:

- initial contacts should be routed through the MSI (eighteen Member States have agreed to implement that guideline);[39]
- MSI should use their normal national procedures when contacting businesses registered for the EU MOSS scheme, and e-mail is to be used for the initial contact (twenty-one Member States are agreeable to this guideline);[40]
- Where there is a contact from the MSC, this should be initiated via the businesses' contact e-mail address (twenty-one Member States agree to this).[41]

For requesting information from traders, the guidelines provide that the best method for exchange of information should be agreed between businesses and the tax authority and should depend on what electronic means is available to both. One possibility is to use a standard audit file for MOSS (SAF-MOSS), in XML format (twenty-one EU Member States are agreeable to this recommendation[42]).

38. Information for businesses signing up for the Mini One Stop Shop: Additional guidelines – auditing under the MOSS, June 2014 http://ec.europa.eu/taxation_customs/resources/documents/taxation/vat/how_vat_works/telecom/one-stop_add_guidelines_en.pdf (see Appendix VII).
39. Countries that will apply this recommendation: BE, BG, DK, EE, ES, FI, HR, IE, LT, LU, LV, NL, PL, PT, RO, SE, SI, UK.
40. Countries that will apply this recommendation: BE, BG, CZ, DK, EE, ES, HR, HU, IE, LU, LV, MT, NL, PL, PT,RO, SE, SI, SK, UK.
41. Countries that will apply this recommendation: BE, BG, CZ, DK, EE, ES, HR, HU, IE, LT, LU, LV, MT, NL, PL, PT, SE, SI, SK, UK.
42. Countries that will apply this recommendation: AT, BE, BG, CZ, DK, EE, ES, FI, HR, HU, IE, LT, LU, MT, NL, PL, PT, SE, SI, SK, UK.

6.4.3 Standard Audit File for MOSS ('SAF-MOSS')

The EU Commission has developed a Standard Audit File for MOSS based on the information businesses are required to keep.[43] The SAF-MOSS builds further on OECD guidance for a Standard Audit file for Tax (or 'SAF-T').[44] The Standard Audit File for MOSS is a file that contains the data required for MOSS data requests. The standardization means that the required data can be exported from the accounting system of the business, quickly, easily and in a predetermined fashion.

Most Member States – apart from Cyprus, France, Germany, Greece, Italy, Latvia and Romania – endorse the use of the Standard Audit File as the preferred method for the submission of data for information exchange. Businesses that can make this available will be in a position to respond quickly and easily to any request. The preferred format for the receipt of this data is XML. The use of the Standard Audit File, though recommended, is not mandatory and it does not have to be submitted in XML. Any appropriate format will do.

6.4.4 Issues That Are Likely to Be Examined during a MOSS Audit

The main issues are likely to be:[45]

- the nature of the supplies;
- the correct application of VAT rates;
- the distribution rules, i.e., whether the business makes the final supply to the customer under Article 9a of the VAT Implementing Regulation;
- the taxable status of the customer;
- how customer location is determined.

6.4.5 Penalties and Statute of Limitations

To resolve any disputes and/or pay any penalties or late payment charges, businesses are expected to deal directly with the tax authorities in the relevant Member State(s) of consumption, and make those payments using the currency designated by that Member State. Disputes need to be resolved at the level of the MSC applying all 'national' procedural rules including statute of limitations.

43. SAF-MOSS XML Schema specifications, DG TAXUD, 4 Nov. 2014, see DG TAXUD dedicated 2015 MOSS webpage http://ec.europa.eu/taxation_customs/taxation/vat/how_vat_works/telecom/index_en.htm.
44. OECD, Guidance on Tax compliance for business and Accounting Software, Guidance Note, May 2005. http://www.oecd.org/tax/administration/34910263.pdf.
45. This list is not exhaustive.

6.5 SUMMARY CONCLUSIONS: IS THE VAT MOSS THE START OF SOMETHING BIG?

The European Commission has, since the 2003[46] and 2011[47] VAT Strategy, been at the forefront of pursuing the OECD destination principle in respect of cross-border B2C supplies of goods and services. The development and roll out of the 2015 VAT MOSS represented a crucial milestone for the European Commission[48] and for the Member State MOSS in this respect, in particular in the framework of its Digital Single Market Strategy[49] for Europe (see Figure 6.5).

Figure 6.5 Partitioning of the Digital Market[50]

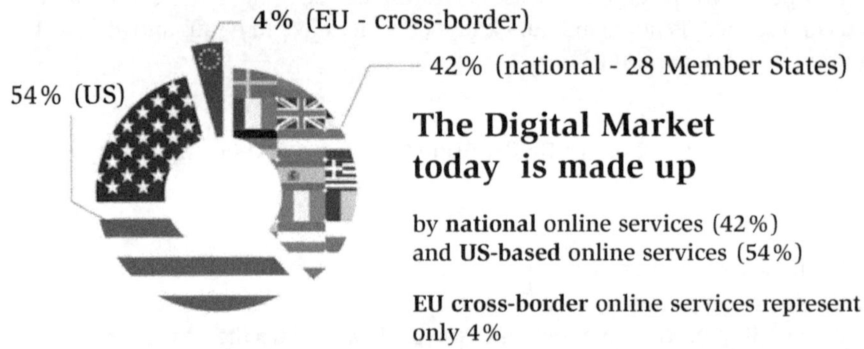

6.5.1 What Works? What Not? What Should Be Reviewed for the Future?

As currently contemplated, the VAT MOSS system provides the possibility for EU and non-EU based digital services providers to appoint one Member State of registration to account for VAT on all their supplies of telecommunications, broadcasting and electronic services into the EU consumer market.

Now the question arises whether the VAT MOSS will indeed significantly reduce the compliance costs and make it a viable option towards a broader one-stop-shop system. We would note a number of concerns. *First,* an important issue which has not

46. Commission Communication on the VAT Strategy (COM (2003) 614 final of 20 Oct. 2003).
47. Communication from the Commission on the future of VAT COM (2011) 851 final.
48. A. Semeta (2012): 'The mini-one-stop-shop for VAT – the start of something big!', World Commerce Review of June 2012.
49. Communication from the Commission to the European Parliament, The Council, the European Economic and Social Committee and the committee of the Regions, COM(2015)192, 6 May 2015, http://ec.europa.eu/priorities/digital-single-market/docs/dsm-communication_en.pdf.
50. European Commission, Digital Single Market, factsheet, May 2015.http://ec.europa.eu/priorities/digital-single-market/docs/dsm-factsheet_en.pdf.

yet been entirely resolved is the audit of the businesses under the MOSS. Current EU legislation and guidance on the VAT MOSS system still envisage that controls and audits are to be carried out by the MSC, although several tools are available to Member States to enhance the coordination of audits. For both EU and non-EU businesses, this may involve up to twenty-eight different tax administrations auditing the same business without any coordination and leading to multiple information requests in multiple languages. Not only could this create disproportionate administrative burdens on business, it could also put at stake the efficiency of the audits themselves as well as the level of voluntary compliance. This is particularly sensitive where non-EU companies are involved and could create unfair distortion of competition between compliant and non-compliant businesses (EU and non-EU).

Appointing the home country of the vendor as single point of contact for the Member States of consumption, as suggested by the Commission guidelines and endorsed by a large number of Member States, is definitely a first step in the right direction. By replacing the VAT audits performed by the destination countries by one VAT audit performed by the home country, the auditing part of the compliance process would be fully streamlined with the reporting part and achieve a significant simplification of the VAT MOSS system.

Second, VAT reporting (and subsequent audit requirements) for digital services businesses are substantially higher than for normal retailers. Indeed, when comparing digital services providers (particularly in B2C) with domestic vendors of similar products, the former appear to be confronted with a complexity caused by the cross-border dimension of their trade, requiring a substantial splitting of their revenues into the correct VAT categories.

Under the current VAT system, the VAT due is determined on a transactional basis.[51] This process implies that digital services providers will have to allocate VAT to the country where the consumer belongs and keep the related audit records, on a transaction-by-transaction basis. Such a process may be very burdensome, especially for companies selling high volumes of low-value digital services for a single price across the EU, since they will have to document all these individual transactions by storing detailed customer and other required information per micro-transaction.

In this respect, one could consider allowing digital services businesses to allocate their VAT receipts and/or store audit information on a gross revenue basis, rather than on a transactional basis. This option could be seen as a precursor for alternative collection models such as a split payment model or a data warehouse model with central VAT monitoring through direct access by the tax authorities to the VAT data warehouse of the digital services business.[52] At the same time, the ten-year record retention period under the VAT MOSS system should be addressed and aligned with the domestic retention rules.

51. Article 1(2) of the Recast VAT Directive states: '*On each transaction, VAT, calculated on the price of the goods or services at the rate applicable to such goods or services, shall be chargeable after deduction of the amount of VAT borne directly after deduction of the amount of VAT borne directly by the various cost components.*'
52. See also: '*Study on the feasibility of alternative methods for improving and simplifying the collection of VAT through the means of modern technologies and/or financial intermediaries*'

Third, even under the VAT MOSS system, businesses still need to comply with twenty-eight sets of VAT rules across the EU. This is particularly problematic when it comes to multiple invoicing requirements in the B2C area, as well as multiple VAT rates applying across the EU.[53] This is causing a barrier to cross-border trade in a Single Digital Market which should be borderless. It also stops innovation, start-ups and SME's to serve customers in the EU twenty-eight Member States and beyond. In this respect, one could consider allowing e-commerce businesses to apply the B2C VAT invoicing rules applicable in their home country under the VAT MOSS, except for the VAT rates, which would still be determined by the destination country. At the same time, work should be done to streamline the VAT rates across the EU, or even introduce common VAT rates for a number of digital supplies.

Finally, there is a call from businesses and a number of Member States for a VAT MOSS threshold. Donato Raponi, Head of the VAT unit at the European Commission, has repeatedly expressed his regret that no threshold has been provided when the 2015 regulations were agreed, back in 2008. However, for a threshold to be implemented, all twenty-eight Member States would have to agree on it. In this respect, one could consider to introduce a B2C digital supplies threshold equal to what we have for distance sales of goods. Alternatively, one could provide for an EU-wide threshold of, for example, EUR 1 million of turnover, below which the 'home country' VAT rules and rates would be applicable, and only if that threshold is crossed in one or more Member States the VAT would become due in the Member State(s) of consumption. The latter idea is currently also being considered as part of the Digital single Market Strategy for cross-border e-commerce in goods, but it would be better to streamline it for both e-commerce goods and digital services.

6.5.2 What Is Next?

The May 2014 report of the Commission Expert Group on the Taxation of the Digital Economy[54] made a number of recommendations to deliver a successful MOSS and laid the foundations for future developments. In short, the Expert Group recommends as a priority that: (1) the VAT MOSS is extended to all B2C supplies of goods and services, (2) that the existing thresholds in respect of distance sales[55] are removed, (3) that the VAT exemption for the import of low value consignments is removed,[56] (4) that these

carried out by PwC for the European Commission, Report dated 20 Sep. 2010, available at http://ec.europa.eu/taxation_customs/resources/documents/common/consultations/tax/future_vat/vat-study_summ_en.pdf.

53. With EU standard VAT rates ranging from 17% (in Luxembourg) up to 27% (in Hungary), the range being even larger when reduced rates apply.
54. Commission Expert Group on Taxation of the Digital Economy, report, 28 May 2014.http://ec.europa.eu/taxation_customs/resources/documents/taxation/gen_info/good_governance_matters/digital/report_digital_economy.pdf.
55. See Article 34 of the Recast VAT Directive, as amended.
56. See Article 23 of Directive 2009/132/EC, which provides Member States the possibility to exempt from VAT good of negligible value imported into the European Union. Member States may set the threshold for exemption between EUR 10 and EUR 22.

transactions together with the transactions below the customs threshold[57] are included within the VAT MOSS system,[58] and (5) that such transactions from third countries benefit from a fast-track customs procedure. The Expert Group considers that, in preparing for the broader One Stop Shop consideration needs to be given to improving the weaknesses of the current legislation and guidance in the area of audit, and in this respect the principle of 'home country control'[59] should be considered.

After the May 2014 report from the Expert Group, the European Commission launched a study on the 'VAT aspects of cross-border e-commerce – options for modernization'[60] in December 2014. On the basis of that study, the European Commission is undertaking an in-depth economic analysis of the VAT aspects of e-commerce as well as evaluating the implementation of the EU 2015 VAT rules and the 2015 VAT MOSS system. The initial feedback will be discussed at a Fiscalis Seminar on 'Modernizing VAT for cross-border E-Commerce', taking place in Dublin, Ireland, in September 2015.

Besides by the EU Commission, the Fiscalis Seminar will be attended by businesses, representative bodies, experts and national tax administrations, and will be a great opportunity to identify the problem areas, best practices and possible improvements.

Extending the VAT MOSS as suggested by the Expert Group will – depending on its functioning and the options chosen for the definitive EU VAT regime[61] – be an important step towards what some call the BOSS or the Bigger One Stop Shop. This would allow any business who needs to comply with VAT in one of the EU Member States, to meet its obligations in its MSI and that business should then also be audited by its 'home' country.

We are looking forward to further contributing to this dialogue and journey in order to help deliver the benefits for all stakeholders.

---

57. Under customs regulations, goods supplied from third countries with a value of less than EUR 150 are not subject to customs duties, but there is still a requirement to collect VAT on such transactions; See Council Regulation (EC) No. 1186/2009 of 16 Nov. 2009 setting up a Community system of reliefs from customs duty.
58. S. Claessens (2015): 'Levelling the location debate: introducing the Digital Single Market for small value consignments', PwC World in beta blog of 25 Jun. 2015 at http://www.worldinbeta.com.
59. 'Home Country Control' is where responsibility for control and auditing falls to the Member State where the business is established, even in respect of supplies where the place of taxation is in another Member State.
60. Report not yet published.
61. 'Study on applying the current principle for the place of supply of B2B services to B2B supplies of goods', a study carried out by PwC for the EU Commission, Final Report dated 10 Jan. 2013 at http://ec.europa.eu/taxation_customs/resources/documents/common/publications/studies/vat_public_sector_exemptions_en.pdf; '*Study on implementing the VAT "destination principle" to intra-EU B2B supplies of goods*', European Commission, Final Report dated 30 Jun. 2015, available at http://ec.europa.eu/taxation_customs/resources/documents/common/publications/studies/ey_study_destination_principle.pdf; Vienna Fiscalis Seminar, 23–25 Jun. 2015.

CHAPTER 7

Internet and the Concept of 'Fixed Establishment' of the Recipient of a Supply of Services: Case C-605/12 *Welmory*

Ben Terra[*]

7.1 INTRODUCTION

Under the EU VAT rules the place where a customer has established his business or has a fixed establishment is decisive in determining where services are (deemed to be) rendered. Defining the concept of the place where the undertaking has established its business does not raise 'problems'. It is clear that the term 'should be understood in its technical sense [that is to say, as referring to] ... the registered office, as indicated by the statutes of the company owning the supplier undertaking'.[1] The concept of a fixed establishment, however, is not the same in all Member States. It is remarkable that the VAT directives do not provide for an accurate definition of a fixed establishment and (until recently) the only guidelines were therefore the judgments of the Court of Justice.

The 2014 *Welmory* case, which is discussed below, should shed some light on internet activities to and from a fixed establishment in another (Member) State than

* Prof. dr.dr.h.c. Ben J. M. Terra teaches at the universities of Amsterdam and Lund.

1. See Advocate General Mancini in Case 168/84 *Berkholz* EU:C:1985:2992. In Case C-73/06 *Planzer Luxembourg* EU:C:2007:397, the Court held that the determination of a company's place of business requires a series of factors to be taken into consideration, foremost amongst which are its registered office, the place of its central administration, the place where its directors meet and the place, usually identical, where the general policy of that company is determined. Other factors, such as the place of residence of the main directors, the place where general meetings are held, the place where administrative and accounting documents are kept, and the place where the company's financial, and particularly banking, transactions mainly take place, may also need to be taken into account. See also Article 10 of the implementing Regulation (EU) No. 282/2011 as amended.

where the business establishment is located. The case deals with a dispute concerning the VAT payable by Welmory sp Z.o.o. (Welmory Poland) during the months of January to April 2010.[2]

Welmory Poland had entered into a cooperation agreement with a Cypriot company, Welmory Ltd. According to the agreement the Cypriot company would run a website in Polish on which auctions could be held. On this website, Welmory Poland would market and sell goods for its own account.

It was however only possible to buy these products if the customers in advance had acquired packets of 'bids', that is, the right to make an offer to purchase goods being auctioned at a higher price than the price last offered. The business model meant in reality that the sale of the products resulted in two transactions: First, Welmory Poland received the purchase price which normally would be below the market value of the goods in question, and secondly the Cypriot company made an income from the sale of the bids.

To run the website, the Cypriot company used employees not employed by the company and it used Welmory Poland's technical equipment. In April 2012, the Cypriot company bought all the shares in Welmory.

Welmory Poland's source of income is, first, the selling price obtained in the online auctions and, secondly, the remuneration received from the Cypriot company corresponding to part of the proceeds of sale of the 'bids' used by the customers in Poland to bid in the auction. Welmory Poland did not pay any VAT since the company was of the opinion that the recipient of the services, the Cypriot company, should pay VAT in Cyprus.

However, the Polish tax authorities found that Welmory Poland should charge Polish VAT on the supply of its services since the Cypriot company has a fixed establishment in Poland to which the services were supplied. Consequently, the *Naczelny Sąd Administracyjny* referred the following question to the European Court of Justice:

> For the purposes of the taxation of services supplied by company A, which is established in Poland, to company B, which is established in another Member State of the European Union, in circumstances where company B carries out its economic activity by making use of company A's infrastructure, is the fixed establishment within the meaning of Article 44 of Council Directive 2006/112/EC of 28 November 2006 on the common system of value added tax situated in the place in which company A is established?

Thus, the question is whether services are rendered to the fixed establishment of the Cypriot company which, based on the cooperation agreement with Welmory Poland, uses personnel and equipment not belonging to the Cypriot company but at least partially to Welmory Poland.

2. Case C-605/12 *Welmory*, Decision of 14 Oct. 2014 available at: http://curia.europa.eu/juris/liste.jsf?language=en&num=C-605/12.

7.2 OPINION OF THE ADVOCATE GENERAL

In her Opinion, delivered on 15 May 2014, AG Kokott started with an overview of the provisions regarding the place of supply of services. In the division of the competence to levy VAT between the Member States the starting point is that for all supplies of services the place of taxation should, in principle be the place where the actual consumption takes place. Obviously, double taxation should be prevented as well as excessive administrative burdens for economic operators. Legal certainty requires that objective and clear-cut criteria apply on the basis of which a supplier of services can determine whether his customer has a fixed establishment in the country.

7.2.1 Case Law regarding Fixed Establishments

The AG continued with an overview of the case law regarding fixed establishments recalling that the Court of Justice in *Berkholz* and subsequent cases has held the business establishment to be the primary point of reference.[3] Regard may be had to another place of establishment if reference to the place where the supplier has established his business is not efficient and does not lead to a rational result for tax purposes or creates a conflict with another Member State. That other establishment must have a certain minimum size and both the human and technical resources necessary for the provision of the services must be permanently present. The AG also recalled that the Court held in *ARO Lease* that when a leasing company does not possess in a Member State either its own staff or a structure which has a sufficient degree of permanence to provide a framework in which agreements may be drawn up or management decisions taken and thus to enable the services in question to be supplied on an independent basis, it cannot be regarded as having a fixed establishment in that State.[4]

The AG also pointed out that the judgment of the Court in the *DFDS* case,[5] which was brought up in the *Welmory* case, can be understood as meaning that where an independent separate legal entity is fully controlled by a parent company it may be regarded as a fixed establishment of the parent company; this could be of importance since the Cypriot company became the sole shareholder of Welmory Poland during the period covered by the dispute. According to the AG, however, *DFDS* exclusively dealt with taxation of travel agents and no general conclusions could be drawn from that case. The AG added to this that the legal certainty of a taxable person requires that an independent legal person is not treated at the same time as a fixed establishment of another legal person.

---

3. Case 168/84 *Berkholz* paragraph 17; Case C-231/94 *Faaborg-Gelting Linien* EU:C:1996:184, paragraph 16; Case C-190/95 ARO Lease EU:C:1997:374, paragraph 15.
4. Case C-190/95 *ARO Lease* paragraph 19.
5. Case C-260/95 *DFDS* EU:C:1997:77.

7.2.2 Implementing Regulation

The AG then turned to the case law referred to above and the new rules of the place of supply introduced by Directive 2008/8/EC and implementing Regulation (EU) No. 282/2011 (see Appendix III). The case law referred to only covers situations dealing with the place where the supplier is established and not where the recipient is established. According to the AG, Article 11 of the implementing Regulation is clear. What is important is no longer whether an establishment is capable of supplying a service, but rather whether it uses services for its own needs. With regard to the capability to supply a service, although irrelevant in the present case, the AG noted that if the Cypriot company would have a fixed establishment it would perform the service of managing the website to which it is contractually obliged. The AG added to this the interesting observation that if, based on a structure requiring personnel and technical equipment, one is capable of using services for one's own needs, it may be presumed that one is at least 'capable' of also supplying services and furthermore that one may question the requirement to be capable of supplying services in the light of Article 43(2) of the VAT Directive which makes Article 44, second sentence, under certain conditions applicable to non-taxable persons. According to the AG legal certainty requires that the business establishment has priority in case of doubt between the business establishment and the fixed establishment She finds confirmation of this approach in Article 44 of the Directive.

Applying the foregoing to the present case, the AG gave a few suggestions to the national court which in the final analysis has to decide whether the Cypriot company has a fixed establishment in Poland.

7.2.3 Outsourced Personnel, Permanence and Identical Use

First of all, referring to AG Poiares Maduro in the *RAL* case,[6] the AG pointed out that for the existence of a fixed establishment it is not required that a taxable person has its own human and technical resources. This does not mean, however, that Welmory Poland as service supplier is to be treated as the fixed establishment of the Cypriot company. Obviously, the requirement for a fixed establishment of possessing a sufficient degree of permanence and a structure adequate in terms of personnel and technical resources to supply services on an independent basis, equally applies when a taxable person makes use of human and technical resources which are not its own. The permanence needs to be proven, *inter alia*, by service and rental contracts which cannot be terminated on short notice. In other words: a taxable person cannot as such be a fixed establishment of another person. However, this does not exclude that a taxable person may have permanent access to the use of personal and technical equipment of another taxable person, which at the same time from a different perspective is the service supplier to the thereby created fixed establishment. If, however, personnel and equipment are identically used by two taxable persons, one may wonder whether there is a supply of a service to a different taxable person. In this respect it needs to be

6. Case C-452/03 *RAL* EU:C:2005:65.

investigated where the Cypriot company performs its activities, whether it performs activities independently in Poland and whether the services supplied by Welmory Poland are used for those activities.

The AG concluded that a precondition for the existence of a fixed establishment as meant in Article 44, second sentence, of the VAT Directive, is an establishment characterized by a sufficient degree of permanence and a structure adequate, in terms of human and technical resources, to receive and use the services, supplied to this establishment, for its own needs. In this connection it is not a requirement that the establishment has its own human and technical resources, if the external resources are available for the establishment in the same way as those of the establishment's own.

7.2.4 The Sale of Bids

As a last point, the AG dealt with the sale of bids and the sale of products. It has been argued that the fundamental problem in the present case is not the question where the services by Welmory Poland are supplied but where the sale of the bids should be taxed since, from an economic perspective, both Welmory Poland and the Cypriot company profit from the sale of the products. The AG left the question whether the sale of bids is falling under Article 44 (supply of services) or under Article 31 (supply of goods) unanswered. She did not exclude the (in my view far-fetched) possibility that the sale of bids is part of the 'the transfer of the right to act as owner of tangible property' and noted that this is certainly the case where bids are bought by the person to whom the goods are sold by auction.

7.2.5 Third Party Payment

In connection with the present case there is another question to be answered. Could it in principle be that that it is not Welmory Poland which supplies services (to the Cypriot Company), but that the Cypriot company is making third party payments to Welmory Poland on an Article 73 of the VAT Directive analysis? According to the AG, this is the case based on settled case law (see *inter alia Naturally Yours*[7] and *Dixons Retail*[8]), provided that there is a direct link between the supply of goods by Welmory Poland and the receipt of payments by the Cypriot company which must in any case be assumed when the payments are based on the quantity of the products sold or the turnover derived from the sale of the products.

7.3 DECISION BY THE COURT

On 16 October 2014, the Court of Justice decided the case.

7. Case 230/87 *Naturally Yours* EU:C:1988:508.
8. Case C-494/12 *Dixons Retail* EU:C:2013:758.

7.3.1 Preliminary Observation, Subject Matter of the Question

As a preliminary observation the Court pointed out that the question, whether the taxable amount which Welmory Poland was required to declare ought to include the remuneration obtained from the Cypriot company corresponding to part of the proceeds of sale of the 'bids' used by the customers in Poland in the auctions, went beyond the subject matter of the question referred for a preliminary ruling. That question relates essentially to the place of taxation of services supplied by the Polish company to the Cypriot company, and hence the interpretation of Article 44 of the VAT Directive and not to the place of taxation of the 'bids' or the determination of the taxable amount. According to the Court, the right to determine the questions to be put to it devolves on the national court alone and the parties to the main proceedings may not change their tenor.[9] The Court thus restricted itself solely to the question asked by the referring court and relating to the determination of the place of taxation of the services supplied by the Welmory Poland to the Cypriot company.

7.3.2 The Relevance of Previous Case Law

The Court raised the question whether its case law on the interpretation of Article 9(1) of the Sixth Directive is still relevant, having regard to the changes made by Article 44 of the VAT Directive, that is that the place of supply of services is no longer determined by reference to the taxable person supplying the services but by reference to the taxable person receiving them.

The Court pointed out that the wording of Article 44 of the VAT Directive is similar to that of Article 9(1) of the Sixth Directive. Furthermore, both Article 44 of the VAT Directive and Article 9(1) of the Sixth Directive are provisions determining the point of reference for tax purposes of supplies of services and pursue the same objective, so that the Court's case law on the interpretation of Article 9(1) of the Sixth Directive can in principle be applied *mutatis mutandis* to the interpretation of Article 44 of the VAT Directive.

That conclusion is borne out by the implementing Regulation, the objective of which, as stated in both recital 4 or 7 in its preamble, is to ensure a more uniform application of the VAT system by laying down rules implementing the VAT Directive, in particular in respect of taxable persons, the supply of goods and services, and the place of taxable transactions. The Court found it apparent from both recital 4 or 7 in the preamble to that regulation that the EU legislature wished to clarify certain concepts necessary for determining criteria relating to the place of taxable transactions, while taking account of the relevant case law of the Court.[10] The Court concluded that for

9. See, *inter alia*, judgment in Case C-316/10 *Danske Svineproducenter* EU:C:2011:863, paragraphs 32 and 34 and the case law cited.
10. The Court added to this that, even though that regulation was not yet in force at the material time, it should none the less be taken into account, clearly neglecting recital 2 to the implementing Regulation providing: 'These implementing measures are legally binding only

answering the question put by the referring court, the Court's case law on Article 9(1) of the Sixth Directive and the implementing Regulation are of relevance.

The Court continued first to determine the primary point of reference in order to establish the place of supply of services, and then to define the criteria which must be satisfied for a taxable person receiving services, such as that at issue in the main proceedings, with its place of business in one Member State, to be regarded as having a fixed establishment in a Member State other than that in which it has established its business.

7.3.3 The Primary Point of Reference

The Court recalled that according to its settled case law on Article 9 of the Sixth Directive, the most appropriate, and thus the primary point of reference for determining the place of supply of services for tax purposes is the place where the taxable person has established his business. It is only if that place of business does not lead to a rational result or creates a conflict with another Member State that another establishment may come into consideration.[11]

According to the Court that interpretation is also valid in relation to Article 44 of the VAT Directive. As was the case under the Sixth Directive, the place where the taxable person has established his business as primary point of reference appears to be a criterion that is objective, simple and practical and offers great legal certainty, being easier to verify than, for example, the existence of a fixed establishment. Moreover, the presumption that the services are supplied at the place where the taxable person receiving them has established his business makes it possible both for the competent authorities of the Member States and for suppliers of services to avoid having to undertake complex investigations in order to determine the point of reference for tax purposes. Furthermore, the business establishment is mentioned in the first sentence of Article 44 of the VAT Directive, whereas the fixed establishment is mentioned only in the following sentence. That sentence, introduced by the adverb 'however', can only be understood as creating an exception to the general rule set out in the previous sentence.

7.3.4 The Concept of Fixed Establishment

According to the Court, in the context of the changes by Article 44 of the VAT Directive, the concept of fixed establishment must therefore be determined in relation to the

from the date of the entry into force of this Regulation and are without prejudice to the validity of the legislation and interpretation previously adopted by the Member States.'

11. See, *inter alia*, judgments in Case 168/84 *Berkholz* paragraph 17; Case C-231/94 *Faaborg-Gelting Linien* paragraph 16; and Case C-190/95 *ARO Lease* paragraph 15. It seems to me that the Court in the present case is more explicit: it is *only* if that place of business does not lead to a rational result or creates a conflict with another Member State that another establishment *may* come into consideration.

taxable person receiving the services. Article 11 of the Implementing Regulation[12] provides that a fixed establishment must be characterized by a sufficient degree of permanence and a suitable structure in terms of human and technical resources to enable it to receive and use the services supplied to it for its own needs (*'les besoins propres de cet établissement'*). So, to be considered, in circumstances such as those in the present case, as having a fixed establishment within the meaning of Article 44 of the VAT Directive, the Cypriot company must have in Poland at the very least a structure characterized by a sufficient degree of permanence, suitable in terms of human and technical resources to enable it to receive in Poland the services supplied to it by the Polish company and to use them for its business, namely, in this case, running the electronic auction system in question and issuing and selling 'bids' (I note that the Court is rephrasing 'for its own needs' by 'for its business' (*'aux fins de son activité économique.'*).

The Court added to this that the fact that a business such as the one carried on by the Cypriot company, consisting in operating a system of electronic auctions which comprises, first, making an auction website available to the Polish company and, secondly, issuing and selling 'bids' to customers in Poland, can be carried on without requiring an effective human and material structure in Polish territory is not determinative. Despite its particular character, such a business requires at least a structure that is appropriate in terms especially of human and technical resources, such as appropriate computer equipment, servers and software.

As a final remark the Court noted that the fact that the economic activities of the two companies, which are linked by a cooperation agreement, form an economic whole and that their results are of benefit essentially to consumers in Poland, is not material for determining whether the Cypriot company possesses a fixed establishment in Poland. The services supplied by Welmory Poland to the Cypriot company must be distinguished from those supplied by the Cypriot company to consumers in Poland. They are distinct supplies of services which are subject to different schemes of VAT.

The Court replied to the preliminary question that a first taxable person who has established his business in one Member State, and receives services supplied by a second taxable person established in another Member State, must be regarded as having a 'fixed establishment' within the meaning of Article 44 of the VAT Directive in that other Member State, for the purpose of determining the place of taxation of those services, if that establishment is characterized by a sufficient degree of permanence and a suitable structure in terms of human and technical resources to enable it to receive the services supplied to it and use them for its business, which is for the referring court to ascertain.

7.4 CONCLUSIONS

The Court follows the reasoning of the AG to a large extent and gives priority to legal certainty. The primary point of reference for determining the place of supply of services

12. See also the judgment in Case C-73/06 *Planzer Luxembourg* EU:C:2007:397, paragraph 54 and the case law cited, which directly inspired the wording of Article 11.

for tax purposes is the place where the taxable person has established his business. To be considered, as having a fixed establishment within the meaning of Article 44 of the VAT Directive, the establishment must have at the very least a structure characterized by a sufficient degree of permanence, suitable in terms of human and technical resources to enable it to receive the services supplied to it and to use them for its business. Presumably, a server is not enough to be treated as a fixed establishment.

It seems to me that the change from the somewhat illusive reference to enable an establishment to receive and use the services supplied to it 'for its own needs' into 'for its business' (economic activity) has clarified the meaning of Article 11, if not it has opened the gate to treat, for example, warehouses, or agencies[13] as fixed establishments. Fortunately, under one caveat, namely that it is only if the place of the business establishment does not lead to a rational result or creates a conflict with another Member State that another establishment may come into consideration.[14] I assume that the suggestions of the AG with regard to outsourced personnel, permanence and identical use have the tacit agreement of the Court. The fact that *DFDS* (although explicitly mentioned in the national court's order for reference), in which the independent status of the subsidiary was disregarded in favour of the *commercial reality*, was not even mentioned by the Court leads us to believe that the *DFDS* judgment only applies in very specific circumstances.

It remains to be seen, whether the suggestions of the AG regarding the sale of bids being part of the 'the transfer of the right to act as owner of tangible property' for which she noted that '*this is certainly the case*' where bids are bought by the person to whom the goods are sold by auction, would have been followed by the Court. As regards the AG's third party payment approach (provided that there is a direct link between the supply of goods by Welmory Poland and the receipt of payments by the Cypriot company which the facts seem to suggest), the Court refers to the distinction between the *services* supplied by Welmory Poland to the Cypriot company and those supplied by the Cypriot company to consumers in Poland, which seems to exclude third party payment.

13. Provided there is a sufficient degree of permanence (see the AG's qualification), suitable in terms of human (see the AG's reference to *RAL*) and technical resources to enable the establishment to receive the services supplied to it and to use them for its business. I submit that the Court when referring to a business such as that carried on by the Cypriot company, consisting in operating a system of electronic auctions which comprises, first, making an auction website available to the Polish company, and second, issuing and selling 'bids' to customers in Poland, implicitly requires (in order to be treated as a fixed establishment) that supplies are made to third parties. This would exclude so-called rep offices from being treated as fixed establishments.
14. Furthermore the fixed establishment may have priority if the place of the business establishment does not reflect the economic reality on a *Paul Newey* analysis (Case C-653/11, EU:C:2013:409), or in cases of fraud considering that *fraus omnia corrumpit* since Joined Cases C-131/13, C-163/13 and C-164/13 *Italmoda* EU:C:2014:2455.

CHAPTER 8
Internet Search Engines: A VAT Analysis

Cristina Trenta[*]

8.1 INTRODUCTION

Search engines are services that index content from the World Wide Web and that can be consulted in order to obtain information about where that said content can be found.[1] Search engines are defined as information location tools in the Directive on Electronic Commerce.[2] This definition has also been confirmed by the European Commission in the Microsoft/Yahoo case:

> An Internet search engine is a tool designed to search for information on the Internet. It consists of a search box in which queries can be typed. The search results of a given query are then usually presented in a ranked list of results. The information searched for may consist of text (including news), maps, images, videos or other types of content. Search engines such as those operated by Microsoft, Yahoo and Google use algorithms to search for information on the Internet and rely on large indexes that try to map the content of the World Wide Web.[3]

Search engines index information automatically, all the time. Results vary among search engines depending on their algorithms and their capability to crawl the web for indexing. Some search engines index only specific types of files, such as those that specialize on image searches, or torrent searches. The most used and most known search engine though, Google, indexes all types of content it can find but still allows to directly filter results according to a number of different criteria, such as for example file-type.

---

* Cristina Trenta, Ph.D. is Senior Lecturer in Tax Law at Örebro University. This chapter is based upon and develops the conclusions drawn in C. Trenta (2013): 'VAT in peer-to-peer content distribution: towards a tax proposal for decentralized networks', Jönköping University, Jönköping International Business School, JIBS Dissertation Series, 2013.

1. Working Party, Opinion 1/2008 on data protection issues related to search engines, Article 29 data protection working party, 00737/EN WP 148, adopted 4 Apr. 2008.
2. Directive 2000/31/EC of the European Parliament and of the Council of 8 Jun. 2000 on certain legal aspects of information society services, in particular electronic commerce, in the Internal Market (Directive on electronic commerce). *OJ L 178, 17.7.2000, at 1–16.* Article 21(2). See also Recital 18.
3. Case no. COMP/M. 5727-Microsoft/Yahoo! Search Business, Regulation (EC) No. 139/2004, Merger procedure, 18/02/2010 paragraph 30.

Google provides a multitude of services, and almost all of them are free of charge for end users.[4] The direct consequence of this is that Google charges no VAT to people using said services. It is not a surprise then that Google and similar companies have generated quite some interest in tax literature and struggle to understand how to reconcile their new business models with traditional taxation profiles.

A recent report underlines the strategic role of the AdWords system, an advertising tool that leverages the amount of user information that is constantly being collected and processed in Google's own successful race to the top.[5] The expert group on taxing the digital economy discussed possible tax implications of search engines, social networks, and other 'free' services that rely on advertising.[6] The OECD as well, in its BEPS Action Plan 1, stresses the tax challenges implied by the so-called digital economy.[7]

Search engines generate revenue through advertisement, either directly or through company-wide strategies that include advertising, or through subscriptions. This latter case especially applies to specialized search engines, for example in law or health care, and here the ordinary rules of VAT apply. For this reason, this contribution will focus on the former group, as they represent the vast majority of free-to-use public search engines on the web, and their taxation profiles are unclear. The goal is to shed some light on whether their business models include profiles of interest to taxation in general, and to VAT in particular, and to open up a debate on taxation and the disruptive changes the digital economy is bringing to our consolidated frameworks.

This contribution details first the economic profiles of search engines, and then moves to defining advertising from a VAT point of view, with special attention being devoted to discussing banner advertising in ECJ case law. The role of users is discussed next, and finally a few preliminary conclusions for the field of VAT are drawn and further research questions are introduced for future discussion.

8.2 THE ECONOMICS OF INTERNET SEARCHING

Generalist Internet search engines such as Google allow end users to search the World Wide Web for any type of content. But they also act as an intermediary between advertisers on one side and their users on the other side, and showing ads to users is what generates revenue.[8] Each side exerts some constraints on the other (see Figure 8.1).[9]

4. C. Anderson (2009): 'The Future of a Radical Price: The Economics of Abundance and Why Zero Pricing Is Changing the Face of Business', Random House, 2009.
5. P. Collin, N. Colin (2013): 'Mission d'expertise sur la fiscalité de l'economie numérique', 2013 at 49 (available at: http://www.hadopi.fr/observation/documentation/rapport-dexpertise-sur-la-fiscalite-de-leconomie-numerique).
6. European Commission, Commission Expert Group on Taxation of the Digital Economy, Report 2014 at 22.
7. OECD, BEPS Public Discussion Draft, Action 1: Address the tax challenges of the digital economy, 24 Mar. 2014–14 Apr. 2014.
8. F. Thépot (2013): 'Market Power in Online Search and Social Networking: A Matter of Two-Sided Markets', 36 World Competition 2 of 2013 at 195–221. See also T. Eisenmann, G. Parker, M.W. Van Alstyne (2006): 'Strategies for two-sided markets', 84 Harvard Business Review 10 of 2006 at 92.
9. M. Armstrong (2006): 'Competition in two-sided markets', 37 RAND J. of Econ. 3 of Autumn 2006 at 668–691.

The OECD maintains that:

> Internet intermediaries bring together or facilitate transactions between third parties on the Internet. They give access to, host, transmit and index content, products and services originated by third parties on the Internet or provide Internet-based services to third parties.[10]

Internet search engines definitely fit this profile.[11]

Figure 8.1 The Internet Search Firm Is an Information Intermediary That Centralizes Communication between Advertisers and Consumers

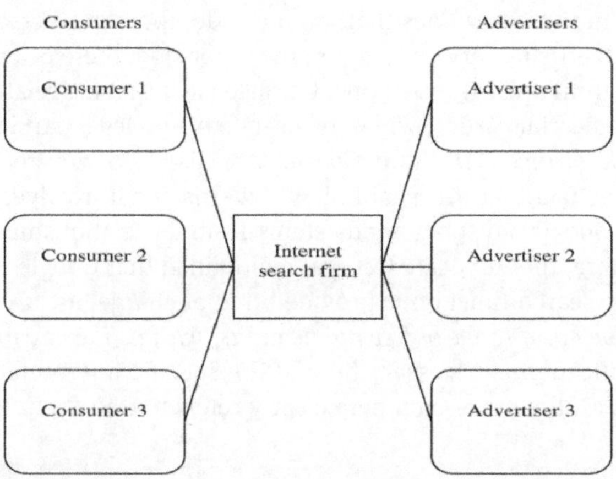

Source: Spulber 2009.

8.3 ADVERTISING

8.3.1 Defining Advertising

Advertising messages that appear on websites are classified at the European level in Annex I (3)(h) of the VAT Council Implementing Regulation (EU) No. 282/2011 (see Appendix III);[12] they are considered advertising space and, according to the VAT Directive, electronically supplied services.[13] At the international level, the OECD (in the 2001 Report of the Technical Advisory Group to Working Party no. 1 of the OECD

10. OECD (2010): 'The Economic and Social Role of Internet Intermediaries', 2010 at 9.
11. D. F. Spulber (2009): 'The Map of Commerce: Internet Search, Competition, and the Circular Flow of Information', 5 J. of Competition L. and Econ. 4 of 2009 at 649 (available at: doi:10.1093/joclec/nhp011).
12. Council Implementing Regulation (EU) No. 282/2011 of 15 Mar. 2011 laying down implementing measures for Directive 2006/112/EC on the common system of value added tax. *OJ L 77, 23.3.2011, at 1–22.*
13. Directive 2006/112/EC, Point (3) of Annex II.

Committee on Fiscal Affairs)[14] defines advertising as the Council Regulation above does, but adds a few clarifications:

> Advertisers pay to have their advertisements disseminated to users of a given web site. So-called 'banner ads' are small graphic images embedded in a web page, which when clicked by the user will load the web page specified by the advertiser. Advertising rates are most commonly specified in terms of a cost per thousand 'impressions' (number of times the ad is displayed to a user), though rates might also be based on the number of click-throughs (number of times the ad is clicked by a user). The Analysis and conclusions of the Working Group was that the payments arising from these transactions would constitute normal business profits falling under Article 7.[15]

It is clear from these few lines that, on one side, there is a person who requests and pays to buy advertising services and, on the other side, there is a business activity that makes profits from those transactions. It is also clear that the relationship involves just these two commercial parties, while the users have no legal part in the agreement.

In the *Google France SARL and Google Inc.* case,[16] Advocate General Poiares Maduro stressed the fact that the legal link of advertisement involves Google and the advertisers only: 'Google's display of ads stems from its relationship with the advertisers.'[17] Furthermore, the Advocate General maintained that Google is to be seen as a tool,[18] and that the search function is provided free of charge, as: '*Google supports its search engine, as well as a range of free applications, with its income from AdWords.*'[19]

A small clarification is necessary here of the specific interpretation of the word 'free' used by the AG: the expression here clearly refers to free of charge, not to free to

14. OECD (2001): 'Tax Treaty Characterisation Issues arising from e-commerce', Technical Advisory Group, Report to Working Party no. 1 of the OECD Committee on Fiscal Affairs.
15. OECD (2001) 'Tax Treaty Characterisation Issues arising from e-commerce', Technical Advisory Group, Report to Working Party no. 1 of the OECD Committee on Fiscal Affairs, Category 17, Advertising, p. 28. See also F. Roccatagliata, P. Valente (2001): 'Internet – Classificazione del reddito e delle prestazioni di servizi', Il Fisco 32 of 2001.
16. Opinion of Mr Advocate General Poiares Maduro in Joined Cases C-236/08 to C-238/08 *Google France SARL and Google Inc. v. Louis Vuitton Malletier SA* (C-236/08), *Google France SARL v. Viaticum SA and Luteciel SARL* (C-237/08) and *Google France SARL v. Centre national de recherche en relations humaines* (CNRRH) SARL and Others (C-238/08), [2010] ECR I-2417.
17. Opinion of Mr Advocate General Poiares Maduro in Joined Cases C-236/08 to C-238/08 *Google France SARL and Google Inc. v. Louis Vuitton Malletier SA* (C-236/08), *Google France SARL v. Viaticum SA and Luteciel SARL* (C-237/08) and *Google France SARL v. Centre national de recherche en relations humaines* (CNRRH) SARL and Others (C-238/08), [2010] ECR I-2417, paragraph 145.
18. Opinion of Mr Advocate General Poiares Maduro in Joined Cases C-236/08 to C-238/08 *Google France SARL and Google Inc. v. Louis Vuitton Malletier SA* (C-236/08), *Google France SARL v. Viaticum SA and Luteciel SARL* (C-237/08) and *Google France SARL v. Centre national de recherche en relations humaines (CNRRH) SARL and Others* (C-238/08), [2010] ECR I-2417, paragraph 89.
19. Opinion of Mr Advocate General Poiares Maduro in Joined Cases C-236/08 to C-238/08 *Google France SARL and Google Inc. v. Louis Vuitton Malletier SA* (C-236/08), *Google France SARL v. Viaticum SA and Luteciel SARL* (C-237/08) and *Google France SARL v. Centre national de recherche en relations humaines (CNRRH) SARL and Others* (C-238/08), [2010] ECR I-2417, paragraph 13.

use. This can be inferred from the Italian text, for example, which uses of the expression 'gratuite' that directly translates into '*free of charge*'. The official French, Spanish and Swedish versions all reinforce this interpretation, which is lost in translation in the English version. The ECJ in the same decision confirmed this view:

> When Internet users enter the name of a trade mark as a search term, the home and advertising page of the proprietor of that mark will appear in the list of the natural results (...) that display, which is, moreover, free of charge.[20]

Thus, by applying the ECJ VAT principles, those services, being free of charge, are outside the scope of VAT. It is worth recalling that in the *Hong Kong* case, the ECJ ruled that the economic activities of taxable persons (...) are necessarily activities which are carried on with the object of obtaining payment of consideration or which are likely to be rewarded by the payment of consideration, because if they are free of charge in all cases they do not fall within the system of value added tax.[21]

8.3.2 Banner Advertisement

According to the principles explained, banner obligations are therefore comparable to the acquisition of a wall display space,[22] and therefore users would be in the same position as the passers-by in a street where the wall display is in place.

The ECJ has already decided that there is no legal relationship between passers-by and a person who performs musical activity in the street.[23] In accordance with this, it would be quite hard to conclude that there is a legal relationship between the users and a search engine because of any banner agreement which the search engine might have concluded with third parties.

Even harder would it be to identify a legal relationship between users and the third party: Google uses banners, and a legal relationship between advertisers and all of Google's users is difficult to maintain. But we know that this relationship between the provider and the consumer is necessary for VAT to be applied. It is possible to say that this is an additional requirement introduced by the ECJ in Tolsma,[24] i.e., that VAT is a tax applied per transaction and not per general relationship.[25]

20. Joined Cases C-236/08 to C-238/08 *Google France SARL and Google Inc. v. Louis Vuitton Malletier SA* (C-236/08), *Google France SARL v. Viaticum SA and Luteciel SARL* (C-237/08) and *Google France SARL v. Centre national de recherche en relations humaines* (CNRRH) SARL and Others (C-238/08), [2010] ECR I-2417, paragraph 97.
21. Case 89/81 *Staatssecretaris van Financiën v. Hong-Kong Trade Development Council* [1982] ECR 1277 paragraph 11.
22. E. Cintolesi, G. Mocci (2001): 'Web economy: aspetti di natura tributaria nella permuta di banners o per lo scambio di link', Il Fisco 26 of 2001.
23. Case C-16/93 *R. J. Tolsma v. Inspecteur der Omzetbelasting Leeuwarden* [1994] ECR I-743.
24. Case C-16/93 *R. J. Tolsma v. Inspecteur der Omzetbelasting Leeuwarden* [1994] ECR I-743, paragraph 14.
25. J. Englisch (2009): 'VAT/GST and Direct taxes: Different purposes', in M. Lang, P. Melz, E. Kristoffersson (Eds.) (2009): 'Value Added Tax and Direct Taxation, Similarities and Differences', IBFD 2009 at pp. 14–15.

Then, in the *Apple and Pear* case,[26] the ECJ ruled that the only argument for qualifying the transaction as a taxable transaction according to the VAT system was the existence of a *'direct link'* between the service and the consideration.

In the case of general search engines, there is no direct link between the service provided by the search engine and the consideration received from the advertising business activity in respect to the users, but there is a direct link between the two business activities, the one selling and the one buying advertisement space.

Similarly, users receive search services without any subscription or obligation to give something in return to the search engines that could be read as a *'direct link'* between the service and the consideration received.[27] For them the services are free of charge and free of mutual obligations.

The ECJ also maintained, in the *Agrardienste GmbH* case, that there is no supply of services in the event that the consumer cannot be identified.[28] This is also true in the case of the normal functioning of search engines: while they can be used being logged in, they surely can be used being logged out and anonymously. As a matter of fact, there is no individual transaction. They cannot therefore be considered as a supply of services within the scope of the VAT scheme in respect of the users' identifiability.[29]

If these principles are applied to web-based search engines and their search functionality, it is clear that the compensation which the Internet search engine owner received for the banner services does not entail any benefit for the users themselves that would open the possibility for them to be considered consumers of a service. Benefits are enjoyed by the entrepreneur who requested and paid for the banner services.[30]

In the *Jürgen Mohr* case[31] Advocate General Jacobs held that compensation can be paid alternatively by either the identifiable customer or by a third party,[32] something the VAT Directive states in Article 73: *'The taxable amount shall include everything which constitutes consideration obtained or to be obtained by the supplier, in return for the supply, from the customer or a third party.'*

Since the other remaining conditions (consumption,[33] identifiable consumer[34] and a direct link) are not fulfilled there is not enough to substantiate a relationship. It

26. Case 102/86 *Apple and Pear Development Council v. Commissioners of Customs and Excise* [1988] ECR 1443.
27. Case 102/86 *Apple and Pear Development Council v. Commissioners of Customs and Excise* [1988] ECR 1443, paragraph 12.
28. Case C-384/95 *Agrardienste GmbH & Co. KG v. Finanzamt Calau* [1997] ECR I-07387, paragraph 24.
29. Case C-384/95 *Agrardienste GmbH & Co. KG v. Finanzamt Calau* [1997] ECR I-07387, paragraph 24.
30. Case C-215/94 *Jürgen Mohr v. Finanzamt Bad Segeberg* [1996] ECR I-959, paragraph 22.
31. Opinion of Mr Advocate General Jacobs in Case C-215/94 *Jürgen Mohr v. Finanzamt Bad Segeberg*, [1996] ECR I-959.
32. Opinion of Mr Advocate General Jacobs in Case C-215/94 *Jürgen Mohr v. Finanzamt Bad Segeberg* [1996] ECR I-959, paragraph 27.
33. Case C-384/95 *Agrardienste GmbH & Co. KG v. Finanzamt Calau* [1997] ECR I-7387, paragraph 13.
34. Case C-384/95 *Agrardienste GmbH & Co. KG v. Finanzamt Calau* [1997] ECR I-7387, paragraph 24.

simply is not possible to maintain that a search engine service is a service provided to users against payment, with a direct link between *'(t)he service provided and the consideration received'*.[35] Therefore, this supply is outside the scope of VAT.[36]

So, even though it is perfectly safe to conclude that internet search engines, such as Google or Yahoo, can be considered to engage in a business (economic) activity when selling banner advertising space, because there is a direct link between that banner service and the consideration received, this has no direct impact on the (anonymous) customers who use the search engines without compensating them for that search service, and without giving them anything in return.

8.4 THE ECONOMIC ROLE OF USERS

While banner agreements[37] as such do not involve the users from a legal point of view, it would not be correct to maintain that users do not have any relevance at all. First of all, there is a passive role which prompts companies to advertise in order to be visible by consumers and increase their sales or brand recognition (see Figure 8.2). But, as users generate traffic and increase the potential profitability of banners for both the seller (directly) and the buyer (indirectly), is there anything else which is relevant for VAT?

Figure 8.2 The Circular Flow of Information Mediated by the Internet Search Firm

Source: Spulber 2009.

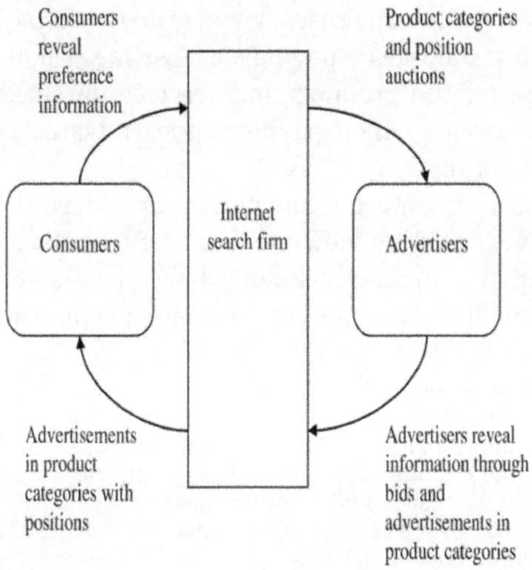

35. Case 102/86 *Apple and Pear Development Council v. Commissioners of Customs and Excise* [1988], ECR 1443, paragraph 11.
36. P. Centore (1998): 'Prestazioni gratuite di servizi fra normativa comunitaria e nazionale', GT – Rivista di giurisprudenza tributaria 3 of 1998 at 220.
37. Banner agreements follow different models. See A. Pezzi (2005): 'Analisi dei modelli di business degli strumenti di ricerca in Internet, Impresa', c.i., no. 2 of 2005 at 224. Fisconline Dottrina. Pezzi lists pay per click, pay per inclusion, pay per positioning.

Very broadly speaking, users have an economic role in that kind of mechanism, because without users visiting the search engine, the banners would be meaningless. This also makes Internet search engines the centre of a circular flow of information.[38] From this perspective, the Internet advertising model is nothing more than an evolution of the traditional media broadcast model. In this context the intermediary gives away content and services for free alongside advertising or branding and co-branding messages.[39] Let us see how literature dealing with TV broadcasting considers this, and how the role of the viewers has been approached by economic literature.

A TV broadcasting platform only works if it attracts viewers.[40] Again, there is a circular economic relationship in place: TV needs viewers, advertisers want viewers as potential consumers, the media company needs advertisers to generate income, but advertisers need TV broadcast to make their products visible and familiar to potential consumers.[41]

Then, is this economic link a link the way VAT doctrine defines it,[42] with a direct connection between viewers and the media company, so that it is possible to say that the viewers are paying for the programme being broadcasted even if it is aired on a freely available channel? Clearly, such a conclusion would allow us to consider internet search engines as services provided to users against payment, and therefore subject to VAT.

Free-to-air television channels (FTV) are generally provided without any subscription. Even though they are classified as free services, they are better categorized conversely as free to receive. In many cases, viewers do in fact pay for them, by various means, either directly, for example by paying a license fee as in the case of the BBC, or indirectly, when paying for the products and services purchased as a result of the banner advertisement, part of which payment goes towards covering the costs of advertising on and sponsoring those FTVs.[43]

Consequently, and from an economic perspective, even though FTVs are a free service they are effectively paid by viewers. It is true that the same could be said in abstract for search engines, indirectly financed by visitors through banner agreements,[44] but an economic link does not automatically become a legal link.

---

38. D. F. Spulber, *ibid.* at 633–682.
39. OECD (2010) 'The Economic and Social Role of Internet Intermediaries', 2010 at 18.
40. P. Martin, T. Valletti (2005): 'Content and advertising in the media: pay-TV versus free-to-air', Mimeo, Imperial College, London, CEPR working paper 4771 of 2005.
41. S. P. Anderson, J. J. Gabszewicz (2005): 'The Media and Advertising: A Tale of Two-Sided Markets', CORE Discussion Paper 2005/88.
42. Case 102/86 *Apple and Pear Development Council v. Commissioners of Customs and Excise* [1988] ECR 1443, paragraph 12.
43. A. Ferrand, L. Torrigiani, A. Camps i Povill (2007): 'Handbook of sports sponsorship: successful strategies', Routledge, 2007 at 135.
44. See for instance, the Swedish Bill 2001/02:150 issued in 2002, asserting the principle that, for search engines, remuneration can be met either directly or indirectly, as in the case of advertisement revenues. Regeringens proposition 2001/02:150, Lag om elektronisk handel och andra informationssamhällets tjänster, Stockholm, 14 Mar. 2002, pp. 56–57: '*(t)he requirement of compensation does not mean that the service has to be paid by those who receive it (...) but would include any form of direct or indirect financial compensation. It is for example given that*

In the *Google France* case, Advocate General Poiares Maduro makes a very compelling case for how easy it is to confuse the two different concepts, even though they are not the same.[45] The AG maintains that '*Google supports its search engine, as well as a range of free applications, with its income from AdWords.*'[46] Then he goes on to explain why, even though a service is a free service, it can still be classified as a service provided upon remuneration:

> There is nothing in the wording of the definition of information society services to exclude its application to the provision of hyperlinks and search engines, that is to say, to Google's search engine and AdWords. The element 'normally provided for remuneration' may raise some doubts as regards Google's search engine, but, as has been pointed out, the search engine is provided free of charge in the expectation of remuneration under AdWords. Since both services are also provided 'at a distance, by electronic means and at the individual request of the recipient of services', they fulfil all the requirements necessary to be regarded as information society services.[47]

Here is where the confusion between economic and legal link becomes apparent. The AG maintains that search engines services can be classified '*(a)s information society services*', but if they are free of charge, as stated early on by the AG himself, they cannot be classified as information society services because Directive 2000/31/EC defines services of the information society as covering '*(a)ny service normally provided for remuneration*'.[48]

The service is either free of charge or it is not, and the mere expectation of remuneration[49] on the part of Google from the AdWords banner programme does not change the fact that the search engine service, legally speaking, is a non-paid-for service for users.

---

marketing online is an information society service, even if only indirectly paid by consumers as a collective entity. Furthermore, such for the recipient free services as search engines, information services etc. financed by e.g. advertising revenue, are included. Also a request of goods or services is covered, even if this request is done for free.'

45. Opinion of Mr Advocate General Poiares Maduro in Joined Cases C-236/08 to C-238/08 *Google France SARL and Google Inc. v. Louis Vuitton Malletier SA* (C-236/08), *Google France SARL v. Viaticum SA and Luteciel SARL* (C-237/08) and *Google France SARL v. Centre national de recherche en relations humaines* (CNRRH) SARL and Others (C-238/08) [2010] ECR I-2417.
46. Joined Cases C-236/08 to C-238/08, Opinion of Mr Advocate General Poiares Maduro, *Google France SARL and Google Inc. v. Louis Vuitton Malletier SA* (C-236/08), *Google France SARL v. Viaticum SA and Luteciel SARL* (C-237/08) and *Google France SARL v. Centre national de recherche en relations humaines* (CNRRH) SARL and Others (C-238/08) [2010] ECR I-2417, paragraph 13.
47. Joined Cases C-236/08 to C-238/08, Opinion of Mr Advocate General Poiares Maduro, *Google France SARL and Google Inc. v. Louis Vuitton Malletier SA* (C-236/08), *Google France SARL v. Viaticum SA and Luteciel SARL* (C-237/08) and *Google France SARL v. Centre national de recherche en relations humaines (CNRRH) SARL and Others* (C-238/08), [2010] ECR I-2417, paragraph 131.
48. Directive 2000/31/EC of the European Parliament and of the Council of 8 Jun. 2000 on certain legal aspects of information society services, in particular electronic commerce, in the Internal Market (Directive on electronic commerce). *OJ L 178, 17.7.2000, p. 1–16.*
49. Opinion of Mr Advocate General Van Gerven in Case C-126/88 *Boots Company plc v. Commissioners of Customs and Excise* [1990] ECR I-1235, paragraph 13.

Search engines can be classified as information society services as per Directive 2000/31/EC, which defines these as covering '*(a)ny service normally provided for remuneration*'.[50] But only banner-related activities are services provided against payment: searching upon user request is totally free of charge.[51]

Further confirmation can be found in the Information Society Directive: Recital 29 of the preamble to Directive 2000/31/EC, clearly illustrates how commercial communications (and hence advertisement) help develop a wide range of new free services in the field. That is, paid-for services and free services can coexist and they do not necessarily come to merge as a rule.

Commercial communications are essential for the financing of information society services and for developing a wide variety of new, charge-free services.[52]

The above conclusions find support in media law literature,[53] and they are also consistent with the ECJ position on these matters, that the same taxable person may well run one activity that falls within the scope of VAT, and another activity that does not[54] and goes untaxed.[55] Search results are '*non transactions*',[56] or '*non supplies*',[57] in this sense, and they fall outside the scope of VAT as they lack every relevant profile to be considered economic activities carried out by a taxable person acting as such.

This conclusion is consistent with the VAT Council Implementing Regulation (EU) No. 282/2011 (see Appendix III)[58] where the use of a search engine[59] is defined recalling Article 7 of the same as well as the VAT Directive:

> (e)lectronically supplied services as referred to in Directive 2006/112/EC shall include services which are delivered over the Internet or an electronic network and the nature of which renders their supply essentially automated and involving

50. Directive 2000/31/EC of the European Parliament and of the Council of 8 Jun. 2000 on certain legal aspects of information society services, in particular electronic commerce, in the Internal Market (Directive on electronic commerce). *OJ L 178, 17.7.2000, p. 1–16.*
51. Joined Cases C-236/08 to C-238/08, *Google France SARL and Google Inc. v. Louis Vuitton Malletier SA* (C-236/08), *Google France SARL v. Viaticum SA and Luteciel SARL* (C-237/08) and *Google France SARL v. Centre national de recherche en relations humaines* (CNRRH) SARL and Others (C-238/08), [2010] ECR I-2417, paragraph 97.
52. Directive 2000/31/EC of the European Parliament and of the Council of 8 Jun. 2000 on certain legal aspects of information society services, in particular electronic commerce, in the Internal Market (Directive on electronic commerce). *OJ L 178, 17.7.2000, p. 1–16. Recital 29.*
53. *O. Castendyk, E.J. Dommering, A. Scheuer (2008): 'European media law', Wolters Kluwer Law & Business, 2008 at 105.*
54. M. Iavagnilio (2007): 'I soggetti passive', L'IVA 2 of 2007 at 17. See Case C-77/01 *Empresa de Desenvolvimento Mineiro SGPS SA (EDM) v. Fazenda Pública* [2004] ECR I-4295.
55. Directive 2008/8/EC, Article 43. 'The purpose of applying the rules concerning the place of supply of services: a taxable person who also carries out activities or transactions that are not considered to be taxable supplies of goods or services in accordance with Article 2(1) shall be regarded as a taxable person in respect of all services rendered to him'. See also Case C-291/07 *Kollektivavtalsstiftelsen TRR Trygghetsrådet v. Skatteverket* [2008] ECR I-8255.
56. C. Cornia (2007): 'Operazioni di finanziamento infragruppo e detraibilità dell'Iva', Rassegna tributaria 5 of 2004 at 1866.
57. A. Schenk, O. Oldman (2007): 'Value added tax: a comparative approach', Cambridge Tax Law Series, Cambridge University Press, 2007 at 113.
58. Council Implementing Regulation (EU) No. 282/2011 of 15 Mar. 2011 laying down implementing measures for Directive 2006/112/EC on the common system of value added tax. *OJ L 77, 23.3.2011, p. 1–22.*
59. VAT Council Implementing Regulation (EU) No. 282/2011, Annex I (3)(i).

minimal human intervention, and impossible to ensure in the absence of information technology.[60]

This definition implies that there is at least one transaction, or better a service as it is defined by the VAT Directive, with a consideration attached. Indeed, Article 2 of the VAT Directive provides that '*the supply of services for consideration*' will '*be subject to VAT*'. The Regulation requires a search activity to be executed against specific consideration, since it recalls the definition of service under the VAT Directive, and it does not refer to every search performed over the Internet via Google or Yahoo! or any similar application, since these configure '*non transactions*', or '*non-supplies*'.

Still, the Council Implementing Regulation is unclear because, when it refers to searches performed against payment, it basically refers to paid-for domain databases, such as the legal databases to which companies, like LexisNexis, license access for a fee.

These services though have already been listed in Annex II of the VAT Directive,[61] where e-services include access to databases, the supply of images, of text and information. The database Directive,[62] correctly defines a database as 'a collection of independent works, data or other materials arranged in a systematic or methodical way and individually accessible by electronic or other means'.[63]

Retrieving information from a database means to access and search through the database, as the VAT Directive implies. The expression used in the Implementing Regulation is meaningless if no further rationale is provided: it either describes what is already regulated by the VAT Directive, or it addresses non-supplies. Moreover, while in media law some authors object to the idea that retrieval software is a separate entity from the data being searched,[64] in VAT law the ECJ has clearly stated more than once that auxiliary transactions follow the tax treatment of the main operations. From the user/provider point of view, access to the search engine is free of charge and therefore a '*non-transaction*'.

8.5 A VAT PERSPECTIVE ON THE ROLE OF USERS

Let us go back to VAT, and let us see whether that economic link can be said to have any relevance and whether the principles that apply to TV broadcasting can be transferred to the Web. Could we maintain, from a VAT perspective, that search engines are really providing services to their users against payment, because the users read the advertisement banners and purchase the advertised goods and services, and

60. Directive 2006/112/EC.
61. Directive 2006/112/EC, Annex II, indicative list of the electronically supplied services referred to in point (k) of Article 56(1).
62. Directive 96/9/EC of the European Parliament and of the Council of 11 Mar. 1996 on the legal protection of databases, *OJ L 77, 27.3.1996 at p. 20–28.*
63. Directive 96/9/EC, Article 1(2).
64. S. Weinstein (2001): 'Copyright, Patents and the Internet' in C. Wild, N. MacEwan, S. Weinstein, N. Geach (Eds.) (2011): 'Electronic and Mobile Commerce Law, An Analysis of Trade, Finance, Media and Cybercrime in the Digital Age', University of Hertfordshire Press, 2011 at 133.

because part of the price paid by the users goes towards covering the advertising cost that in turn finances the 'free' search engines?

It seems that we can indeed conclude that online users play the role of viewers in the TV model, and from an economic perspective the parallel stands. From a VAT point of view though, users, once again, do not have a role in the advertising agreement for banners. The ECJ has made it very clear that a legal relationship between the parties who are involved in the operation is required for a transaction to be relevant for VAT purposes.[65]

Not only that, but in EU law an economic link between the service provider and the recipient has to exist, albeit that the payment does not need to be direct,[66] for a service to be considered against remuneration, and this is how it is for VAT as well, where consideration could be paid by the customer or by a third party.[67] In the field of EU law, a debate has been going on for a while on whether or not TV advertisement could be said to be paid by TV viewers.

In the UK, viewers of free-to-air television do not pay for their programmes, but only pay a license fee in respect of the services offered by the BBC, which has now the responsibility to levy it.[68] Commercial TV companies take advantage of this fee indirectly, because the fee, so to speak, gets viewers to turn on their TV sets, which again makes it attractive for other companies to advertise their products and services, which allows the commercial TV companies to make money on advertising. Can such a situation be read as an indirect payment from the viewers to commercial free-to-air TV channels?

According to the Treaty, services are services if they are provided for remuneration.[69] In EU law, as we can read in the Humbel case, '*(s)tate education, however, like health care, is largely financed from state taxes*',[70] meaning that such services cannot be considered as normally provided for remuneration according to the particular meaning purported by the Treaty. Therefore, those services fall outside the scope of the Treaty even in the event that they are to be paid for individually.[71]

The conclusion holds true also for VAT law, where in the *Republic of Finland* case[72] the Advocate General did not believe that the relationship between the person providing public legal assistance and the client is a direct and necessary link:

65. Case C-16/93 *R. J. Tolsma v. Inspecteur der Omzetbelasting Leeuwarden* [1994] ECR I-743.
66. L. Woods (2004): 'Free Movement of Goods and Services within the European Community', Ashgate Publishing, 2004 at 165.
67. Opinion of Mr Advocate General Jacobs in Case C-215/94 *Jürgen Mohr v. Finanzamt Bad Segeberg* [1996] ECR I-959, paragraph 27. Directive 2006/112/EC, Article 73.
68. L. Woods, *ibid.*, 2004 at p. 165.
69. TFEU, Article 57, Services shall be considered to be 'services' within the meaning of the Treaties where they are normally provided for remuneration.
70. Opinion of Mr Advocate General Sir Gordon Slynn in Case 263/86 *Belgian State v. René Humbel and Marie-Thérèse Edel* [1988] ECR 5365.
71. L. Woods, *ibid.*, 2004 at p. 166.
72. Opinion of Mr Advocate General Ruiz-Jarabo Colomer in Case C-246/08 *Commission of the European Communities v. Republic of Finland* [2009] ECR I-10605.

> the payment received by the Administration does not correspond to the actual value of the service, not even with that provided for by law (which the private lawyer receives), but is a percentage of that value.[73]

Part of the services is factually financed by public contribution. Thus, in both VAT law and EU law if a service is paid for by the state[74] it cannot be considered a service provided against payment, because the direct link,[75] between the service and the consideration received, is lacking:

> (i)n the public offices, however, it is unlikely that the link between the contribution payable by the recipient and the assistance provided meets the criterion of 'direct and necessary' required by the case-law.[76]

Since the BBC is a public service paid by a license fee, which is a type of tax,[77] it is not possible to argue that the BBC is a service provided against remuneration, and it is therefore not possible to argue that the commercial TV channels are provided upon remuneration as well. This also means that the relationship between commercial TVs and the various businesses buying advertising does not involve viewers.

Similarly, on the Web we have search engines on one side and business buying advertising on the other. Users pay for a broadband connection to a telecommunication company to be online and access, among other services, the search engines. But that payment has nothing to do with Google or Yahoo!: these are totally different companies providing different services.

The broadband connection is considered by the VAT Directive as a telecommunication service, a '(p)rovision of access to global information networks'[78] done against payment. This view has been also confirmed in VAT Council Implementing Regulation (EU) No. 1042/2013.[79] Advertisement on search engines, however, is classified as an

---

73. Opinion of Mr Advocate General Ruiz-Jarabo Colomer in Case C-246/08 *Commission of the European Communities v. Republic of Finland* [2009] ECR I-10605, paragraph 48.
74. P. Centore (2009): 'Enti non commerciali: profili iva nazionali e comunitari', Enti non-profit 11 of 2009. Opinion of Mr Advocate General Ruiz-Jarabo Colomer in Case C-246/08 *Commission of the European Communities v. Republic of Finland* [2009] ECR I-10605, paragraph 48.
75. Case 102/86 *Apple and Pear Development Council v. Commissioners of Customs and Excise* [1988], ECR 1443, paragraph 11.
76. Opinion of Mr Advocate General Ruiz-Jarabo Colomer in Case C-246/08 *Commission of the European Communities v. Republic of Finland* [2009] ECR I-10605, paragraph 48.
77. Italian doctrine distinguishes different forms of Government revenue, including 'imposta' (impost), 'tassa' (tax) and contributo (contribution). Taxes are paid by taxpayers as consideration for a particular service rendered by a public body. Therefore taxes have a general, community goal, and specific goals. Imposts are a forcible withdrawal of wealth operated by a public body for the provision of general services that are neither divisible nor generalizable. Contributions are a forcible, one-off withdrawal of wealth directed at people who are benefiting from specific public works. See C. Arena (1947): 'Principi di Scienza delle Finanze e Statistica Economica', 3rd ed. of 1947.
78. Directive 2006/112/EC, Article 24. '*Telecommunications services shall mean services relating to the transmission, emission or reception of signals, words, images and sounds or information of any nature by wire, radio, optical or other electromagnetic systems, including the related transfer or assignment of the right to use capacity for such transmission, emission or reception, with the inclusion of the provision of access to global information networks.*'
79. Council Implementing Regulation (EU) No. 1042/2013 of 7 Oct. 2013 amending Implementing Regulation (EU) No. 282/2011 as regards the place of supply of services *OJ L 284, 26.10.2013,*

electronic supply of services by the VAT Council Implementing Regulation (EU) No. 282/2011 (see Appendix III).[80]

One final case involves the user who buys an item being advertised, contributing somewhat to covering costs. Is such a situation for some reasons similar to the *Agrardienste GmbH* case,[81] in which the ECJ ruled that for a VAT relevant consumption to occur, a *'benefit capable of being regarded as a cost component of the activity of another person in the commercial chain'*[82] must be present.

It is my opinion that the answer lies in the fact that there are two different contracts: one for advertisement, involving two business activities, and the other involving the individual user and the advertising business activity, for the sale of an item. But the only way to qualify a transaction as provided against payment according to the VAT system is the *'direct link'* between the service received and its consideration.[83]

While in this triangulation there is an economic flow, this does not necessarily mean that consideration is being paid and that there is a direct link between the user and the advertiser on the search engine.[84] Figure 8.3 shows the way in which the different players are connected: while we have a direct link between the advertising service received and its consideration,[85] no direct link exists between users (here 'audience') and the advertising providers (here 'media').[86]

Figure 8.3 Links between Platform, Audience, and Advertisers

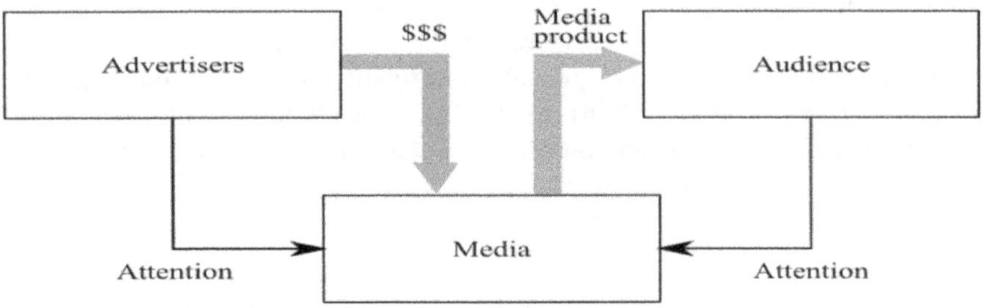

Source: Adapted from Farmer 2008.

p. 1–9. See the newly inserted Article 6a(g) of the Regulation, where access to the Internet, including the World Wide Web is classified as telecommunication services.

80. Council Implementing Regulation (EU) No. 282/2011 of 15 Mar. 2011 laying down implementing measures for Directive 2006/112/EC on the common system of value added tax. *OJ L 77, 23.3.2011, p. 1–22, Annex I (h).*
81. Case C-384/95 *Agrardienste GmbH & Co. KG v. Finanzamt Calau* [1997] ECR I-7387.
82. Case C-384/95 *Agrardienste GmbH & Co. KG v. Finanzamt Calau* [1997] ECR I-7387, paragraph 23.
83. Case 102/86 *Apple and Pear Development Council v. Commissioners of Customs and Excise* [1988] ECR 1443, paragraph 12.
84. M. E. Van Hilten (1999): 'The legal Character of VAT', in 'Selected Issues in European Tax Law. The Legal Character of VAT and the Application of General Principles of Justice', Foundation for European Fiscal Studies, Erasmus University Rotterdam, Kluwer Law International, 1999, p. 7.
85. Case 102/86 *Apple and Pear Development Council v. Commissioners of Customs and Excise* [1988] ECR 1443, paragraph 12.
86. J. Farmer (2014): 'Web 2.0 and Two-sided Markets', at http://20bits.com/ 2008. Accessed 2 Sep. 2014.

8.6 CONCLUSIONS

Mainstream search engines may generate business profits from advertisement transactions. When that happens, the advertising party buys paid services on which VAT is levied, and the search engine pays taxes in accordance with the rule of business profit. This situation in consistent with the principles of VAT neutrality,[87] preventing VAT from being applied twice on the same transaction and, at the same time, from being imposed when goods or services pass into consumption.

Article 2 of the VAT Directive provides that *'the supply of services for consideration'* will *'be subject to VAT'*. This rule can be described as the rule of 'only once': VAT can be applied to any transaction only once.[88] The transparency that distinguishes and qualifies a VAT system cannot be achieved without an effective application of this principle, which is also expressed in the text of the VAT Directive.

Indeed, Article 59(a),[89] for the specific purposes of territoriality, admits derogative solutions with the specific goal to avoid double taxation or non-taxation. The fact that this principle is inserted within a specific territoriality rule, which is one of the basic principles of VAT, does not diminish its general importance.[90]

This situation does not involve users from a legal point of view, but only from an economic perspective, and this is not enough to substantiate the hypothesis that searching is done against consideration according to the specific meaning this has in VAT law, and that therefore users would have to pay VAT.[91] It is also clear that the relationship involves just these two commercial parties, while the users have no legal part in the agreement.

8.7 FURTHER RESEARCH

The above conclusions clarify how Internet search engines lack any additional VAT profile for the provision of free search to their users when this is financially sustained through advertisement, sponsored links, or sponsored ads. Nevertheless, if this is straightforward enough from a VAT perspective, a few ambiguous elements emerged from the analysis in terms of consumption taxation liability.

Article 2 of the VAT Directive provides that the supply of services for consideration will be subject to VAT. This statement excludes entire categories of online

87. The principle is clearly stated in Directive 2006/112/EC, Article 1(2). *'On each transaction, VAT, calculated on the price of the goods or services at the rate applicable to such goods or services, shall be chargeable after deduction of the amount of VAT borne directly by the various cost components'.*
88. P. Centore (2011): 'Il campione gratuito in bilico fra imponibilità e non soggezione IVA, GT', Rivista di giurisprudenza tributaria 2 of 2011 at 97.
89. Council Directive 2008/8/EC of 12 Feb. 2008 amending Directive 2006/112/EC as regards the place of supply of services, *Official J. L 044, 20 February 2008 at 11–22, Article 59a.*
90. P. Centore (2002): 'Niente IVA in entrata e niente IVA in uscita: il principio dell'only once', Corriere tributario 28 of 2002 at 2556.
91. *A different conclusion would also go against the principle that VAT is applied only once.*

services that are not funded even by advertising, and are nevertheless provided for free by most service providers.

The emergence of Internet-based social media and peer-to-peer technology have made it possible for one person to easily share commercial information, products, or services, with very large audiences, with a comparably small economic effort and, in the case of peer-to-peer technology, without having to participate in all transactions. If social media enable businesses to talk to their customers, they also enable customers to talk about said businesses directly to one another. Because of this, different forms of advertising are emerging. Here follows a brief list with no pretence of being exhaustive.

A supermarket has been opened recently in Copenhagen where goods can be had for free.[92] Its business model is based on the concept of 'tryvertising'. Registered customers visiting the supermarket can have goods for free, with an obligation to try them and then write a review and post it online. While there are limitations to the number of products one can obtain for free each month, and profiles can be shut down if reviews are not coming in timely, this is definitely a new approach. But is this also a transaction against payment, a barter scheme, falling within the purpose of VAT?[93]

While here the answer might be easy enough to ascertain, if slightly complicated to manage, more nuanced situations can be listed if we move online. Many of the social services available on the Internet are offered for free, sometimes without support of advertising. These include blogs, microblogs, photo sharing services, messaging services, and so on, and they all somehow profit from the added value of users sharing content. If anything, large numbers of users mean an increase in visibility which usually turns into an increase in the general value of the company. Does this have any implications for taxation?

Another example is GotuitTV Media.[94] An established player in the field of on-demand video, Gotuit has started a video portal providing several services using user-generated materials as well as direct access for free to a variety of mainstream content (music, news, sports, and entertainment). What is the service here? What about audio-visual content that can be (and is) generated by private individuals who distribute and share it via the Internet, possibly anonymously, and which is then modified, sometimes substantially, by other users? It is clear to see how difficult it becomes to determine who is who, who has what role, who has the responsibility for the content, and where the threshold is to be set for *'a service against consideration'* according to the VAT Directive.

These new venues and revenue models all seem to explore a continuum of intersecting possibilities, fuelled by variations in the distribution technology they use, and based on user participation, which is precisely what the current VAT framework does not regulate. This also means that we cannot restrict the conversation to a specific

92. Copenhagen Post (2014): 'Copenhagen to get its first free supermarket', 12 Aug. 2014; *BBC news (2014): 'Denmark: Free supermarket swaps food for reviews'*, 13 Aug. 2014.
93. C. Trenta *ibid.*, 2013 at pp 227–338, 339–368.
94. Business Wire (2010): 'Digitalsmiths Acquires Gotuit', 23 Nov. 2010. http://www.businesswire.com/news/home/20101123005186/en/Digitalsmiths-Acquires-Gotuit. Accessed 10 Jul. 2014.

type of business model, for example, the traditional e-commerce model, nor to one single contractual scheme.[95]

Article 2 of the VAT Directive provides that the supply of services for consideration will be subject to VAT: it means that free supplies do not fall within its scope, but this provision is very often at odds with the hybrid and fuzzy nature of contemporary online services. In the field of economics it has been argued that when two or more groups of agents interact via a network platform, surplus is created:[96] the potential fiscal impact of this should not be underestimated. If traditional VAT rules are inadequate to explain or regulate phenomena such as social media, co-production, or peer-to-peer, we should not refrain from further investigation of new and unbiased approaches.

95. As of July 2015, the European Commission has launched a public consultation to end September 2015 concerning Directive 2010/13/EU on Audio-visual Media Services (AVMSD). The Commission is specifically positing that currently a number of audio-visual services do not fall within the AVMSD scope and that the growth of alternative distribution channels such as streaming and peer-to-peer is rapidly changing the media landscape. See European Commission, 'Commission seeks views on Europe's audio-visual media rules', https://ec.europa.eu/digital-agenda/en/news/commission-seeks-views-europes-audiovisual-media-rules. See also Directive 2010/13/EU of the European Parliament and of the Council of 10 March 2010 on the coordination of certain provisions laid down by law, regulation or administrative action in Member States concerning the provision of audio-visual media services (Audio-visual Media Services Directive). *OJ L 95, 15.4.2010*, at 1–24.

96. M. Armstrong (2006): 'Competition in two-sided markets', 37 RAND J. of Econ. 3 of Autumn 2006 at 668–691.

CHAPTER 9

VAT and Virtual Reality: How Should Cryptocurrencies Be Treated for VAT Purposes?

Oskar Henkow[*]

9.1 INTRODUCTION[1]

Value Added Tax (VAT) systems are challenged by the Internet age. Especially when the virtual reality meets the European VAT system (which is in itself not a wonder of clarity) and in a financial services setting (which is also a very intangible discipline), things tends to be especially complicated. The following two quotes are colourful expressions of these respective complications:

> 'Beyond the everyday world, ..., lies the world of VAT, a kind of fiscal theme park in which factual and legal realities are suspended or inverted.'[2]
> 'Trying to get to grips with banking [...] is akin "to trying to get your hands around a piece of jelly".'[3]

So what happens when you try to get a grip on a piece of jelly in a fiscal theme park but it is not really happening because it is all in the virtual world? That is essentially what this article is about.

---

* Oskar Henkow is Associate Professor at the Department for Business law at Lund University School of Economics and Management in Sweden.

1. I was lucky to have two occasions to discuss the topic of the present contribution within a short period of time, at a conference in Brussels in May and in Vienna in September. The contributions submitted for the conference proceedings for these two occasions are very similar.
2. *Royal & Sun Alliance Insurance Group plc v. Customs and Excise Commissioners* [2001] STC 1476 (CA) at [54] per Sedley L.
3. A. Tait (1988): 'Value Added Tax; International Practice and Problems', IMF, 1988 at p. 100.

The article discusses primarily the EU VAT system. EU VAT could be defined as a general, indirect tax on consumption expenditure, levied at all stages of the production and distribution chain.[4] It shares its characteristics with the Goods and Services Tax (GST) systems applicable in the new world (in a broad sense).[5] In these systems, there are a number of requirements that must be fulfilled in order for the tax to be levied. Broadly speaking, and in respect of what is relevant for the topic of this contribution, there are three basic requirements:

- There has to be a supply of goods and/or services.
- The supply has to be made on a market, i.e., by a trader (taxable person): homework and private individuals' sales are not included within the scope of the tax.
- The supply has to be 'for consideration', i.e., there has to be a nexus between the supply and the consideration paid in respect of the supply.

The requirements are defined and applied differently depending on their legal context. The EU VAT system rests heavily on generic definitions of the concepts without reference to national, legal definitions.[6] In other VAT/GST systems, concepts tend to be defined based on their national legal context: references are made to other national laws to define who is a trader etc.

Independent of how the requirements are defined in the national context, there is a need in all VAT/GST systems to define what is transpiring in order to be able to subsume reality, be it virtual or not, under the national rules.

9.2 THE VIRTUAL REALITY AND VAT

The virtual reality is not, at first sight, easy to grasp and put in a VAT context. The types of transactions involving the Internet can however be grouped together which makes it easier to see, first, what issues arise for VAT purposes and second, whether there really is any expenditure for consumption on a market present that should result in a VAT charge.

First, the Internet is used as a tool in the process of selling and buying real-life goods and services. When buying books, furniture, clothes, a ticket to the movies, a train ticket etc. from a goods or services supplier, the Internet is used as a tool for marketing, ordering and paying. There are issues arising with regard to the place of taxation in a destination-based VAT (it may be difficult to know where the customer is resident), and issues regarding the capacity in which the trader is acting (as a disclosed

4. See B. Terra (1988): 'Sales Taxation', Kluwer, 1988.
5. Such as New Zealand, Australia, South Africa, Singapore etc.
6. Community concepts, they are called.

or undisclosed agent or simply as a provider of a platform). However, the supplies take place in real life and the issues arising are no different from when the Internet is not used (mail-ordering, booking tickets by calling and reserving etc.).

Consumers also use Internet platforms to sell real-life goods and services. Here, the Internet platform provider may provide an electronic service, an intermediary service or actually resell whatever is sold through the platform. Issues arise as regards *inter alia* the place of supply, the capacity in which the Internet platform provider is acting and the status of the consumer (whether he has turned into a trader and should charge VAT or not).

Second, in addition to a tool for marketing, ordering and payment, the Internet is used for the distribution of content. Producers and consumers purchase content and software solutions on the Internet from content providers. One example is when you purchase e-books, films or other content from an online 'bookstore'. Other examples include membership fees on social networks, payments for online and offline games made to traders etc. This is what is most often referred to as e-commerce. Here, a number of issues arise, *inter alia* as regards the VAT treatment, the place of supply and the services of intermediaries.[7]

Importantly, there may not even be a trader involved. Content may be shared, peer-to-peer, without an intervening content provider. In peer-to-peer networks, the provider of the content may also be a consumer. The computer capacity of participating peers is used for sharing the content. Actually, this phenomenon is not only present as part of (illegal) consumer sharing of film and music. The technique is used by large firms, such as Skype, when delivering their service.[8]

In peer-to-peer content sharing, there seems, in the normal circumstances, not to be the necessary nexus (at least not from an EU VAT perspective) between the services provided and any payments made (in cash or in kind). The requirements are very strict, payments have to be made directly for services or goods provided and inducement payments are not taxed, but no one is requiring payment in order to supply content.[9]

7. It seems to me that Article 9a of Council Implementing Regulation (EU) No. 282/2011 of 15 Mar. 2011 laying down implementing measures for Directive 2006/112/EC on the Common System of Value Added Tax, as amended, latest by Council Implementing Regulation (EU) No. 1042/2013 of 7 Oct. 2013 amending Implementing Regulation (EU) No. 282/2011 as regards the place of supply of services will to a large extent clarify matters as regards intermediaries in the EU.
8. See C. Trenta (2013): 'VAT in peer-to-peer content distribution: towards a tax proposal for decentralized networks' (Doctoral dissertation). Jönköping: Jönköping International Business School at pp. 66–74.
9. For example, in Case 102/86 *Apple and Pear Development Council v. Commissioners of Customs and Excise* EU:C:1988:120, the Court did not find a link present despite the fact that the payments were clearly linked to supplies made and at least made for the inducement of supplies. Similarly, in Case C-16/93 *Tolsma* EU:C:1994:80, the payments made to a street musician was not seen as consideration, despite the fact that such payments clearly, from time to time, constitute consideration for services performed. See further, B. Terra, J. Kajus (2014): 'A Guide to the European VAT Directives', 2014, Ch. 8.4.4 and 8.4.5. It is clear that whether or not the content-sharing is lawful does not impact the assessment, see P. Rendahl (2011): 'Imposing EU VAT on Unlawful Digital Supplies?', EC Tax Rev., 2011–2014 at pp. 192–202.

The fact that the contract conditions for receiving the service or content stipulate that you have to participate in the P2P network and actually, if need be, may distribute and/or provide content, does not change the analysis. Contract conditions as such are neither, it seems to me, in the normal course of events, seen as constituting separate services supplied by the recipient of a supply for a consideration.[10] And as a peer does not involve himself in a peer-to-peer network with the purpose of supplying, it seems doubtful whether the activity constitutes exploitation of property for the purposes of obtaining income (and thus an economic activity) also due to the fact that it is not explicitly paid for.[11]

Similar issues arise as regards peer-to-peer networks for sharing real-life assets. Here, however, the presence of a consideration for the use of the asset may yield a different result.

Lastly, with the use of Internet, new so-called virtual currencies or virtual money have been created. These are currencies that are not present in the form of legal tender, i.e., bank notes and coins, but solely as electronic codes in computer systems. Virtual currencies are defined by the ECB as a type of unregulated, digital money, which is issued and usually controlled by its developers, and used and accepted among the members of a specific virtual community.[12]

Virtual currencies have, depending on their interaction with traditional, 'real' money and the real economy, been grouped in three categories by the ECB (see Figure 9.1).[13]

---

10. In situations concerning findings of facts, such as this one, the circumstances determine what has occurred. The statements here are based on what in my view is clear from a general assessment of how P2P networks function. It may be that the facts merit another finding in an individual case. Compare also the reasoning of the Court in Case C-283/12 *Serebryannay vek* EU:C:2013:599 and Joined Cases C-53/09 and 55/09 *Loyalty Management UK and Baxi Group* EU:C:2010:590. In Case C-277/05 *Société thermale d'Eugénie-Les-Bains* EU:C:2007:440, the Court refused to see a separate supply of a reservation service in the reservation of a hotel room, relying on the contractual circumstances which entail conditions etc. without there necessarily being supplies made (other than the supply regulated by the contract). In Case C-305/01 *MKG Kraftfahrzeuge-Factoring* EU:C:2003:377, the contract covered several supplies, one of which was a factoring services provided by the recipient of a debt. Thus, the Court did not in that case find a separate supply hidden in the contract terms of a sale of debts but simply applied the supplies stipulated in the contract to the case at hand.
11. See, for the same view, P. Rendahl (2011): 'Imposing EU VAT on Unlawful Digital Supplies?', 20 EC Tax Review 4 of 2011 at 192–202. See also C. Trenta *ibid.*, (2013) for an explorative view on how the peer-to-peer phenomenon could and should be incorporated into the VAT system. Appendices contains the evaluation of the direct link and peer-to-peer networks.
12. European Central Bank (2012): 'Virtual Currency Schemes', October 2012, [published online ISBN: 978-92-899-0862-7 (online)], p. 6.
13. The categorization has been made by the ECB, see European Central Bank (2012): 'Virtual Currency Schemes', October 2012, [ISBN: 978-92-899-0862-7 (online)]. The description has been adapted slightly to suit the present article and the VAT context.

Figure 9.1

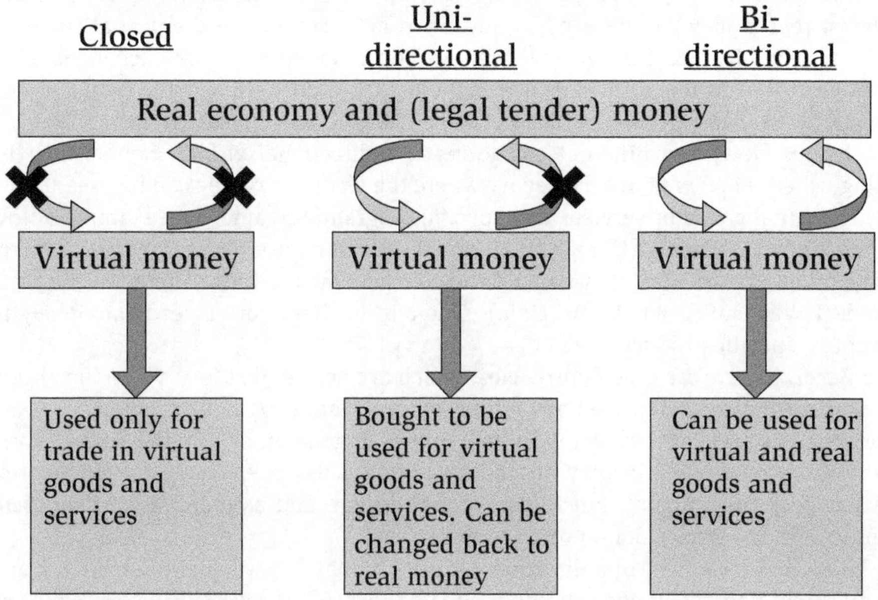

First, sometimes games have their own currency that is used to buy goods or services within the game. When the game is virtual, virtual goods and services are bought. These virtual currencies have nothing to do with either the real economy or with real money. As such, this kind of 'money' is not a new phenomenon, at least not to anyone familiar with traditional board games such as Monopoly. What is new is the virtual setting, but that does not change anything for VAT treatment purposes. Closed systems of virtual money are irrelevant for VAT purposes.

Second, in some games, and with regard to some social networks, it is possible to buy currency with real money. For example, paying to the game's organizer a sum of EUR 1,50 could provide the player with virtual money to be used in the game. The virtual money could however not be changed back to real money. There is a unidirectional flow of money from the real economy to the virtual currency. Examples of such systems are manifold, Facebook credits (FC) being an obvious example.[14] Essentially, what is purchased with real money is not equivalent to money at all (see further section 9.4 on the definition of money). The player is buying a possibility to enjoy an electronic service. Consequently, the payment made is a (pre)payment for the

14. Smurfs, Hay Day, Clash of Clans are examples of games for tablets that use some kinds of unidirectional virtual currencies.

supply of (a more full version of) a game/software. Note that similar systems exist as regards vouchers, air miles etc.[15]

Lastly, there are virtual currencies that are bidirectional in character. In these systems, real money can be used to buy a virtual currency but the virtual currency could also be changed back to real money. The uniqueness is the exchangeability. Here, the virtual currency could be used not only to buy something in the virtual world, but also as an investment, that could later be changed back to real money.

In my view, two different categories of bidirectional virtual money must be distinguished. First, we have a category where the virtual currency can be used to buy specific virtual goods or services in a specific programme/game. One example of this are the Linden Dollars (L$) in Second Life, which can be used to buy virtual property in the online platform but they can also be changed back to USD. Another example is World of War craft Gold (WOW Gold). One aim of these currencies is obviously to promote a specific product (a game).

Second, there are cryptocurrencies, which are neither tied to any specific virtual programme or game, nor issued by a trader selling a platform/game or similar. They are intended to be used as consideration for supplies in general, be it in the virtual world or the real world. They display no additional characteristics. The best-known cryptocurrency is the 'bitcoin', but there are many more and as many as 275 different cryptocurrencies have been reported to exist.[16]

The VAT treatment of bidirectional virtual money is particularly interesting and the question, how this money should be treated for VAT purposes, is discussed in the remainder of this chapter.

9.3 TREATMENT OF MONEY, DEBTS AND VOUCHERS IN EU VAT

The EU VAT Directive[17] contains only one provision explicitly dealing with 'currency, bank notes and coins used as legal tender' namely Article 135(1)(e) of the VAT Directive, which exempts from VAT:

> transactions, including negotiation, concerning currency, bank notes and coins used as legal tender, with the exception of collectors' items, that is to say, gold, silver or other metal coins or bank notes which are not normally used as legal tender or coins of numismatic interest.

15. Compare European Central Bank (2012): 'Virtual Currency Schemes', October 2012, [published online ISBN: 978-92-899-0862-7 (online)], pp. 16–17, where trade in air miles is discussed and air miles classified as a unidirectional virtual currency.
16. https://en.wikipedia.org/wiki/Cryptocurrency. 'Cryptocurrency', visited 9 Aug. 2014. Except for bitcoins there are Litecoin, Peercoin, Ripple, Darkcoin, Namecoin Mastercoin, Primecoin, Vertcoin and so forth.
17. Council Directive 2006/112/EC of 28 Nov. 2006 on the Common System of Value Added Tax (as amended, latest by Council Directive 2013/42/EU of 22 Jul. 2013 amending Directive 2006/112/EC on the Common System of Value Added Tax, as Regards a Quick Reaction Mechanism against VAT Fraud and Council Directive 2013/42/EU of 22 Jul. 2013 amending Directive 2006/112/EC on the Common System of Value Added Tax, as Regards a Quick Reaction Mechanism against VAT Fraud).

According to Article 45 of the Implementing regulation:[18]

> The exemption provided for in point (e) of Article 135(1) of Directive 2006/112/EC shall not apply to platinum nobles.

Also exempt from VAT is, according to Article 135(1)(d):

> transactions, including negotiation, concerning deposit and current accounts, payments, transfers, debts, cheques and other negotiable instruments, but excluding debt collection.

There is consequently in the legal texts a lack of definitions, because the concept of currency etc. is not defined in the VAT Directive.

The VAT Directive should be interpreted in its EU law context, and concepts and definitions in other areas of EU law are therefore relevant. There are numerous EU legal instruments relevant to money.[19] In the *Money Laundering Directive*, money as such is not defined.[20] Instead, reference is made to the laundering of property, which is broadly defined.[21] The *Payment Services Directive*, regulating the provision of payment services in the EU, does not contain a definition of money either.[22] Rather, it explicitly includes, and excludes, particular types of payment activities.[23]

The text closest to a definition of 'money', for the purposes of EU law, I have been able to find is the definition present in the *Electronic Money Directive* (regulating rules for the pursuit of the activity of issuing electronic money).[24] Article 2(2) of the *Electronic Money Directive* contains a definition of electronic money:

> 'electronic money' means electronically, including magnetically, stored monetary value as represented by a claim on the issuer which is issued on receipt of funds for the purpose of making payment transactions as defined in point 5 of Article 4 of Directive 2007/64/EC, and which is accepted by a natural or legal person other than the electronic money issuer.

A payment transaction is defined in point 5 of Article 4 of the Payment Services Directive as an act, initiated by the payer or by the payee, of placing, transferring or

18. Council Implementing Regulation (EU) No. 282/2011 of 15 Mar. 2011 laying down implementing measures for Directive 2006/112/EC on the Common System of Value Added Tax, as amended, latest by Council Implementing Regulation (EU) No. 1042/2013 of 7 Oct. 2013 amending Implementing Regulation (EU) No. 282/2011 as regards the place of supply of services.
19. See recital 3 to the Payment Services Directive for a list of the most relevant with regard to payments.
20. Directive 2005/60/EC of the European Parliament and of the Council of 26 Oct. 2005 on the prevention of the use of the financial system for the purpose of money laundering and terrorist financing (referred to here as the Money Laundering Directive).
21. Article 3(3) of the Money Laundering Directive.
22. Directive 2007/64/EC of the European Parliament and of the Council of 13 Nov. 2007 on payment services in the internal market amending Directives 97/7/EC, 2002/65/EC, 2005/60/EC and 2006/48/EC and repealing Directive 97/5/EC (Text with EEA relevance).
23. Articles 2 and 3 of the Payment Services Directive.
24. Directive 2009/110/EC of the European Parliament and of the Council of 16 Sep. 2009 on the taking up, pursuit and prudential supervision of the business of electronic money institutions amending Directives 2005/60/EC and 2006/48/EC and repealing Directive 2000/46/EC (referred to here as the E-money Directive).

withdrawing funds, irrespective of any underlying obligations between the payer and the payee.

I have not been able to find any further definitions of money or currency that could be of help. It can be concluded, however, that cryptocurrencies do not meet the definition of being electronic money in the Electronic Money Directive.[25]

In the sphere of EU VAT law, the Court of Justice of the EU, the CJEU, has commented on the use of money in a wider context in several judgments. First, the CJEU has held that a taxable person who only pays the consideration (due in respect of a supply of services) in cash, or who undertakes to do so, does not himself make a supply of services.[26]

It also follows, from the very provisions defining the material scope of VAT (Articles 1 and 2 of the VAT Directive) that only money transferred as consideration for a supply falls within the scope of VAT (but does not constitute a supply in itself). Pure transfers of money, not linked to any supply, are not taxed. This is clear from several cases from the CJEU, concerning lump sum payments, not amounting to consideration for any supplies,[27] or the exchange of currencies, where the exchanged values are not consideration in itself (but the exchange rate applied may entail a consideration for the exchange service).[28] This is actually conforming to EU law in general, where the transfer of money is the transfer of neither a good nor a service.[29] The case law extends to situations of transfers, not of money itself, but of debts[30] and capital contributions and share issues.[31] The sale of shares, however, amounts to a supply for consideration in the eyes of the Court, and so does a transfer of insurance contracts.[32]

In addition, the Court's case law on, essentially, non-financial rights needs to be considered. The Court has ruled, *inter alia*, on the taxable amount in relation to vouchers used for rebates and as payment, on the value of services performed in return for promotion gifts and vouchers,[33] and on the various services involved in the distribution of a promotion scheme.[34] In *Astra Zeneca UK*, the question was whether the provision of a retail voucher by a company to its employees constituted a supply of services effected for consideration.[35] The vouchers in question enabled the employees to purchase goods or services in specific shops. The Court found that the vouchers

25. European Central Bank (2012): 'Virtual Currency Schemes', October 2012, [published online ISBN: 978-92-899-0862-7 (online)], p. 16.
26. Case C-409/98 Mirror Group EU:C:2001:524, paragraph 26.
27. See Case C-419/02 BUPA EU:C:2006:122, Case C-107/13 FIRI EU:C:2014:151, Société thermale d'Eugénie-Les-Bains, but also Case C-151/13 *Le Rayon d'Or* EU:C:2014:185.
28. Case C-172/96 *First National Bank of Chicago* EU:C:1998:354.
29. Case C-358/93 *Bordessa and others* EU:C:1995:54. But, in customs law, counterfeit currency has been (implicitly) treated as a good! See Case C-343/89 *Witzemann v. Hauptzollamt München-Mitte* EU:C:1990:445.
30. Case C-93/10 *GFKL Financial Services* EU:C:2011:700.
31. Case C-465/03 *Kretztechnik* EU:C:2005:320.
32. Case C-29/07 *SKF* EU:C:2009:665 and Case C-242/08 *Swiss Re Germany Holding* EU:C:2009:647 respectively.
33. Case C-126/88 Boots Co Ltd EU:C:1990:136, Case C-33/93 *Empire Stores* EU:C:1994:225, Case C-317/94 *Elida Gibbs* EU:C:1996:400 and further B.Terra, J. Kajus *ibid.*, 2014, Ch. 13.2.2.
34. Joined Cases C-53/09 and C-55/09 *Loyalty Management UK* (C-53/09), *Baxi Group* (C-55/09) EU:C:2010:590.
35. Case C-40/09 *Astra Zeneca UK* EU:C:2010:450.

conferred a future right to goods or services that was as yet indeterminate as to its object.[36] The Court also found that the vouchers were obtained for consideration. There was a direct link between the provision of retail vouchers by Astra Zeneca to its employees and the part of the cash remuneration which the employees had to give up as consideration for that provision.[37] The 'sale' of the voucher to the employees in exchange for a reduction in salary was therefore a (taxed) supply of services, the right to future supplies.

In *Lebara*, the Court dealt with a specific type of phone cards, which could only be used to make international telephone calls to destinations, and at rates, determined in advance.[38] Accordingly, the cards allowed access only to services of one type, the nature and quantity of which were determined in advance and which were subject to a single rate of tax.[39] The Court found that the expression 'telecommunication services' was broad enough to encompass the sale and resale of such cards.

Lastly, in *Granton Advertising*, Granton cards, a type of rebate cards, were discussed.[40] The cards were purchased from Granton Advertising and could be used when obtaining goods or services from affiliated businesses which had agreed to grant a rebate if the card was presented. Consequently, the cards conferred on its holder only a right to obtain reductions in the prices of goods and services offered by the affiliated businesses.[41]

The Court noted that the VAT treatment of the Granton cards depended on the legal and financial characteristics of those cards.[42] As the cards solely entitled the holder to a price reduction, they were not financial instruments (securities or debt instruments) for the purposes of the exemptions for financial services in the VAT Directive.[43]

Even though the Granton cards entitled their holder to price reductions, they did not constitute, in themselves, a payment instrument for the purpose of EU VAT. Even if such cards were transferrable and could be resold at a certain price, they did not operate as a way of transferring money, unlike payments, transfers and cheques.[44] The sale of the cards was therefore not exempt from VAT.

As can be seen, the Court relies on the legal and financial classification of the instrument/voucher in question. Typically, a rebate voucher, giving the holder a right to price reductions on the purchase of goods and services, is simply a right, and the sale of the voucher is taxed (*Granton Advertising*).[45] A voucher entailing the right to receive unidentifiable goods and services is typically seen as a right/service, not as money (*Astra Zeneca UK*). And, lastly, a voucher entailing a right to a specific service is in principle seen as a prepayment for that specific service (*Lebara*).

36. Case C-40/09 *Astra Zeneca UK*, paragraph 25.
37. Case C-40/09 *Astra Zeneca UK*, paragraph 29.
38. Case C-520/10 *Lebara*, EU:C:2012:264.
39. Case C-520/10 *Lebara*, paragraph 28.
40. Case C-461/12 *Granton Advertising*, EU:C:2014:1745.
41. Case C-461/12 *Granton Advertising*, paragraph 31.
42. Case C-461/12 *Granton Advertising*, paragraph 17.
43. See (now) Article 135(1)(d) and (f) of the VAT Directive.
44. Case C-461/12 *Granton Advertising*, paragraph 37.
45. Chargeability arising when the supply is made, compare *Société thermale d'Eugénie-Les-Bain*.

These conclusions on the typical treatment of the various kinds of vouchers could be compared to the Commission's proposal as regards the treatment of vouchers.[46] The Commission defines a voucher as an instrument carrying a right to receive a supply of goods or services, or to receive a price discount or rebate with regard to a supply of goods or services and where there is a corresponding obligation to fulfil this right.[47] Three types of vouchers are distinguished. First, single-purpose vouchers (SPV) are vouchers carrying a right to receive a supply of goods or services where the supplier's identity, the place of supply and the applicable VAT rate for these goods or services is known at the time of issue of the voucher. Essentially, SPV's are thus *Lebara*-type of pre-payments.[48] Second, a voucher carrying a right to receive a price discount or rebate with regard to a supply of goods or services is a discount voucher. Granton Cards are a type of discount vouchers.[49] Lastly, a voucher, other than a discount or rebate voucher, which does not constitute a SPV, is a multi-purpose voucher (MPV). The type of voucher discussed in *Astra Zeneca UK* seems to be essentially an MPV. Payment services are excluded from the definition.[50]

According to the proposal, the distribution of an MPV should be seen as a service performed by the acquirer of the MPV to the seller, when the sale is made from another person than the issuer and the price is below the nominal value of the voucher.[51] When the MPV is redeemed against goods and services, the redeemer is liable to pay the VAT on the supply. The provision of the MPV at redemption, which in itself is the provision of a right and therefore a barter situation, is ignored. The underlying supply governs the VAT treatment.[52]

The taxable person who issued the MPV does not always redeem MPV's. In such a situation the issuer will reimburse the redeemer. According to the Explanatory Memorandum to the Proposal, the reimbursement falls outside the scope of VAT.[53]

Of primary interest, in the present perspective, is the distinction between MPVs and money. According to the proposal, a payment service within the meaning of the Payment Services Directive, should not be regarded as a voucher.[54] That reference creates a number of questions. For example, would a change to the Payment Services

46. Proposal for a Council Directive amending Directive 2006/112/EC on the common system of value added tax, as regards the treatment of vouchers, COM(2012) 206 final (below referred to as the Proposal).
47. Article 30a(1) of the Proposal contains the definitions of the various types of vouchers.
48. More or less there are potential differences which are not discussed here.
49. The Granton cards were discount vouchers paid for. Consequently, the new taxable transaction created in the proposal, see Article 1 of the Proposal adding an Article 25(e) to the VAT Directive, is not applicable as it only relates to free discount vouchers. The primary interest of the present article is virtual currencies. Free discount vouchers are not of interest as regards such currencies and they are therefore not discussed here.
50. Article 30a(2) of the Proposal.
51. See Article 1 of the Proposal adding an Article 25(d) to the VAT Directive. The nominal value is defined in Article 74a(2) of the Proposal as everything that is received, or to be received, by the issuer of the voucher, i.e., the face value of the voucher minus any rebates granted to the final holder of the MPV exchanging it for goods or services.
52. See Article 30b of the Proposal.
53. Explanatory Memorandum to the Proposal, p. 14.
54. See Article 30a(2) of the Proposal.

Directive also result in a change in the VAT treatment, or was the reference static? And would that mean that paper cheques and similar instruments were MPVs as they are explicitly excluded from the scope of the Payment Services Directive and hence not money?[55] And how would that interpretation align with existing case law of the Court of Justice of the EU?

In the discussions of the proposal in the Council, the link to the Payment Services Directive has obviously been debated and under a Greek Presidency compromise text the reference is dropped.[56] According to the definition of a voucher as it now reads, a voucher is an instrument where there is an obligation to accept it as consideration or part consideration for a supply where the goods or services to be supplied *or* the identities of the potential suppliers are either indicated on the instrument itself or on related documentation, including the terms and conditions of usage of the instrument.[57] According to the Presidency Note, the word *or*, emphasized in the definition above, was chosen rather than *and*, because 'the Presidency believes that the two requirements (goods or services to be supplied-identities of potential suppliers) for the distinction between vouchers and means of payment should not be required to apply simultaneously'.[58] Consequently, if the proposal is adopted, we will get a negative definition of means of payments in the VAT Directive.

9.4 VIRTUAL CURRENCIES AND THEIR VAT TREATMENT

What happens then when the virtual reality and virtual currencies in particular meet the VAT reality? Already in section 9.2 above, some conclusions were discussed in general as regards virtual currencies. It is apparent from that discussion that the most problematic virtual currencies are bidirectional virtual currencies. Before discussing these in relation to their VAT treatment, there will be a brief discussion of what money is, from an economic perspective. I note that the Court in *Granton Advertising* points out that a legal and financial classification should be made. The financial benchmark of money is now discussed.

Money serves three functions: it is a store of value, a unit of account and a means of payment.[59] As a store of value money it preserves purchasing power between different periods of time. Money has a fixed value, and as such it functions as a unit of account and simplifies price comparisons. Money also guarantees the double coincidence of wants and facilitates trade, functioning as a means of payment. These three

55. See Article 3(g) of the Payment Services Directive.
56. Council of the European Union, Brussels, 27 Mar. 2014, 8268/14, FISC 62, pp. 5–6.
57. Council of the European Union, Brussels, 27 Mar. 2014, 8268/14, FISC 62, pp. 5 (my emphasis).
58. Council of the European Union, Brussels, 27 Mar. 2014, 8268/14, FISC 62, p. 6.
59. I have discussed these functions in O. Henkow (2008): 'Financial Activities in European VAT', Kluwer Law International, 2008 at Ch. 2.6.1. It should be noted that money was not created because there was a need to guarantee the double coincidence of wants, and thus to ease trade (as suggested in economic literature and by me in Ch. 2.6.1.1). Rather, an historical assessment of money suggests that money was created to fund war, see Graeber (2011): 'Debt: the first 5,000 years', Melville House Publishing, 2011.

functions are all functions that money serves. There are no additional functions relevant to the VAT discussion.[60]

From a financial benchmark point of view, money should therefore be understood as including all assets or items that solely display these three functions, and no others. If we consider the two types of bidirectional virtual currencies discussed in section 9.2, we can see that only cryptocurrencies display solely the three functions in question.[61] The other categories of bidirectional virtual money also serve other functions, such as promotion and/or giving access to certain specific features in on-line games and platforms. These are MPVs under the new definition and not means of payment as defined in the compromise text of the Greek Presidency.

In my view, it is important to distinguish cryptocurrencies in EU VAT, not only as a financial benchmark but also because of the character of the VAT. The pure transfer of wealth is not, in itself, any production or consumption activity. A pure transfer of wealth cannot therefore fall within the scope of a tax on consumption expenditure, as there is no consumption (or production) involved.[62] Money represents such pure transfers of wealth, and if the fundamental characteristics of the VAT system should be preserved, all other items that display the exact same features must thus, when transferred, also fall outside the scope of VAT. But, equally important, all items having also consumption characteristics must be treated as falling within the scope of VAT.[63] Trade in these pure financial assets should be treated as outside the scope of VAT. Otherwise there is a break of the characteristic of VAT as a tax on consumption, as it taxes also pure savings and transfers. This is the reason that an MPV should also display other characteristics than those of money. The changes made in the Greek Presidency's text are therefore most welcome.

From a non-VAT, legal perspective, it is clear that cryptocurrencies are not legal tender. They are not money in the traditional sense of the word. They are not issued by a central monetary authority and not under supervision of any authority.[64] The control and risk related policies and regulations all distinguish cryptocurrencies from real money.[65]

Consequently, there is no clear alignment between essential financial characteristics of cryptocurrencies (they serve the three functions of money, and no more) and their legal classification (they clearly are not money). The treatment in different

60. Ignoring the functions money has in public finance, where the liquidity, i.e., issuance of money, is a key function.
61. According to the ECB, it could be questioned whether they function as a store of value, see European Central Bank (2012): 'Virtual Currency Schemes', October 2012, [published online ISBN: 978-92-899-0862-7 (online)], p. 11. They also point to the fact that it is not intended to be a store of value but only a means of exchange, at p. 27. The fact remains that it serves these functions.
62. See, in detail, O. Henkow (2008): 'Financial Activities in European VAT', Kluwer Law International, 2008 at pp. 76 et seq.
63. The distinction between pure financial investments and other assets is discussed in Henkow, Financial Activities in European VAT, Ch. 2.X.X.
64. Compare section 3 above and discussion of money in EU law and European Central Bank (2012): 'Virtual Currency Schemes', October 2012, [published online ISBN: 978-92-899-0862-7 (online)], pp. 24–27.
65. See ECB, p. 16.

national systems seems to vary. Some countries essentially treat bitcoins as a kind of debt instrument,[66] others see them as an alternative means of payment that is taxed (non-financial).[67] Some commentators have suggested that bitcoins are a type of MPVs and should be treated as such.[68]

The Swedish Supreme Administrative Court has now asked the question of the correct VAT treatment of bitcoins to the CJEU.[69] The national court asks whether there is a supply for consideration when a person exchanges a virtual currency for a traditional currency and vice versa. The national court also asks whether any of the financial services exemptions in Article 135(1) of the VAT Directive are applicable.

I note that, under the original proposal of the Commission as regards the treatment of vouchers, the classification of cryptocurrencies as a type of MPV has merits. However, it seems clear that it is not an MPV under the proposal as worded following the amendments made in the Council. A cryptocurrency neither denotes the goods or services to be supplied, nor the identities of potential suppliers. On the contrary, it meets the definition of being money-equivalent under the amended voucher proposal as explained by the Greek Presidency.[70] That would be consistent with the financial characteristics of the functions served by cryptocurrencies. The promotional aim that a voucher should have under the new definition is also in conformity with this.

In my view, the Court of Justice's judgment will depend upon what aspects should take precedence. If the functional, financial perspective should take precedence, and in my view the principle of fiscal neutrality speaks for the conclusion that it should, cryptocurrencies should be treated as equivalent to any other debt instrument, independent of the differences it has from a legal perspective with such instruments. Essentially, from a functional perspective, using cryptocurrencies is a method of settling a debt, storing wealth and comparing value, and no more. But, from a more legal perspective, there is a basis to distinguish cryptocurrencies as an unregulated, alternative means of payment that should not be covered by the exemption for transactions concerning debts. I presume no government is especially keen on cryptocurrencies because they are a product of anarchy and operate outside the control of government (and you cannot pay taxes in cryptocurrencies). To treat them as a taxed right would seem to put a stick in the wheels of the system, which may be welcomed by some.

66. HM Revenue & Customs Brief 09/14: 'Tax treatment of activities involving Bitcoins and other similar cryptocurrencies.'
67. As reported by the IBFD, Tax News Service [online] report of 8 Apr. 2014, Estonia, Taxation of bitcoin transactions.
68. B. Terra, J. Kajus (2014): 'A Guide to the European VAT Directives', IBFD Amsterdam, 2014, n. 504.
69. Pending Case C-264/14 *Hedqvist*.
70. See section 9.3 *in fine* above.

CHAPTER 10

Consumption Taxation of Cloud Computing: Lessons from the US Subnational Retail Sales Tax Experience

*Walter Hellerstein**

10.1 INTRODUCTION AND PRELIMINARY CAVEATS

If one is looking for an appropriate focus for examining the challenges that the digital economy poses for VATs, it would be hard to find a better candidate than cloud computing. Indeed, in its Base Erosion and Profit Shifting (BEPS) initiative, the OECD identifies cloud computing as one of the principal new business models that give rise to the tax challenges of digital economy,[1] and these include, specifically, the challenge of 'how to ensure the effective collection of VAT/GST'.[2] Equally important, for my purposes, cloud computing is a business model that creates enormous challenges for the US subnational retail sales tax (RST), challenges that the RST is beginning to confront and address.[3] Accordingly, cloud computing provides an ideal vehicle for exploring the question to which this article is devoted, namely the lessons, if any, that US RST's experience with the challenges raised by the digital economy may have for the VAT's approach to the same or similar challenges.

At the outset, it appropriate to identify the limitations of any effort to extract useful lessons from the US RST experience for VATs. Although there is general

* Walter Hellerstein is Distinguished Research Professor & Francis Shackelford Distinguished Professor in Taxation Law at the University of Georgia, US.

1. OECD (2014): 'BEPS Action 1: Address the Tax Challenges of the Digital Economy' (Public Discussion Draft) (OECD 2014), paragraphs 79–84, available at http://www.oecd.org/ctp/tax-challenges-digital-economy-discussion-draft-march-2014.pdf.
2. OECD (2013): '*Action Plan on Base Erosion and Profit Shifting*' (OECD 2013), at 14–15, available at www.oecd.org/tax/beps.htm.
3. W. Hellerstein, and Jon Sedon (2012): 'State Taxation of Cloud Computing: A Framework for Analysis', 117 J. of Tax'n 1 of 2012 at 11–31. The following discussion draws freely from this article.

agreement, at least among academic observers, that an ideal VAT and an ideal RST would (at the end of the day) tax supplies or sales in the same appropriate way, namely, imposing a uniform levy on final consumption,[4] there are a number of features of RSTs, and in particular the US RST, that should lead one to be cautious about drawing lessons from the US RST for VATs. First, because RSTs are in principle single-stage taxes imposed only on the final sale for private consumption, they may have limited relevance for the taxation of business purchases under the staged collection process that is the hallmark of VATs.[5] Second, although the US RST in principle should apply only to final consumption, in point of fact roughly 40% of US RST falls on business,[6] which may limit the relevance of the US RST for a VAT that in principle should not impose a tax burden on business. Finally, and perhaps most significantly for an analysis of issues raised by cloud computing, the US RST, unlike VATs, is generally limited to sales of tangible personal property and applies only selectively to services that are specifically identified for taxation.[7] Accordingly, the considerable attention that the US RST regimes devote to determining whether a particular cloud computing offering should be treated as the taxable sale or lease of tangible personal property or as a non-taxable service has limited relevance to VATs, which typically draw no such distinction.

Despite these differences, there are general lessons that the US RST's experience with cloud computing contains for VAT regimes' approach to cloud computing.

10.2 WHAT IS CLOUD COMPUTING?

Like most discussions of cloud computing, this article adopts the definition of cloud computing provided by the US National Institute of Standards and Technology (NIST).[8] According to the NIST, cloud computing is a model for enabling ubiquitous, convenient, on-demand network access to a shared pool of configurable computing resources (e.g., networks, servers, storage, applications, and services) that can be rapidly provisioned and released with minimal management effort or service provider interaction.[9]

4. See, e.g., OECD (2014): 'International VAT/GST Guidelines' (OECD 2014) paragraph 1.2 available at http://www.oecd.org/ctp/consumption/international-vat-gst-guidelines.pdf ('*The overarching purpose of a VAT is to impose a broad-based tax on consumption, which is understood to mean final consumption by households.*'); Ch. E. McLure Jr., W. Hellerstein (2004): 'Congressional Intervention in State Taxation: A Normative Analysis of Three Proposals,' 31 State Tax Notes 9 of 2004 at 721–735, 727 ('*A neutral system of sales taxation would follow these … tenets: (a) all sales to consumers would be taxed uniformly; (b) all sales to businesses would be exempt….*').
5. OECD (2014): 'International VAT/GST Guidelines', paragraph 1.5 ('The central design feature of a VAT, and the feature from which it derives its name, is that the tax is collected through a staged process.').
6. See J.R. Hellerstein, W. Hellerstein, J.A. Swain (2015): 'State Taxation', Vol. II (3d ed. 2015 rev.), ¶ 12.03.
7. *Ibid.*, ¶ 12.06.
8. See, e.g., A. Bal (2012): 'Tax Implications of Cloud Computing – How Real Taxes Fit into Virtual Clouds,' 66 Bulletin for International Taxation 6 of June 2012 at 335–339, 335, note 1; OECD (2014): 'BEPS Action 1: Address the Tax Challenges of the Digital Economy', cited above, paragraph 79, note 13.

The five 'essential characteristics' of cloud computing are:

- On-demand self-service;
- Broad network access;
- Resource pooling;
- Rapid elasticity; and
- Measured service.[10]

As the NIST further observes, however, cloud computing is 'an evolving paradigm'.[11]

There are three 'models' of cloud computing. The Software as a Service (SaaS) model allows a customer to access a provider's applications on a cloud infrastructure (i.e., the collection of hardware and software that enables the essential characteristics of cloud computing described above).[12] Under the SaaS model, a customer does not manage or control the underlying cloud infrastructure, with limited exceptions. The Platform as a Service (PaaS) model allows a customer to deploy its created or acquired applications on a cloud infrastructure using programming languages, libraries, services, or tools supported by the provider. As with the SaaS model, the customer does not manage or control the underlying cloud infrastructure. However, the customer has control over the deployed applications and, potentially, configuration settings for the

---

9. The NIST Definition of Cloud Computing, National Institute of Standards and Technology, Special Publication 800-145, available at http://csrc.nist.gov/publications/nistpubs/800-145/SP800-145.pdf.
10. *Ibid.*, The NIST explains the 'essential characteristics' as follows:

    On-demand self-service. A consumer can unilaterally provision computing capabilities, such as server time and network storage, as needed automatically without requiring human interaction with each service provider.
    Broad network access. Capabilities are available over the network and accessed through standard mechanisms that promote use by heterogeneous thin or thick client platforms (e.g., mobile phones, tablets, laptops, and workstations).
    Resource pooling. The provider's computing resources are pooled to serve multiple consumers using a multi-tenant model, with different physical and virtual resources dynamically assigned and reassigned according to consumer demand. There is a sense of location independence in that the customer generally has no control or knowledge over the exact location of the provided resources but may be able to specify location at a higher level of abstraction (e.g., country, state, or datacentre). Examples of resources include storage, processing, memory, and network bandwidth.
    Rapid elasticity. Capabilities can be elastically provisioned and released, in some cases automatically, to scale rapidly outward and inward commensurate with demand. To the consumer, the capabilities available for provisioning often appear to be unlimited and can be appropriated in any quantity at any time.
    Measured service. Cloud systems automatically control and optimize resource use by leveraging a metering capability at some level of abstraction appropriate to the type of service (e.g., storage, processing, bandwidth, and active user accounts). Resource usage can be monitored, controlled, and reported, providing transparency for both the provider and consumer of the utilized service.

    Ibid.
11. *Ibid.*
12. The ensuing description of cloud computing relies on the NIST discussion in *ibid.*

application-hosting environment. The Infrastructure as a Service (IaaS) model allows a customer access to processing, storage, networks, and other computing resources, where the customer can deploy and run software, including operating systems and applications. Under the IaaS model, the customer does not manage or control the underlying cloud infrastructure, but has control over operating systems, storage, and deployed applications. Providers of SaaS and PaaS are often called 'application service providers.' 'Application services' generally refer to services that allow customers to access software on the provider's system, typically by means of a web browser.

To a casual observer, the definition of cloud computing, the identification of its essential characteristics, and the description of the three models may provide little clarity as to what is, and what is not, cloud computing. At its core, cloud computing allows users remote access to software, storage, or even hardware. While this simplified overview may be helpful for the layperson, it is apparent that cloud computing is *not* usually the equivalent of using software, storage, or hardware as most of us are accustomed to thinking about those terms. To illustrate this difference, assume an individual wants to purchase word processing software and goes to a store or a web site to purchase an 'off-the-shelf' (prewritten) computer program. To ensure that the software will work on the individual's computer, one would need to make certain that the computer system meets the minimum specifications – a certain amount of disk space, a compatible operating system, a minimum processor speed, etc. By contrast, suppose that a similar word processing application were available in the cloud. There would be no concerns about the computer's disk space, operating system, or processor speed because the application service provider is providing the necessary storage, operating system, and processing. As a technological matter, the infrastructure supplied by the application service provider is a necessary component of the cloud computing and cannot be separated from the underlying software.

10.3 LESSONS FROM THE US RST EXPERIENCE: THE DANGERS OF 'REASONING BY ANALOGY' IN *DESIGNING CONSUMPTION TAX REGIMES FOR CLOUD COMPUTING*

One of the fundamental characteristics of legal thinking is its embrace of reasoning by analogy. Indeed, the required reading of Edward Levi's classic tract, *An Introduction to Legal Reasoning*,[13] by generations of American laws students[14] impresses upon them the significance of this central feature of the study and practice of law. The states' efforts to deal with the problems raised by cloud computing under their RSTs provide a classic illustration of the powerful influence of analogical reasoning in the application of existing laws to new fact patterns. It also demonstrates the difficulties that such reasoning can create and a cautionary tale for those designing rules for the application of consumption taxes to cloud computing. Indeed, if there is an single overarching lesson for VATs in the US VATs experience with cloud computing it is this: *be careful*

13. E.H. Levi (1949): 'An Introduction to Legal Reasoning' (Chicago: University of Chicago Press 1949).
14. Including this one, back in the Mesozoic era.

about 'reasoning by analogy' in designing consumption tax regimes for cloud computing.

10.3.1 Introductory Note: The Role of 'Use' Taxes in the US RST Regimes

To fully appreciate the US RST regimes' approach to cloud computing, one must have at least a rudimentary understanding of the federal constitutional limitations on the states' power to tax distance sales and the consequent role of 'complementary use taxes' in these regimes. Under the US Supreme Court's interpretation of the Commerce Clause of the Federal Constitution,[15] the states lack the constitutional power to impose a sales tax on goods or services purchased in other states or in interstate commerce because 'to impose a tax on such a transaction would be to project its powers beyond its boundaries and to tax an interstate transaction'.[16] The constitutional prohibition on the states' taxation of sales consummated outside their borders or in interstate commerce created a troublesome gap in their consumption tax structures. The gap created two concerns. First, states feared the loss of business that local merchants would suffer when prospective customers made out-of-state or interstate purchases to avoid in-state sales tax liability. Second, states feared the loss of revenue they would incur as a result of the diversion of sales tax to non-tax states. To deal with this potential loss of business and revenue, states enacted 'complementary' or 'compensating' use taxes on the use of goods purchased outside the state and brought into the state for use.

Compensating use taxes are functionally equivalent to sales taxes. They are typically levied upon the use, storage, or other consumption in the state of tangible personal property that has not been subjected to a sales tax. The use tax imposes an exaction equal in amount to the sales tax that would have been imposed on the sale of the property in question if the sale had occurred within the state's taxing jurisdiction. The state overcomes the constitutional hurdle of taxing an out-of-state or interstate sale by imposing the tax on a subject within its taxing power – the use, storage, or consumption of property within the state.[17] In principle, then, the in-state purchaser stands to gain nothing by making an out-of-state or interstate purchase free of sales tax because it will ultimately be saddled with an identical use tax when the property is brought into the taxing state. Taken together, the sales and use tax provides a uniform scheme of taxation on goods purchased within the state and goods purchased outside

15. The Commerce Clause by its terms is simply an affirmative grant of power to Congress to 'regulate Commerce with foreign Nations, and among the several States, and with the Indian Tribes.' US Const. Article I, § 8, cl. 3. Nevertheless, the US Supreme Court has long construed the clause as imposing implicit restraints on state authority, even when Congress has not acted. Under this so-called negative or dormant Commerce Clause doctrine, the Court has consistently struck down taxes that, in the Court's judgment, discriminate against or otherwise burden interstate commerce. See generally J.R. Hellerstein, W. Hellerstein, J.A. Swain (2015): 'State Taxation', cited above, Vol. I, Ch. 4.
16. *McLeod v. J.E. Dilworth Co.*, 322 US 327, 328 (1944).
17. See *Henneford v. Silas Mason Co.*, 300 US 577 (1937) (sustaining constitutionality of state use tax scheme).

the state for 'storage, use, or consumption' within the state. Every one of the forty-five states (and the District of Columbia) that imposes a sales tax also imposes a compensating use tax.

Because the use tax is complementary to the sales tax, it generally applies only to the use of goods and, in some states, to services[18] that have not already been subjected to sales tax. Consequently, the use tax applies principally to goods and services purchased outside the state.[19] The use tax also applies, however, in other situations. First, when a taxpayer purchases an item under a resale certificate, and therefore pays no sales tax on the purchase, but subsequently withdraws the item from inventory for its own use, most states impose a use tax on the item when it is utilized by the taxpayer.[20] Second, when a taxpayer manufacturers an item that it uses in its own business (e.g., if General Motors uses its own cars in its business), many states impose a tax upon the taxpayer's own use of the item. Third, many business taxpayers, especially larger purchasers, will register with states under 'direct pay' permits under which they agree to 'self-assess' a use tax on all taxable goods and services they purchase.[21] By notifying their suppliers that they have direct payment authority, these purchasers avoid paying sales or use tax to individual suppliers upon their purchase of the goods or services.[22] Finally, a use tax will apply to a taxpayer's use of a taxable good or service if a sales tax should have been imposed and collected upon the original purchase, but was not – for whatever reason.

18. Some states (e.g., New Mexico, Ohio, and Texas) apply their use tax to taxable services; other states (e.g., California) do not; and still other states (e.g., New York) apply their use tax only to some of the services they tax. See generally J.R. Hellerstein, W. Hellerstein, L.A. Swain (2015): 'State Taxation', cited above, Vol. II, ¶ 16.14 (describing application of use tax to services).
19. Although a use tax therefore discriminates on its face against interstate commerce, because it applies to goods and services purchased outside (but not within) the state, the practical effect of the use tax, when considered in conjunction with the sales tax for which it compensates, is the imposition of a non-discriminatory tax on all taxable goods and services used in the state.
20. This is analogous to the concept of 'self-supplies' or 'input tax adjustments' under a VAT, though a VAT treats an 'application to own use' as a self-supply only in more limited circumstances, such as when an input tax credit/deduction has been claimed for goods/services that are later used to make exempt supplies or for private purposes.
21. This is analogous to the 'reverse charge' for inbound services under a VAT. The difference is, of course, that since a VAT is not a tax on business, VAT reverse charge for inbound services is generally counter-balanced by a corresponding input tax credit/deduction, so that no actual tax is payable unless the services will be used to make exempt supplies or for other purposes for which a credit/deduction is denied.
22. The Federation of Tax Administrators describes the direct payment process as follows: '*Direct pay is an authority granted by a tax jurisdiction that generally allows the holder of a direct payment permit to purchase otherwise taxable goods and services without payment of tax to the supplier at the time of purchase. (Also in the case of exempt transactions, it allows a holder to purchase without issuing exemption certificates.) Suppliers are to be furnished a written notification of the purchaser's direct pay authority (often a numeric designation). The holder of the direct payment permit is to timely review its purchases and make a determination of taxability and then reports and pays the applicable tax due to the tax jurisdiction. The permit holder's tax determination and adequacy of payment are subject to audit by the tax jurisdiction.*'Federation of Tax Administrators (2000): 'Model Direct Payment Permit Regulation,' Report of the Steering Committee (June 2000), p. ii, available at http://www.taxadmin.org/fta/pub/DPay.pdf. According to the cited report, thirty-three of the forty-five states with sales and use taxes provide for the direct payment of tax.

In order to avoid double taxation of multistate transactions, every state imposing a use tax allows a credit against its use taxes for sales or use tax paid to other states. It is clear that such a credit is now required by federal constitutional law, at least if a state provides a credit against (or exemption from) the state's use tax for goods or services purchased within the state and taxed under the state's sales tax (as all states do). Otherwise there would be discrimination against out-of-state purchases.

10.3.2 Jurisdiction over the Parties to a Cloud Computing Transaction

The initial question that the US RST regimes must address, at least from a practical perspective, is whether there is personal jurisdiction over (or nexus with) one or both[23] of the parties to the cloud computing transaction, a question that may turn on the jurisdictional implications of the cloud computing transaction itself.[24] If the provider or purchaser[25] has nexus with the state (whether as a result of the cloud computing transaction or other activities), the next question is whether the transaction is taxable in that particular state.[26]

10.3.2.1 Purchaser's Nexus

From the purchaser's perspective, there are at least two issues to consider. First, if the purchaser is considered to own or lease tangible personal property in a state in which it would not otherwise have nexus as a result of a cloud computing transaction, it arguably satisfies the physical-presence requirement that the US Supreme Court's dormant Commerce Clause jurisprudence has established for the states' ability to

23. The suggestion that there are only two parties to a cloud computing transaction may oversimplify reality, because a cloud computing transaction often involves more than one service provider. See Part 3. For present purposes, however, the issues raised by consumption taxation of cloud computing are complex enough without introducing this additional complexity, and we shall assume throughout this discussion, unless otherwise indicated, that the transaction involves only a single purchaser and provider (at least in a contractual sense).
24. We say 'from a practical perspective,' because one could just as easily say that that the initial question is whether the state subjects the cloud computing transaction to tax, whether or not there is jurisdiction over the parties to the transaction. Typically, however, taxpayers first determine whether there is jurisdiction to enforce a tax before determining whether the substantive taxing provisions reach the transactions under consideration. See generally W. Hellerstein (2003): 'Jurisdiction to Tax Income and Consumption in the New Economy: A Theoretical and Comparative Perspective,' 38 Georgia Law Review 1 of 2003 at 1–70.
25. The purchaser's nexus with the state may be of little significance in the business-to-consumer (B2C) context, because individual consumers are no more likely voluntarily to remit a use tax on the purchase of cloud computing services than they are to remit a use tax on the purchase of a book in connection with a distance sale from Amazon.com. In business-to-business (B2B) transactions, however, a business with nexus in the state may well take its tax payment and collection obligations seriously, particularly if it is a large business that is routinely audited by state taxing authorities. Moreover, the purchaser of cloud computing services in a B2B transaction may also be a seller in a B2C transaction, so that it must be attentive to the possibility that a purchase of cloud computing services in the B2B transaction will trigger tax collection nexus with respect to a B2C transaction in the same state.
26. See 10.3.3.

enforce sales and use tax collection obligations.[27] Needless to say, whether an interest in tangible personal property causes the purchaser to have nexus in a particular state is fact-sensitive. On the one hand, a taxpayer that leases dozens of servers in a particular state almost certainly has created nexus with that state, as would a taxpayer that leases any other type of tangible property in the state. On the other hand, we doubt that a taxpayer that purchases software application services, and acquires no interest in the servers on which the software is hosted, would establish even a *de minimis* physical presence in the state where the software is hosted.[28]

Even if the purchaser's own activities do not create nexus in the state, the purchaser of cloud computing services must consider whether the service provider's activities create nexus for the purchaser. This could occur, for example, if the cloud provider performs activities in a state on behalf of the purchaser that are significantly associated with the purchaser's ability to establish and maintain a market in the state for its sales.[29]

10.3.2.2 Provider's Nexus

Providers of cloud services face thorny nexus issues as well. We doubt that software in digital form, even if characterized by a state as tangible personal property for sales or use tax purposes, becomes tangible personal property for purposes of *Quill*'s physical-presence test,[30] thereby providing a basis for imposing sales or use tax collection responsibility upon the provider at the 'location' of the software. If, however, the provider owns servers or leases server space, the issue becomes more difficult, because servers are indisputably tangible.

10.3.2.3 State Guidance

Only a handful of states have thus far addressed the nexus consequences of cloud computing transactions for sales and use tax purposes. In 2011, Texas enacted a law addressing the nexus consequences for purchasers of 'Internet hosting' services, the definition of which is quite broad, potentially encompassing a multitude of cloud services.[31] The law provides that a person whose only activity in the state is conducted

27. See *Quill Corp. v. North Dakota*, 504 US 298 (1992).
28. This assumes, of course, that accessing software hosted in the state is the taxpayer's only activity, such as it is, in the state. Even if a state were to deem the software to be 'tangible personal property' for purposes of the state's sales and use tax provisions, we doubt that the state, by its mere say-so, could transform digital property into tangible property and provide the state with the argument that it has satisfied *Quill's* physical presence test on the basis of the out-of-state purchaser's licensing of 'tangible' software in the state. If we are wrong, the question would then arise as to whether the purchaser's interest amounted to more than 'a few floppy diskettes.' See *Quill*, 504 US at 315 n. 8.
29. See *Tyler Pipe Industries, Inc. v. Washington. Department of Revenue*, 483 US 232 (1987).
30. See n. 27 above.
31. Tex. Tax Code § 151.108 (Westlaw 2015). 'Internet hosting' is defined as 'providing to an unrelated user access over the Internet to computer services using property that is owned or

as a user of Internet hosting is not engaged in business in Texas.[32] In a publication, the Texas Comptroller summarized the impact of the law by explaining that:

> if an out-of-state company leases or owns servers in Texas which it uses to do business, it has nexus. But, if the out-of-state company purchases Internet hosting services from an unrelated seller located in Texas who provides the service by use of servers that the seller owns or leases in Texas, and that is the only contact the out-of-state company has with Texas, no nexus is created.[33]

The comptroller further noted, however, that *purchasers* who buy Internet hosting services for use in Texas from a seller who is not engaged in business in Texas continue to be responsible for remitting use tax.[34]

A Washington law provides a similar nexus safe harbour. For sales and use tax purposes (among others):

> the department of revenue may not consider a person's ownership of, or rights in, computer software ... including computer software used in providing a digital automated service; master copies of software; digital goods or digital codes residing on servers located in this state in determining whether the person has substantial nexus with this state.[35]

The Virginia Tax Commissioner addressed a taxpayer's question as to whether purchasing 'managed hosting' services or 'co-location hosting' services that utilized servers located in Virginia could cause the taxpayer to have nexus for sales and use tax purposes.[36] Under the 'managed hosting' service model, a third party would provide power and bandwidth connections, other web hosting services, and Internet servers dedicated exclusively to the taxpayer's websites. Under this model, the servers would be owned by the third party. Under the 'co-location hosting' service model, the web hosting company would provide similar services, but the servers would be owned or leased by the taxpayer. The commissioner concluded that, under either of the scenarios, the taxpayer would not have nexus with Virginia if the taxpayer's only presence was the use of computer servers in the state. However, in a more recent ruling, the commissioner concluded that the ownership of several servers in the state 'would appear to create nexus'.[37]

---

leased and managed by the provider and on which the user may store or process the user's own data or use software that is owned, licensed, or leased by the user or provider.' *Ibid.*, § 151.108(a).

32. *Ibid.*, § 151.108(b). The law is presumably a response to a Texas regulation, which provided that that a person has nexus with Texas for sales tax purposes if the person 'derives receipts from a rental or lease of tangible personal property that is located in this state or owns or uses tangible personal property that is located in this state, including a computer server or software.' 34 Tex. Admin. Code § 3.286(a)(2)(E) (Westlaw 2015).
33. Texas Comptroller, 'Tax Policy News,' July 2011, available at http://www.window.state.tx.us /taxinfo/taxpnw/tpn2011/tpn1107.html.
34. *Ibid.*
35. Wash. Rev. Code § 82.32.532(1) (Westlaw 2015).
36. Va. Public Document Ruling 00-53 (Va. Tax Comm'r, 14 Apr. 2000).
37. Va. Public Document Ruling 12-36 (Va. Tax Comm'r, 12 Mar. 2012).

The Missouri Department of Revenue concluded that a taxpayer purchasing data storage, data manipulation, or data processing services performed by a Missouri provider would not have nexus with Missouri.[38] Guidance promulgated by the Kansas Department of Revenue provides that an owner or lessor of a server located in Kansas is considered to be 'doing business' in the state, and as such, is required to register with the state and collect and remit sales tax.[39] The critical question in Kansas, it would seem, is whether a purchaser of cloud services could be considered to be an owner or lessor of a server located in Kansas. The guidance, perhaps not surprisingly, leaves this critical question unanswered.

10.3.3 The US RSTs' Approach to the Taxability of Cloud Computing Transactions

The US state RST regimes have approached the taxability of cloud computing transactions for sales and use tax purposes in the same manner as they have approached the taxability of transactions involving other goods, services, or intangibles under the sales and use tax. Accordingly, in determining the taxability of a cloud computing transaction, state tax administrators generally have inquired whether there is: (1) a sale or use of (2) a taxable good, service, or intangible (3) in the state. The challenge the states have encountered in analysing cloud computing transactions is that these complex and unfamiliar transactions often do not fit easily into existing statutory classifications that determine taxability in a state.

10.3.3.1 'Sale' or 'Use'

Cloud computing can raise difficult questions as to whether the transaction in question constitutes a taxable 'sale' or 'use.' A 'sale' for sales tax purposes is typically defined as '[a]ny transfer of title or possession, or both, exchange, barter, license, lease, or rental, conditional or otherwise, in any manner or by any means whatsoever, of tangible personal property for a consideration'.[40] Assuming that a cloud computing transaction involves 'consideration' for 'tangible personal property', there may be a question whether there is a 'transfer of title or possession'. For example, on several occasions, the Tennessee Department of Revenue has concluded that a service that allowed customers to access software remotely over the Internet did not constitute a 'sale' because there was no 'transfer.'[41] However, the New York Department of Taxation and Finance concluded that the access of a taxpayer's software by its customers constitutes a 'transfer of possession' because customers gain 'constructive possession' of the software, and have 'the right to use, or control or direct the use' of

38. Mo. Letter Rul. 3819 (Mo. Dep't of Revenue, 11 Apr. 2007).
39. Kan. Info. Guide EDU-71R (Kan. Dep't of Revenue, 23 Jul. 2010).
40. See, e.g., Fla. Stat. § 212.02(15)(a) (Westlaw 2015); see also N.Y. Tax Law § 1101(b)(5) (Westlaw 2015).
41. Tenn. Dep't of Revenue Letter Ruling 07-35 (Tenn. Dep't of Revenue, 26 Nov. 2007).

the software.[42] The Utah Tax Commission similarly determined that fees received for 'web services' constituted a sale because the company at issue 'in substance grants subscribers the right to use the Company's proprietary software under a lease or contract'.[43]

Even if no 'transfer' occurs, one might consider certain cloud computing transactions to constitute taxable 'licenses', 'leases', or 'rentals' of tangible personal property. For example, the Arizona Department of Revenue has characterized hosted software transactions as 'leases' or 'rentals' of tangible personal property.[44] The Wisconsin Tax Commission has likewise suggested that a sale of application services may constitute the lease of tangible personal property.[45]

In addition to the question of whether cloud computing transactions constitute 'sales', 'leases', or 'licenses', the question also arises whether such transactions amount to a taxable 'use' of tangible personal property. 'Use' is often defined as 'the exercise of any right or power over tangible personal property…'.[46] It is entirely possible that a seller of cloud computing may not be making a taxable 'sale' (due to a lack of a transfer of title or possession), but that the purchaser could be making a taxable use. For example, the Nebraska Department of Revenue cautions that, although certain cloud computing transactions may not be taxable (as described above), an application service provider is still responsible for paying sales or use tax on its purchase of software if the software resides on a computer in Nebraska.[47]

10.3.3.2 Tangible Personal Property, Service, or Intangible?

A transaction generally will be subject to sales or use tax if it constitutes a sale or use of: (1) tangible personal property, (2) an enumerated taxable service, or (3) another item specifically identified as taxable that might ordinarily be considered an intangible, for example, an extended warranty.

10.3.3.2.1. Distinguishing between Sales of Tangible Personal Property and Sales of Services in the Cloud Computing Context

The distinction between tangible personal property and services has traditionally been the touchstone of taxability under the US RST. For that reason, there probably is no sales and use tax issue on which more ink has been spilled than the effort to draw that

42. N.Y. Advisory Opinion TSB-A-09(33)S (N.Y. Dep't of Tax'n & Fin., 13 Aug. 2009) (citing N.Y. Sales & Use Tax Reg. § 526.7).
43. Utah Private Letter Rul. 10-011 (Utah State Tax Comm'n, 24 Feb. 2012).
44. See, e.g., Ariz. Taxpayer Info. Rul. LR11-010 (Ariz. Dep't of Revenue, 22 Jun. 2011); Ariz. Taxpayer Info. Rul. LR10-007 (Ariz. Dep't of Revenue, 24 Mar. 2010); Ariz. Private Taxpayer Rul. LR04-007 (Ariz. Dep't of Revenue, 31 Aug. 2004).
45. Wis. Private Letter Rul. W1025002 (Wis. Dep't of Revenue, 24 Mar. 2010); Wis. Private Letter Rul. W0921002 (Wis. Dep't of Revenue, 6 Mar. 2009).
46. See, e.g., Fla. Stat. § 212.02(20) (Westlaw 2015); N.Y. Tax Law § 1101(b)(7) (Westlaw 2015).
47. Neb. Info. Guide 6-511-2011 (Neb. Dep't of Revenue, 27 Jul. 2011).

line.[48] It therefore should come as no surprise that the distinction plays a central role in determining the taxability of cloud computing. The traditional tests for distinguishing sales or rentals of tangible personal property from sales of services – 'the true object', 'dominant purpose', and 'essence of the transaction' tests[49] – have understandably informed the efforts of state tax authorities to draw this line in the context of cloud computing. For example, the Colorado Department of Revenue addressed the question of whether a hosted software solution for sending, receiving, and tracking large digital files over the Internet was subject to tax.[50] The department first noted that Colorado 'imposes sales and use tax on the sale, use, storage, and consumption of tangible personal property, which includes standardized software, but does not impose sales or use tax on services'.[51] The department further observed that the state Supreme Court had identified the criterion for drawing the distinction between taxable sales of tangible personal property and non-taxable sales of services,[52] namely, 'whether the "true object, dominant purpose, or essence" of the transaction is, in fact, corporeal tangible personal property or an intangible right or service'.[53] The department found that the 'essence' of the service at issue was similar to the email services of several well-known providers.[54] Although customers might be considered to 'use' the servers of those providers (and the software provided), the department concluded that such providers are 'most commonly understood to be providers of a service, not lessors of computer servers or software'.[55]

A ruling by the Massachusetts Department of Revenue further illustrates the application of the familiar tests for distinguishing between sales or rentals of tangible personal property and sales of services in the context of cloud computing. The department examined a service that enables customers to access financial information about businesses 'to mitigate credit and supplier risk, increase cash flow and drive increased profitability'.[56] The core service offering allows customers to search and 'create customizable reports containing summary trade data, basic credit scores, legal filings, and general company information'.[57] Customers can purchase 'upgraded' data packages – for an additional fee – that provide access to more data. Additionally, customers can purchase certain 'workflow add-ons' that allow customers to automate credit decisions, enter account information and establish rules to trigger labelling (e.g., flag an account for review if a credit indicator hits a certain level), manage risk exposure, create customizable credit applications, and pass information between the

48. See J.R. Hellerstein, W. Hellerstein, J.A. Swain (2015): 'State Taxation', cited above, Vol. II, ¶ 12.08 and Ch. 13.
49. See *ibid.*, ¶ 13.06.
50. Colo. Private Letter Rul. PLR-11-7 (Colo. Dep't of Revenue, 20 Dec. 2011).
51. *Ibid.*
52. See *Leanin' Tree v. City of Boulder*, 72 P.3d 361 (Colo. 2003).
53. Colo. Private Letter Rul. PLR-11-7 (Colo. Dep't of Revenue, 20 Dec. 2011) (citing *Leanin' Tree*, 72 P.3d at 365).
54. *Ibid.*
55. *Ibid.*
56. Mass. Letter Rul. 11-2 (Mass. Dep't of Revenue, 4 Mar. 2011).
57. *Ibid.*

taxpayer and customer systems. The department observed that the object of the taxpayer's core service offering and upgraded data packages was to obtain database access rather than use the software, and, accordingly, the service offering and data packages were not taxable. At the same time, however, the department concluded that the object of the workflow add-ons was to access the taxpayer's software and was therefore taxable. On similar facts, the Indiana Department of Revenue concluded that the core service offering and data packages constituted non-taxable services, but the workflow add-ons were taxable as prewritten computer software.[58]

10.3.3.2.2. Cloud Computing as Canned/Prewritten Computer Software

Most state statutes include canned or prewritten software in the definition of 'tangible personal property' for sales tax purposes.[59] A few state statutes, however, simply subject such software to tax without explicitly providing whether it is tangible personal property, a service, or an intangible.[60] Although all cloud computing models differ in significant respects from traditional sales of computer software, some states have determined that certain cloud services constitute canned or prewritten computer software and, as such, are subject to the state's sales and use tax.

One of the most puzzling trends in the taxation of cloud computing is how casually state taxing authorities have concluded that certain cloud services constitute canned or prewritten computer software and thus generally are classified as tangible personal property under the state statutes. As noted above, all cloud services deliver more than just the use of software – the cloud provider's operating system, servers, and other hardware usually are vital to the provision of cloud services. Yet the state taxing authorities that have deemed cloud computing services to be canned or prewritten computer software have done so with little or no analysis of the underlying service offering. For example, the taxing authorities in Arizona, New York, Pennsylvania, and Utah have summarily concluded that various cloud services constitute canned or prewritten computer software.[61] Although taxing authorities' analysis of cloud transactions may appear overly simplistic, the fault may lie in part with taxpayers (or their advisors) insofar as they have described the service offering in far too simplistic a manner. For example, if a taxpayer describes its service offering simply as 'hosted software,' rather than describing the infrastructure necessary to provide the service, it is understandable to why a taxing authority might treat the service as canned or prewritten software.

58. Ind. Rev. Rul. 2011-05 ST (Ind. Dep't of Revenue, 11 Oct. 2011).
59. See, e.g., Mich. Comp. Laws section 205.51a (q) (Westlaw 2015); Ohio Rev. Code Ann. section 5739.01(YY) (Westlaw 2015).
60. See, e.g., Tenn. Code Ann. § 67-6-231(a) (Westlaw 2015); Wash. Rev. Code § 82.04.050(6)(a) (Westlaw 2015).
61. See, e.g., Ariz. Taxpayer Info. Rul. LR11-010 (Ariz. Dep't of Revenue, 22 Jun. 2011); N.Y. Advisory Opinion TSB-A-11(17)S (N.Y. Dep't of Taxation & Fin., 1 Jun. 2011); Penn. Sales & Use Tax Rul. SUT-10-005 (Penn. Dep't of Revenue, 8 Nov. 2010); Utah Private Letter Rul. 10-011 (Utah State Tax Comm'n, 24 Feb. 2012).

10.3.3.2.3. *Cloud Computing as Tangible Personal Property (without Regard to Whether It Constitutes Canned/Prewritten Computer Software)*

A state might conclude that certain cloud computing services constitute sales or rentals of tangible personal property without treating the services as canned or prewritten computer software.[62] For example, if a taxpayer rents a particular server, it is likely that the transaction will be treated as the rental of tangible personal property. However, state treatment of data storage or hosting sales is less consistent. In one ruling, the Utah Tax Commission treated data and information storage (which the commission presumed could occur over shared or dedicated servers) to be 'the lease of disk space and server equipment and hardware' and thus taxable.[63] Similarly, several states have indicated that hosting services are taxable as rentals of tangible personal property.[64] Conversely, several states have analysed hosting services as non-taxable services.[65]

10.3.3.2.4. *Cloud Computing as a Service*

If a state does not characterize a particular cloud computing transaction as involving a taxable sale of tangible personal property,[66] it frequently will be because the state has concluded that the cloud computing transaction constitutes a service. The question then becomes whether the service is taxable or not. The basic problem of distinguishing between sales of taxable and non-taxable services is analogous to the problem of distinguishing between sales of tangible personal property and sales of services.[67] Moreover, the tests that state taxing authorities employ for drawing these lines in both contexts are similar in which they typically look for the 'object' of the transaction in light of the relevant statute. For example, two state taxing authorities have addressed the question of whether data backup and recovery services are taxable or non-taxable services.[68] The facts at issue in each ruling are essentially the same. The taxpayers provided a service to ensure the safe storage of customers' data, enabling customers to replace the data if the original data is lost or stolen. In each case, software was downloaded by customers (at no charge), and the software would function only in conjunction with the taxpayer's service. Under these facts, the Utah Tax Commission concluded that the primary object of the transaction was for a customer to preserve and protect existing data - a service that was not taxable in Utah.[69] The provision of

62. As we have observed above, most states characterize canned or prewritten software as tangible personal property and taxable for that reason whereas a few states tax canned or prewritten software without regard to its characterization as tangible personal property, a service, or an intangible.
63. Utah Private Letter Rul. 06-004 (Utah State Tax Comm'n, 27 Jul. 2006).
64. See, e.g., Ariz. Private Taxpayer Rul. LR09-007 (Ariz. Dep't of Revenue, 3 Dec. 2009); Ind. Letter of Finding 04-20091023 (Ind. Dep't of Revenue, 1 Dec. 2011).
65. See 10.3.3.2 D.
66. Or as taxable simply because it is canned or prewritten, regardless of its characterization.
67. See 10.3.3.2 A.
68. N.Y. Advisory Opinion TSB-A-05(40)S (N.Y. Dep't of Taxation & Fin., 26 Oct. 2005); Utah Private Letter Rul. 07-013 (Utah State Tax Comm'n, 21 Dec. 2007).
69. Utah Private Letter Rul. 07-013 (Utah State Tax Comm'n, 21 Dec. 2007).

software to customers to access the backup service was considered to be 'merely incidental to the provision of the service'.[70] As such, the software was consumed by the taxpayer rather than being 'resold'.[71] The New York Department of Taxation and Finance concluded that the taxpayer was not making a sale of a taxable information service, because a customer would not receive any new information from the taxpayer; rather, it would receive a copy of its own data.[72] The department further concluded that even though the taxpayer was not selling software, it was nevertheless making a taxable use of the software in the course of providing its non-taxable service.

10.3.3.3 In What State Does the 'Sale' or 'Use' Occur?

One of the most perplexing issues with respect to sales and use taxation of cloud computing transactions is the determination of where the sale or use occurs. Recall that most states that have determined that a particular SaaS/hosted software transaction is subject to sales or use tax have done so on the theory – and fiction – that the transaction constitutes the sale of tangible personal property, often based on the determination that the transaction involves canned or prewritten software, which is treated as tangible personal property.[73] Accordingly, in that context, the issue of determining where the sale or use occurs is a difficult one in large part because the application of the traditional rules for determining where a sale of tangible personal property occurs can be awkward at best when applied to cloud computing. Traditionally, sales of tangible personal property are sourced to their 'destination,' which normally means the place of 'delivery' or where title passes.[74] However, when software or hardware is accessed remotely, where delivery occurs is not self-evident. Two different sourcing regimes have emerged among states with respect to cloud computing transactions: location of the server on which the software is located and location of the user.

10.3.3.3.1. Location of the Server

Several states have determined that hosted software transactions occur at the location of the server on which the hosted software is stored. For example, prior to a change in the law, the Utah State Tax Commission concluded on several occasions that sales of hosted software should be attributed to the state where the server that housed the

70. *Ibid.*
71. *Ibid.*
72. N.Y. Advisory Opinion TSB-A-05(40)S (N.Y. Dep't of Taxation & Fin., 26 Oct. 2005). The department also observed that the data being stored was not considered 'tangible personal property,' so the charge for the storage was not subject to tax. Furthermore, the data was stored on the taxpayer's equipment, which the taxpayer operated and maintained. Accordingly, subscription charges were not receipts from the rental of equipment.
73. See 10.3.3.2 B. and 10.3.3.2 C.
74. See J.R. Hellerstein, W. Hellerstein, J.A. Swain (2015): 'State Taxation', cited above, Vol. II, ¶ 18.02.

software was located.[75] In a letter ruling addressing a company's provision of hosted software to clients, the Commission observed:

> Company's clients might possess the software when the software is downloaded onto the Company servers if the clients are leasing server space. However, because the Company's servers are not located in Utah, the clients do not possess the software in Utah and the sales transactions are not taxable by Utah. The clients' remote access of the software without downloading the software onto a computer located in Utah does not create possession of the software in Utah. Instead, such access is akin to merely going to an Internet site and viewing a database without downloading the software.[76]

In a Tennessee ruling, the department of revenue concluded that although the granting of a license to use computer software constituted a taxable 'sale,' a taxpayer's remote access of software located on a server outside of Tennessee was not taxable by Tennessee.[77]

Determining the place of taxation for sales of cloud computing services by reference to the location of the server on which software is hosted has its advantages. First, any serious issue over whether the seller has nexus with the state will probably be avoided if the seller has tangible personal property in the state (e.g., a server). Second, the location of the server is likely to be known by the seller. Third, the location of the server may be a single location, at least with regard to a particular customer. Collectively, these features tend to support the 'location of the server' regime from the standpoint of administrative ease, although the 'single location' assumption may be problematic because of the widespread use of multiple servers in cloud-based applications.

Whatever its administrative advantages, however, the 'location of the server' regime makes no sense from a tax policy standpoint, assuming that the retail sales tax should reflect the destination principle.[78] The destination would ordinarily be the customer's location, not the seller's. The location of a server (or other hardware of the seller) is likely to correspond to the customer's location only in unusual circumstances and is thus a poor choice for attributing sales of cloud computing services, aside from its administrative benefits.

10.3.3.3.2. Location of the User

A number of state taxing authorities have attributed hosted software transactions to the location of the customer. New York has considered the source of hosted software sales

75. See, e.g., Utah Private Letter Rul. 09-003 (Utah State Tax Comm'n, 7 Apr. 2009); Utah Private Letter Rul. 08-12 (Utah State Tax Comm'n, 21 Jan. 2009); Utah Private Letter Rul. 08-002 (Utah State Tax Comm'n, 4 Aug. 2008, superseded 10 Jun. 2009, rescinded effective 1 Dec. 2010).
76. Utah Private Letter Rul. 09-003 (Utah State Tax Comm'n, 7 Apr. 2009).
77. Tenn. Dep't of Revenue Letter Ruling 11-58 (Tenn. Dep't of Revenue, 10 Oct. 2011).
78. See OECD (2014): 'International VAT/GST Guidelines', (OECD 2014) paragraph 1.11, available at http://www.oecd.org/ctp/consumption/international-vat-gst-guidelines.pdf.

on several occasions.[79] In each case, the New York Department of Taxation and Finance determined that the situs of the sale was the location of the customer's employees who used the software. In the event that the customer's employees who used the software were located both in and outside New York, the department concluded that tax should be collected based upon the portion of the receipts attributable to the customer's employee-users located in New York.

Utah enacted a law providing rules for determining the location of sales of computer software when there is no transfer of a copy of the software to the purchaser.[80] Such sales are generally attributed to a state based upon 'an address for or other information on the purchaser if (a) the address or other information is available from the seller's business records; and (b) use of the address or other information from the seller's records does not constitute bad faith'.[81] A Utah letter ruling addressing the sale of hosted software summarized this law as providing that the locations of sales are based on the addresses of the purchasers.[82] Guidance promulgated by the Arizona Department of Revenue likewise reflects the view that fees derived from sales of hosted software should be sourced to the location of the consumer.[83]

A Hawaii letter ruling considered sales and licenses of software used outside Hawaii.[84] Although the ruling does not offer a detailed description of the services or products at issue, the Hawaii Department of Taxation strongly implied that the transaction involves SaaS.[85] The department concluded that regardless of whether the software is considered 'a product, a service, or some combination of the two', the

79. See, e.g., N.Y. Advisory Opinion TSB-A-11(17)S (N.Y. Dep't of Taxation & Fin., 1 Jun. 2011); N.Y. Advisory Opinion TSB-A-09(44)S (N.Y. Dep't of Taxation & Fin., 24 Sep. 2009); N.Y. Advisory Opinion TSB-A-09(41)S (N.Y. Dep't of Taxation & Fin., 22 Sep. 2009); N.Y. Advisory Opinion TSB-A-09(33)S (N.Y. Dep't of Taxation & Fin., 13 Aug. 2009); N.Y. Advisory Opinion TSB-A-09(8)S (N.Y. Dep't of Taxation & Fin., 2 Feb. 2009).
80. Utah Code Ann. § 59-12-211(12) (Westlaw 2015).
81. *Ibid.*
82. Utah Private Letter Rul. 10-011 (Utah State Tax Comm'n, 24 Feb. 2012).
83. See, e.g., Ariz. Taxpayer Info. Rul. LR11-011 (Ariz. Dep't of Revenue, 22 Jun. 2011); Ariz. Taxpayer Info. Rul. LR11-010 (Ariz. Dep't of Revenue, 22 Jun. 2011); Ariz. Taxpayer Info. Rul. LR10-007 (Ariz. Dep't of Revenue, 24 Mar. 2010); Ariz. Private Taxpayer Rul. LR04-007 (Ariz. Dep't of Revenue, 31 Aug. 2004).
84. Haw. Letter Rul. 2012-06 (Haw. Dep't of Taxation, 23 Mar. 2012).
85. In the course of its letter, the department raised a host of questions relevant to the analysis of cloud computing such as:
    - Should SaaS be treated like electronically delivered software?
    - Is a license agreement imperative, and what happens if there is none?
    - Is SaaS simply a 'license to use'?
    - Is SaaS an information service or database?
    - What if tangible backup copies are provided to the licensee?
    - What if the agreements provide for periodic updates?
    - Is a sale sourced to the customer's billing/shipping address?
    - Is a sale sourced to where the hosting server is located, because the software is 'used' in that state?
    - Is a sale sourced to where users access it? What if it's not known where the users are?

    Ibid.

transaction was exempt from Hawaii general excise tax because the software is consumed entirely outside of Hawaii and the taxpayer has no customers in the state.[86]

Just as the 'location of the server' regime had its advantages and disadvantages, so the 'location of the user' regime has its advantages and disadvantages, although they are largely the 'flip side' of the server regime. First, from a tax policy standpoint, the customer-location rule reflects the destination principle that is widely accepted as the appropriate rule for implementing the retail sales tax and other consumption taxes.[87] Furthermore, attributing hosted software to the customer's location would result in equivalent treatment between cloud computing and transactions involving the sale of prewritten computer software in tangible form. There is no policy justification for taxing the customer's purchase of say, tax compliance software that is delivered on a disc (or, indeed, downloaded onto the customer's computers) at the customer's location while not taxing the customer's purchase of an 'online' version of the same tax compliance software, which involves the use of hosted software in the 'cloud,' at the same location. Second, at least in circumstances in which the customer owes use tax and is responsible for and likely to be compliant with its own tax obligations – namely, in the B2B context – the customer will be in a position where it can attribute the tax to its proper location, which it is likely to know.

Nevertheless, the 'location of the user' regime is not without its own problems. The seller might not have the requisite information to determine the purchaser's location, particularly if the 'user' for purposes of the attribution rule is the location of the ultimate user rather than the purchaser.[88] Furthermore, even if the seller has the requisite information about the purchaser, if the seller has no nexus with the state, tax collection of B2C transactions relying on purchaser compliance is likely to be no more effective in the cloud computing contexts than in other contexts. 'Taxing honesty' has not proven to be a winning tax strategy.

10.4 CONCLUDING OBSERVATIONS

The key lesson from the efforts of the US states to 'reason by analogy' in applying their RST regimes to cloud computing transactions is that any effort to force the complex reality of cloud computing into the Procrustean bed of our existing tax rules may well

86. *Ibid.*
87. See J.R. Hellerstein, W. Hellerstein, J.A. Swain (2015): 'State Taxation' cited above, Vol. II, ¶ 18.02[1]; OECD (2001): 'Taxation and Electronic Commerce: Implementing the Ottawa Framework Conditions', at 24.
88. The problem here is analogous to the problem faced by the online advertising provider in N.Y. TSB-A-09(8)C, involving the sourcing of receipts for purposes of the sales factor of the New York corporate franchise (income) tax. The taxpayer provided online advertising services to customers and asked the New York Department of Taxation and Finance for guidance on sourcing its receipts for sales factor purposes. The department concluded that the 'governing principle' is to source receipts to New York on the basis of the number of people who view or read the advertisement in New York. In addition, the department noted that if the taxpayer 'does not have any way of knowing where a prospective customer is when (s)he views or reads an advertisement on the Web site, [the taxpayer] may use some reasonable method…subject to the approval of the Tax Department'. *Ibid.*

be doomed to failure. Sales and use taxes are transaction-based taxes. The very notion that taxpayers and tax administrators will be capable of deconstructing cloud computing transactions for purposes of our existing tax rules, based on the characterization and location of software and hardware, for a 'transaction' that involves computing resources that are pooled to serve multiple consumers using a multi-tenant model, with different physical and virtual resources dynamically assigned and reassigned according to consumer demand and with simultaneous interactions between cloud providers and purchasers employing multiple servers located throughout the country if not the world, borders on the fanciful.

While some cloud computing transactions are considerably less complex and may well be amenable to traditional state tax analysis, we need to acknowledge that our existing tax regime simply may be incapable of accommodating many cloud computing transactions in an administrable fashion. Hence, eventually, the US states may be compelled to take a different, and ultimately simpler, approach to these issues, e.g., by assigning the sale based on some practical proxy for the 'location' of the transaction, such as the location of the provider or purchaser. Those charged with the design of VAT regimes for cloud computing transactions would be well-advised to embrace this more practical approach from the outset, thereby recognizing the wise observation that, at the end of the day, that 'tax administration *is* tax policy'.[89]

89. M. Casanegra de Jantscher (1990): 'Administering the VAT,' in M. Gillis, C.S. Shoup, G.P. Sicat, (eds.) (1990): 'Value Added Taxation in Developing Countries', Washington: World Bank, 1990 at 171–179, at 179 (emphasis in original).

CHAPTER 11

Methodological Notes on a Changing Legislative Landscape

Pernilla Rendahl[*]

11.1 INTRODUCTION

The digital economy, or electronic commerce, has created new business opportunities and new, or at least renewed, legal issues which arise alongside technological developments. From a taxation perspective one of the core questions is whether the digital economy should be taxed and if so, how it should be taxed. More specific questions are whether the current tax structures are suitable and efficient for creating a level playing field between traditional and digital commerce? Should there be a level playing field between these two forms of commerce or are there reasons to make a distinction between them? Is there a level playing field between different forms of electronic commerce and should there be one? Are risks of double taxation and non-taxation eliminated in cases in which more than one jurisdiction can claim the right to tax a transaction or an income?

Even though there are many interesting and still somehow unanswered questions of both a legal and a political nature, this note covers some of the changes in the legislative landscape concerning e-commerce and examines some of the different legislative materials that can be used to help solve basic questions such as what is to be taxed and which country has the jurisdiction to tax the income arising out of the transactions taking place within the digital economy. These fundamental questions are essential for avoiding double taxation and unintended non-taxation.

The reason for considering methodological questions that arise when working on these legal questions is that academics, including myself, tend to put forward the need

* Rendahl is Associate Professor (Docent) in Tax Law at the School of Business, Economics and Law of the University of Gothenburg. She can be reached at: pernilla.rendahl@law.gu.se.

for international coordination to solve legal questions in the digital economy.[1] International coordination typically results in soft law tools such as the 'International VAT/GST Guidelines' issued by the OECD and the 'Explanatory Notes' on the 2015 EU VAT rules on telecommunications-, radio and television broadcasting services and electronically supplied services issued by the European Commission (for the text see Appendix V).[2]

The aim of this article is to flag a few methodological questions concerning the impact of these two soft law tools and the practical demands created by decisions that need to be made more or less automatically by business platforms for electronic commerce. The scope of the methodological questions is, however, limited to an overview or systematization of issues that may be considered in different contexts when solving some of the legal questions brought forward above. This article also covers an overview of the role which soft law has or may have when courts interpret and apply rules to a specific case.[3] At the end of this article, a few concluding remarks are made.

11.2 INTERNATIONAL COORDINATION BY SOFT LAW

When discussing international coordination as a tool for finding common ground or best practices in cross-border situations it may be discussed in terms of policies, practices or principles. Some aim at finding administrative or formal solutions, while others aim at coordinating or harmonizing substantive understandings of legal concepts. These policies or principles thereafter need to be implemented into legal provisions or applied by national administrations and courts in both a general and a specific context. The effects which soft law may have and whether and how it may become 'hard law', are questions that need further analysis not only from an international tax law perspective. There may also be conflicts between coordination and cooperation and accepted principles of international law. Questions that arise on the possible effects of soft law are therefore closely linked to questions on compliance with international coordination from a state perspective.[4] The scope of this article is less far reaching and uses soft law as a concept to describe the ongoing international

1. See e.g., A. Cockfield, W. Hellerstein, R. Millar and C. Waerzeggers (2013): 'Taxing Global Digital Commerce', Kluwer Law International, 2013 at 506–509; P. Rendahl (2009): 'Cross-Border Consumption Taxation of Digital Supplies', IBFD Doctoral Series No. 18, 2009 at 400–401; B. Westberg (2002): 'Cross-Border Taxation of E-Commerce', IBFD 2002 at p. 242.
2. See OECD (2014): 'International VAT/GST Guidelines, Global Forum on VAT' and European Commission (2014): 'Explanatory Notes on the EU VAT changes to the place of supply of telecommunications, broadcasting and electronic services that enter into force in 2015' (see Appendix V).
3. Soft law is a relative concept and for further discussions of soft law in a wider perspective, see e.g., A.T. Guzman, T. L. Meyer (2010): 'International Soft Law', 2 J. of Legal Analysis 1 of 2010 at pp. 171–225.
4. For a further discussion of the compliance-based theory of international law see A.T. Guzman (2014): 'A Compliance Based Theory of International Law', 90 California Law Review 6 at 1823; For a further discussion of the international common law theory see A.T. Guzman, T. L. Meyer (2010): 'International Soft Law', 2 J. of Legal Analysis 1 of 2010 at 171–225.

developments in the OECD and the EU.[5] In the end a legal solution aims at solving a legal problem in a specific case. The outcome depends on the regulatory context, the administrative context and also on the validation of a specific situation.

The regulatory context refers to the implementation of internationally agreed principles or practices into national legal provisions, because imposing tax on transactions or income generally requires a legislative basis in accordance with the principle of legality. Of course, the legislative or regulatory context is different in different countries, which means that principles or practices that are agreed at an international level need to be vague enough to fit variations in national contexts while still being precise enough to actually attain the goal of the coordination. Whenever legal traditions are similar or share a common historic background, it may be easier for different national systems to have the same understanding of an agreed policy or principle and to implement it in accordance with its objective.

The common law countries can be used as an example, as they share a common legal background, but even so there are differences between common law countries in how principles are implemented and used in interpretation. One such example is the use of neutrality as a policy tool in Canada and the use of neutrality as an interpretative tool in the United Kingdom, giving effect to the case law from the ECJ.[6] Equally the Scandinavian countries can be used as an example where similarities between the legal orders may support the implementation of an internationally agreed principle. The implementing procedures in these countries are, however, not common, which means that it remains up to the specific country to implement an internationally agreed principle in a suitable way. Between EU Member States there are possibilities to use common legislative instruments, such as directives, to support the implementation of an internationally agreed principle. The Member States then have an obligation to comply with the objectives set out in the EU directive. But where internationally agreed soft law is implemented through soft law at regional level, as is the case sometimes within the EU (see, for instance, the Code of Conduct on Business Taxation and the Explanatory notes on E-commerce taxation), questions on how to give effect to EU soft law at national level arise alongside questions on how to implement soft law arising from international coordination. What effects are these competing or overlapping international and regional materials given by the courts?

The administrative context refers to how tax authorities implement internationally agreed principles or practices into national guidelines or recommendations. These can be developed based on regulatory national provisions or be implemented directly on the basis of regional or international soft law materials. They may have different legal value depending on which form is chosen and in which national context they are developed. In Sweden the Tax Authority issues notes on how it treats different legal situations. These notes are non-binding but serve as guidance and are thus a form of

5. For another discussion of soft law and hard law see e.g., A. Christians (2007): 'Hard Law & Soft Law in International Taxation', University of Wisconsin Law School, Legal Studies Research Paper Series, Paper No. 1049 of May 2007.
6. See P. Rendahl (2009): 'Cross-Border Consumption Taxation of Digital Supplies', IBFD Doctoral Series No. 18, 2009 at p. 84 and e.g., Case TC04249 from the VAT Tribunal, [2015] UKFTT 0036 (TC).

national soft law. Courts may follow the positions given by the Tax Authority, but are not obliged to do so.

Validation of a specific situation depending on evidence brought before the court is the final stage in a case concerning the effects of international coordination through soft law. If a specific situation cannot be proven or if an evidence of a certain cost cannot be shown, it affects the decision in a specific case. It is not a direct consequence of international coordination, but is equally affecting the outcome in an individual case. The validation is an example of coordination of formal rules or provisions affecting the procedures and practices in a tax case, whereas it may not affect the actual interpretation of a tax provision. This means that alongside the coordination of tax provisions allocating tax rights between states, coordination of information exchange and procedural provisions is equally important for reaching the goal of the coordination. Thus, international coordination means that two or more countries need to reach a similar or the same result in both contexts and give recognition to cases by a common standard.

The Ottawa Taxation Framework Conditions can be used as an example of international coordination of principles in a non-legally binding way. The principles need to be clear enough in meaning to avoid misinterpreting their purpose. Otherwise, the goal of coordination is lost. They also have to be vague or flexible enough to be adaptive into national rules or recommendations, and to fit into the legal system of the respective countries, coordinating their legislation. How this is best done at a national level is out of the scope of this note, but one key issue is to respect the division of powers and the principle of legality. Imposing a legal obligation on individuals and companies, even if someone else, in principle, carries the actual tax burden, should be done through constitutionally valid measures.[7]

Other types of international coordination are the OECD Model and the transfer pricing guidelines.[8] Interestingly, the Model is a soft law tool, used as a basis for bilateral and multilateral tax treaties (such as the Nordic Tax Treaty) which are, however, not soft law tools, but binding treaties between states that concern other issues besides allocation of the tax base between two or more jurisdictions. They also provide tools to tax administrations such as mutual agreement procedures and procedures to reach mutual decisions on how to treat a company or an individual in a situation of double taxation. This difference between the international context for income tax purposes (international soft law transformed into international hard law) and the international context for VAT/GST purposes (international soft law that may be transformed into legally binding regional or national law) needs to be kept in mind

7. From the perspective of how to design tax law, see e.g., D. Bently (2004): 'Tax Law Drafting: the principled method', 14 Revenue L. J. 1 of 2004 at 1–4: V. Thuronyi (2000): 'Drafting Tax Legislation' in V. Thuronyi (ed.) (2000): 'Tax Law Design and Drafting', International Monetary Fund, Kluwer Law International 2000 at 71–94.
8. For an analysis of the transfer pricing guidelines as one example of soft law, see e.g., A. Vega (2012): 'International Governance through Soft Law: The Case of the OECD Transfer Pricing Guidelines', Max Planck Institute for Tax Law and Public Finance, Working Paper 2012-05 of July 2012.

for the rest of this article, which primarily deals with international coordination for VAT/GST purposes.[9]

Within the EU there is also another type of international coordination by means of harmonization of the national laws of the Member States, based on the EU Treaties. This is primarily done by directives, but from the spring of 2014 it also has taken the form of Explanatory Notes in the VAT area. This note does not cover the full EU perspective on how EU law is given effect at national level, but focuses on the use of these Explanatory Notes.[10] Their effect within the EU is mainly discussed in section 11.5 within the context of the Member States' obligation of a proper application of EU law at national level.

A final remark to be made on international coordination is that the national perspective on what is law (and what is not) needs to be understood as relative, depending on the legal traditions in the respective countries. Therefore also the discussion of the contents of soft law is relative: a specific soft law tool may be given different effects in different legal traditions and questions on equality between different types of soft law tools may be difficult to argue. Likewise, discussions on what is international (and what is not), may give rise to different answers in different national contexts. Hence, these differences need to be understood when discussing international coordination and soft law. This also means that all of these perspectives cannot be covered in this particular article. This article merely aims at identifying and systemizing methodological questions arising from the use of soft law in international coordination, providing a base for further discussion.

11.3 SPECIFIC DEMANDS IN THE CONTEXT OF ELECTRONIC COMMERCE

Many authors have written about taxing electronic commerce or digital commerce. Some say it is possible to tax electronic commerce in the traditional way, but others have suggested new taxes or argue that no taxes should be imposed at all.[11] The advantages and disadvantages of these different suggestions are not discussed in this article. This article discusses the current increased use of soft law tools as a means for further international coordination. One question that needs to be discussed, though, is whether there are specific demands arising from the particularities of electronic commerce compared to traditional commerce? Electronic commerce and particularly digital commerce is instant and to a large degree carried out between anonymous

9. See P. Rendahl (2009): 'Cross-Border Consumption Taxation of Digital Supplies', IBFD 2009 at 62: T. Ecker (2013): 'A VAT/GST Model Convention', IBFD 2013 at 72.
10. There are several books and articles discussing the effects of EU law at national level in the Member States, see e.g., U. Bernitz (2012): 'Europarättens genomslag', Norstedts Juridik 2012; A. von Bogdandy (2008): 'Pluralism, direct effect, and the ultimate say: On the relationship between international and domestic constitutional law', 6 Intl J. of Constitutional L. 3–4 of 2008 at 397–413; P. Craig, G. de Burca (2011): 'EU Law Text, Cases and Materials', Oxford University Press 2011.
11. See e.g., the Permanent Internet Tax Freedom Act, H.R. 3086, 15 Jul. 2014; A.J. Cordell (1996): 'New Taxes for a New Economy', 2 Government Information in Canada/Information gouvernementale au Canada, No. 4.2; C. Trenta (2013): 'VAT in Peer-to-peer Content Distribution', JIBS Dissertation Series, No. 90, 2013.

parties. Most important, perhaps is the fact that the customers want to be able to use the purchased materials as soon as the materials are accessible or downloaded. This is different from traditional supplies or even supplies that are purchased (but not delivered) through electronic means, because in those cases the goods still need to be delivered by traditional logistic means.

One of the main questions for the supplier is what (price) information is to be given to the customer and one of his main problems is that he carries the risk if that information is incorrect. The customer, and in particular consumers without the right to deduct input VAT, need an instant price inclusive of taxes. If there is a mistake in calculating that tax, the company selling the goods or services, carries the burden of that mistake. One simple ratio could then be that the more complex a tax provision is, or the more difficult it is to allocate the correct tax to a particular transaction, the higher the risk for the company supplying the goods or services. The question of what degree of risk companies or taxable persons should or should not be expected to carry is complex. Perhaps a larger company can carry a larger risk than a smaller company or perhaps the risk carried by taxable persons when it comes to consumption taxation should be kept to a minimum – minimizing the costs that cannot be carried forward to the final consumer?

One, perhaps less obvious way to decrease the risk that may increase compliance costs is to use presumptive tax methods. At EU level a presumptive method is used by the Commission in its Explanatory Notes to give practical solutions to the question how to allocate the tax base from the moment that the destination principle becomes applicable for B2C digital supplies (1 January 2015), including electronically supplied services, telecommunication services and radio- and television broadcasting services.

11.4 THEORETICAL COMPARISON OF TWO SOFT LAW TOOLS

11.4.1 The EU Explanatory Notes on Digital Supplies

The alleged purpose of the Explanatory Notes is to give more detailed guidance on the practical application of the provisions of Council Implementing Regulation (EU) No. 1042/2013 of 7 October 2013 amending Implementing Regulation (EU) No. 282/2011 as regards the place of supply of services (the Explanatory Notes).[12] It is difficult to generalize the content of the Explanatory Notes. They provide specific presumptions for several provisions of the Regulation so as to facilitate their practical application. A few examples are discussed here that show the particular difficulties with electronic commerce (presumptions on definitions, the use of intermediaries, customer location and status).

Some presumptions cover the definitions of the three types of supplies (telecommunication supplies, electronically supplied services and radio and television broadcasting services). One positive aspect of these definitions is that they give further

12. Explanatory Notes on the EU VAT changes to the place of supply of telecommunications, broadcasting and electronic services that enter into force in 2015, 3 Apr. 2014, at 3.

guidance on the concept of radio and television broadcasting services, which was lacking just a few years ago. That concept only covers the distribution of radio and television programmes for simultaneous, or quasi-simultaneous, listening or viewing on the basis of a programme schedule, and the content needs to be provided by and under the editorial responsibility of a media service provider.[13] One difficulty in applying this definition is to distinguish these services from on-demand services falling under the definition of electronically supplied services. The guidance given by the Explanatory Notes puts forward that, if the service is supplied to an individual against payment instead of to a general public, there is a presumption that it concerns an electronically supplied service. A radio and television broadcasting service therefore needs to be transmitted to a general or regional public, and the fact that the customer needs to pay for the service, does not restrict the scope of the concept: radio and television broadcasting services.[14] There may, however, still be difficulties in applying this to an actual case if services are bundled with non-digital supplies. The Explanatory Notes refer to the criterion developed by the Court of Justice in several cases and conclude that such decisions heavily depend on the facts and then need to be decided on a case-by-case basis.[15] When using a presumptive method, it is, however, possible also to use such guidance for creating a more uniform interpretation of facts. For example certain factors can be indicators for when supplies are artificially split or are seen as one single service from an economic point of view.

Other presumptions cover more complex supplies that involve intermediaries. The Explanatory Notes bring forward five different scenarios providing presumptions for how different contractual agreements influence the production- and distribution chain.[16] Companies can use presumptions as they build up their business platforms if they are specific enough. Specific or detailed presumptions can be used in a similar manner as a list of factors asking a customer to check boxes online leading to a result in line with the current tax provision. Questions arise, however, on the responsibility for the providers if the information given is incorrect or if different countries use different presumptions in a cross-border situation. In such cases, a presumptive method does not solve problems of double taxation or non-taxation: it just moves the problem from one legal criterion to another. The difference is which legal basis the legal criterion has: an EU regulation, an EU directive, a national law, case law or soft law.

The Explanatory Notes also provide guidance in situations where one or more of the intermediaries in the production- and distribution chain rebut the presumption,[17] but that guidance does not cover radio- and television broadcasting services because the definition of those services includes editorial responsibility, thus limiting the possibility of using intermediaries.[18]

In addition to this the Explanatory Notes cover several examples of provisions (that should apply both in B2B and in B2C cases), on how customer location and

13. *Ibid.*, at 16–17.
14. *Ibid.*, at 19.
15. *Ibid.*, at 21.
16. *Ibid.*, at 23–32.
17. *Ibid.*, at 35–42 describes scenario six to ten.
18. *Ibid.*, at 43–44.

customer status could be decided. These are too detailed to be discussed here, but there is a common theme for the presumptions. They are detailed giving facts that presume a certain legal treatment, but at the same time they aim at being flexible enough to cover technological developments in what is supplied and how supplies are made. They also provide presumptions on how to validate or give proof for a certain presumption to apply.[19] The requirements, of which documents or information can be used, should, however, not be seen as limiting. Since there is an obligation for suppliers to know what they could have known about the customer, an immediate reaction is to build a platform for electronic commerce with the capacity of collecting plenty of documentation since tax authorities and courts in the different Member States still can interpret what the different facts mean differently, in particular when the possibility to rebut a presumption is used by a supplier.[20] Where room for interpretation of not only legal concepts but also legal facts is given, the presumptions thus may increase complexity and uncertainty rather than reaching its aim of explaining the application of provisions in complex situations. Another practical difficulty is to provide platforms with technical solutions for companies coping with the presumptions and gathering required information.

When discussing presumptive methods, it may be useful to clarify different forms of those methods. The Explanatory Notes mainly use the rebuttable form of the presumptive method, providing guidelines for increasing predictability for taxable persons by aiming for coordinating the practical application of the VAT provisions. They are not binding. Non-rebuttable methods can equally be non-binding, even if it is preferred that they are binding (questions may otherwise occur whether they actually are non-rebuttable or rebuttable).[21] Even if non-rebuttable methods are used these can be combined with a possibility for a taxable person to present better data or other circumstances that could validate another tax decision. Non-rebuttable presumptive methods may result in a minimum tax or exclusive tax. A minimum tax result means that the result of the method is that tax liability for a taxable person does not go below the result of the presumptive provisions. An exclusive tax, on the other hand, means that the presumptive methods lead to a tax liability for a taxable person that cannot lead to a higher liability irrespective whether other provisions may lead to a higher liability.[22] Another distinction can be made on the basis of whether the presumptions are mechanical or whether they allow discretion. The more discretion a presumption leaves to tax officials, the more likely it is that the presumptions are rebuttable.[23]

The balance between the different types of presumptive methods affects the question whether the presumptive methods fulfil the aim which the Explanatory Notes are assumed to have. The perspective of that aim is practical. From a theoretical perspective a number of questions arise. Increasing the practical applicability of provisions is an advantage both from a practical and theoretical perspective. It may

19. *Ibid.*, at 66.
20. *Ibid.*, at 66.
21. See Thuronyi, V (2000): 'Presumptive Taxation' in V. Thuronyi (ed.) (2000): 'Tax Law: Design and Drafting', Kluwer Law International 2000 at 403–404.
22. *Ibid.*, at 404.
23. *Ibid.*, at 405.

lower compliance costs for taxable persons and increase predictability. However, if courts at national and EU level do not give effect to the presumptions, they may equally cause distortions and complexity, decreasing both neutrality and legal certainty. The use of presumptive methods therefore needs to be combined with the doctrine of proper application, not yet fully developed by the Court of Justice in combination with re-evaluating the effects of EU law following from Article 267 EU and case law developing the doctrines of indirect effect of EU law before national courts.[24]

11.4.2 International VAT/GST Guidelines

The International VAT/GST Guidelines (the Guidelines), currently being developed by the OECD constitute another soft law tool, not directly comparable with the EU Explanatory Notes discussed above in 11.4.1. The Guidelines are not connected to legally binding substantive provisions in the way in which the Explanatory Notes are. The Guidelines are developed through multilateral cooperation between both OECD Member States and Partners. The aim of the Guidelines is to reduce uncertainty and the risk of double taxation and unintended non-taxation, resulting from inconsistencies between jurisdictions in cross-border situations. It is also clarified that the Guidelines do not aim to provide detailed prescriptions for national legislation, but that they respect the sovereignty of national jurisdictions to design and apply national laws.[25]

The Guidelines do not use a presumptive method in a similar manner as the Explanatory Notes do. The approach chosen in the Guidelines derives from the principles defined in the Ottawa Taxation Framework Conditions, serving not only as fundamental principles but also as a means for evaluating different regulatory choices.[26] The use of the Ottawa Taxation Framework Conditions may, however, end up in detailed presumptions, either implemented at national level or by further development of the Guidelines at international level. There is no contradiction between the two. As an example, the main rule for allocating taxing rights between jurisdictions is combined with a presumption in cases in which a customer has more than one establishment. In those cases it is the jurisdiction where the service or the intangible is used that has the taxing rights.[27] The presumption is based on the principle of taxing supplies where consumption takes place, following the destination principle.

One further question is, whether, since the presumption is characterized as a proxy, there is a difference between a presumptive method and a proxy method? Presumptions refer to validation of circumstances or facts. If a taxable person acts in accordance with a presumption, lower requirements for proof or evidence may apply compared to when he or she chooses to rebut the presumption. A proxy is not necessarily linked to an assumption of facts or indicators leading to a certain conclusion, but is closer to a legal criterion or concept used to achieve a desired outcome.

24. See Case C-337/95 *Dior* [1997] ECR I-6013, paragraph 25 and Case C- 282/10 *Dominguez* [2012] Judgment of 24 Jan. 2012, p. 24–25 with subsequent references to additional case law.
25. See OECD, International VAT/GST Guidelines, Global Forum on VAT 17–18 Apr. 2014 at 4.
26. *Ibid.*, at 5–6.
27. *Ibid.*, at 27.

Another comparison between the Explanatory Notes and the Guidelines is that the Guidelines use commentaries, explaining the meaning of the suggested concepts and approaches. The Explanatory Notes explain how the provisions found in directives and regulations and connected with the Explanatory Notes may be applied by using presumptions.

11.5 INTERPRETATION AND APPLICATION BY AUTHORITIES AND COURTS

The effects of soft law depend on its usefulness for authorities when they administer the tax and for the courts when they interpret and apply legal provisions. In the area of international direct tax law, the OECD Model and its commentaries, including the transfer pricing guidelines, have been given effect in different jurisdictions.[28] These soft law tools are, however, often implemented partially in relation to legal provisions, thus creating a constitutional link between the soft law derived from the international level and the legal provisions adopted at national level. The effects of the VAT/GST guidelines is not connected in the same way to legal provisions at the national level, hence it is more uncertain to predict which effects these guidelines may have in interpreting and applying legal provisions at the national level.

Within the EU several doctrines have been developed to ensure the effects of EU law at national level, but the effects of the Explanatory Notes are uncertain at this point. Questions on whether or not they are able to fulfil their aim of facilitating the practical application of the rules is yet to be seen, because the legal provisions to which they are connected only entered into force on 1 January 2015. As far as the interpretation of the legal provisions at EU level is concerned, Article 267 EC clarifies that it is the Court of Justice that has the interpretative rights. This is supported by the doctrines developed by the Court of Justice in cases like *van Gend en Loos*[29] and *Costa v. ENEL.*[30] These doctrines are well discussed in literature and therefore not discussed in detail in this chapter. As regards the responsibility of national courts when interpreting European legal provisions, it is clear that, in case of doubt, they have an obligation to ask for a preliminary ruling from the Court of Justice (following Article 267 EC and case law like *Broekmeulen*).[31] As far as the application of EU law in individual cases is concerned this falls within the scope of the obligations for the national courts in the Member States within the doctrine of *proper application* as explained in the *Dior* case.[32] The proper application refers to the obligations for national courts to give effect to EU law when

28. See e.g., K. Vogel (2000): 'The Influence of the OECD Commentaries on Treaty Interpretation, Bulletin' 2000 at 617–618; D. A. Ward et.al. (2005): 'The Interpretation of Income Tax Treaties with Particular Reference to the Commentaries on the OECD Model', IFA and IBFD 2005; A. Vega (2012): 'International Governance through Soft Law: The Case of the OECD Transfer Pricing Guidelines', Max Planck Institute for Tax Law and Public Finance, Working Paper 2012-05 of July 2012.
29. Case 26/62 *van Gend en Loos* [1963] ECR I.
30. Case 6/64 *Costa v. ENEL* [1964] ECR 585.
31. Case 246/80 *Broekmeulen* [1981] ECR I-7791.
32. Case C-337/95 *Dior* [1997] ECR I-6013.

applying EU law or national provisions implementing EU law in individual cases.[33] The doctrine builds upon the principle of cooperation between the Court of Justice and the national courts as expressed in the *CILFIT* case on ensuring a uniform interpretation and proper application of EU law at national level.[34]

Explanatory Notes given by the World Customs Organisation (WCO) have been given relevance by the ECJ in interpreting the Common Customs Tariff. These notes have been adopted through an international convention and approved by a Council decision on behalf of the EU (EEC at the time).[35] This does, however, not mean that the Explanatory Notes in the area of VAT will be given the same effect. The non-binding effects of Explanatory Notes may, however, not prevent them to be referred to as a useful interpretative tool.[36] It is for the ECJ to give further guidance on the legal effects of both the Explanatory Notes and if the OECD guidelines will have effect within the EU as well.

11.6 CLOSING REMARKS

This note aimed at identifying and systematizing methodological issues arising from the use of soft law as a tool for international coordination and to give an overview for further discussions. The legal effects of the Guidelines and the Explanatory Notes from the EU are still uncertain. I can therefore not answer the question of whether the choice of using soft law in the area of VAT does affect the interpretation and application of the VAT rules at national level. There are, however, a few arguments that can be flagged as a basis for further discussion both nationally and internationally. To affect the policy level, a theoretical model based on principles may be sufficient to reach the desired result of the coordination. As far as the interpretation of legal provisions at national level implementing soft law is concerned, there is a difference between regionally based materials (as within the EU) and internationally based materials (as within the OECD). Besides that difference there also is a difference in the level of detail. If concepts or criteria are used creating a common understanding or if presumptions are used, it also affects the validation of certain circumstances or facts. In practice this affects the documentary requirements for companies and how automatic computer systems assist in that process. It is not without difficulties for companies to find suitable platforms coping with the administrative demands of the VAT. A proxy model based on principles as used in the Guidelines may affect the interpretation of legal provisions but is more limited as far as interpreting the facts or circumstances in a case is concerned. Since one of the causes for double taxation and non-taxation also is different interpretations of facts, the presumptive method is more far reaching. Perhaps a combination of the two is necessary, but such methods also need to discuss the

33. *Ibid.*, at 25.
34. Case 283/81 *CILFIT* [1982] ECR 3415 p. 7.
35. See the International Convention on the Harmonised Commodity Description and Coding System, concluded in Brussels on 14 Jun. 1983 and approved on behalf of the European Economic Community by Council Decision 87/369/EEC of 7 Apr. 1987 (OJ 1987 L 198, p. 1).
36. See Case C-2/13 *Humeau Beaupréau* [2014] ECR I-000, Judgment of 6 Feb. 2014, p. 32–33.

degree of discretion and how that may affect the practical application of the provisions. The Explanatory Notes do leave unanswered questions yet for companies to answer in their platforms. Hence, if presumptive methods are combined with uncertainty requiring interpretation of concepts at yet another level, the aim of simplifying and increasing predictability with the Explanatory Notes is hampered. E-commerce demands 'click-made' decisions putting more pressure on proactive provisions or presumptions where perhaps little or no discretion is given. Too mechanical presumptions may, however, raise other issues affecting a reasonable balance between certainty and efficiency.

Another issue to put forward is how the changing legislative landscape using more soft law tools affects certainty in terms of legality. What is constitutionally valid and what is not? Is this a form of self-regulation, because taxable persons are more involved in the development of the soft law tools, compared to their more limited role in developing national legal provisions? Of course, this varies between different countries and their procedures for adopting legislation, but even so, international coordination would benefit from discussing also these methodological questions. If tax authorities cooperate more, perhaps also courts need to be more aware of decisions of other court on similar provisions, creating a common interpretation or common interpretative methods for provisions based on internationally coordinated materials?

Appendices

APPENDIX I

Council Directive 2002/38/EC of 7 May 2002 Amending and Amending Temporarily Directive 77/388/EEC as Regards the Value Added Tax Arrangements Applicable to Radio and Television Broadcasting Services and Certain Electronically Supplied Services, O.J. 15 May 2002, L 128

Full text:

THE COUNCIL OF THE EUROPEAN UNION,
Having regard to the Treaty establishing the European Community, and in particular Article 93 thereof,
Having regard to the proposal from the Commission[1],
Having regard to the opinion of the European Parliament[2],
Having regard to the opinion of the Economic and Social Committee[3],
Whereas:

(1) The rules currently applicable to VAT on radio and television broadcasting services and on electronically supplied services, under Article 9 of the sixth Council Directive 77/388/EEC of 17 May 1977 on the harmonisation of the laws of the Member States relating to turnover taxes - Common system of

(1) OJ C 337 E, 28.11.2000, p. 65.
(2) OJ C 232, 17.8.2001, p. 202.
(3) OJ C 116, 20.4.2001, p. 59.

value added tax: uniform basis of assessment[(4)], are inadequate for taxing such services consumed within the Community and for preventing distortions of competition in this area.

(2) In the interests of the proper functioning of the internal market, such distortions should be eliminated and new harmonised rules introduced for this type of activity. Action should be taken to ensure, in particular, that such services where effected for consideration and consumed by customers established in the Community are taxed in the Community and are not taxed if consumed outside the Community.

(3) To this end, radio and television broadcasting services and electronically supplied services provided from third countries to persons established in the Community or from the Community to recipients established in third countries should be taxed at the place of the recipient of the services.

(4) To define electronically supplied services, examples of such services should be included in an annex to the Directive.

(5) To facilitate compliance with fiscal obligations by operators providing electronically supplied services, who are neither established nor required to be identified for tax purposes within the Community, a special scheme should be established. In applying this scheme any operator supplying such services by electronic means to non-taxable persons within the Community, may, if he is not otherwise identified for tax purposes within the Community, opt for identification in a single Member State.

(6) The non-established operator wishing to benefit from the special scheme should comply with the requirements laid down therein, and with any relevant existing provision in the Member State where the services are consumed.

(7) The Member State of identification must under certain conditions be able to exclude a non-established operator from the special scheme.

(8) Where the non-established operator opts for the special scheme, any input value added tax that he has paid with respect to goods and services used by him for the purpose of his taxed activities falling under the special scheme, should be refunded by the Member State where the input value added tax was paid, in accordance with the arrangements of the thirteenth Council Directive 86/560/EEC of 17 November 1986 on the harmonisation of the laws of the Member States relating to turnover taxes - arrangements for the refund of value added tax to taxable persons not established in Community territory[(5)]. The optional restrictions for refund in Article 2(2) and (3) and Article 4(2) of the same Directive should not be applied.

(9) Subject to conditions which they lay down, Member States should allow certain statements and returns to be made by electronic means, and may also require that electronic means are used.

---

(4) OL L 145, 13.6.1977, p. 1. Directive as last amended by Council Directive 2001/115/EC (OJ L 15, 17.1.2002, p. 24).

(5) OJ L 326, 21.11.1986, p. 40.'

(10) Those provisions pertaining to the introduction of electronic tax returns and statements should be adopted on a permanent basis. It is desirable to adopt all other provisions for a temporary period of three years which may be extended for practical reasons but should, in any event, based on experience, be reviewed within three years from 1 July 2003.

(11) Directive 77/388/EEC should therefore be amended accordingly,

HAS ADOPTED THIS DIRECTIVE:

Article 1

Directive 77/388/EEC is hereby temporarily amended as follows:

1. in Article 9:
   (a) in paragraph (2)(e), a comma shall replace the final full stop and the following indents shall be added: '- radio and television broadcasting services, - electronically supplied services, inter alia, those described in Annex L.'
   (b) in paragraph 2, the following point shall be added: '(f) the place where services referred to in the last indent of subparagraph (e) are supplied when performed for non-taxable persons who are established, have their permanent address or usually reside in a Member State, by a taxable person who has established his business or has a fixed establishment from which the service is supplied outside the Community or, in the absence of such a place of business or fixed establishment, has his permanent address or usually resides outside the Community, shall be the place where the non-taxable person is established, has his permanent address or usually resides.'
   (c) in paragraph 3, the introductory phrase shall be replaced by the following: '3. In order to avoid double taxation, non-taxation or the distortion of competition, the Member States may, with regard to the supply of services referred to in paragraph 2(e), except for the services referred to in the last indent when supplied to non-taxable persons, and also with regard to the hiring out of forms of transport consider:'
   (d) paragraph 4 shall be amended as follows: '4. In the case of telecommunications services and radio and television broadcasting services referred to in paragraph 2(e) when performed for non-taxable persons who are established, have their permanent address or usually reside in a Member State, by a taxable person who has established his business or has a fixed establishment from which the service is supplied outside the Community, or in the absence of such a place of business or fixed establishment, has his permanent address or usually resides outside the Community, Member States shall make use of paragraph 3(b).'

2. in Article 12(3)(a), the following fourth subparagraph shall be added: 'The third subparagraph shall not apply to the services referred to in the last indent of Article 9(2)(e).'
3. the following Article shall be added:
   'Article 26c Special scheme for non-established taxable persons supplying electronic services to non-taxable persons'

A. Definitions

For the purposes of this Article, the following definitions shall apply without prejudice to other Community provisions:

(a) 'non-established taxable person' means a taxable person who has neither established his business nor has a fixed establishment within the territory of the Community and who is not otherwise required to be identified for tax purposes under Article 22;
(b) 'electronic services' and 'electronically supplied services' means those services referred to in the last indent of Article 9(2)(e);
(c) 'Member State of identification' means the Member State which the non-established taxable person chooses to contact to state when his activity as a taxable person within the territory of the Community commences in accordance with the provisions of this Article;
(d) 'Member State of consumption' means the Member State in which the supply of the electronic services is deemed to take place according to Article 9(2)(f);
(e) 'value added tax return' means the statement containing the information necessary to establish the amount of tax that has become chargeable in each Member State.

B. Special scheme for electronically supplied services

1. Member States shall permit a non-established taxable person supplying electronic services to a non-taxable person who is established or has his permanent address or usually resides in a Member State to use a special scheme in accordance with the following provisions. The special scheme shall apply to all those supplies within the Community.
2. The non-established taxable person shall state to the Member State of identification when his activity as a taxable person commences, ceases or changes to the extent that he no longer qualifies for the special scheme. Such a statement shall be made electronically.
   The information from the non-established taxable person to the Member State of identification when his taxable activities commence shall contain the following details for the identification: name, postal address, electronic addresses, including websites, national tax number, if any, and a statement that

the person is not identified for value added tax purposes within the Community. The non-established taxable person shall notify the Member State of identification of any changes in the submitted information.

3. The Member State of identification shall identify the non-established taxable person by means of an individual number. Based on the information used for this identification, Member States of consumption may keep their own identification systems.

   The Member State of identification shall notify the non-established taxable person by electronic means of the identification number allocated to him.

4. The Member State of identification shall exclude the non-established taxable person from the identification register if:
   (a) he notifies that he no longer supplies electronic services, or
   (b) it otherwise can be assumed that his taxable activities have ended, or
   (c) he no longer fulfils the requirements necessary to be allowed to use the special scheme, or
   (d) he persistently fails to comply with the rules concerning the special scheme.

5. The non-established taxable person shall submit by electronic means to the Member State of identification a value added tax return for each calendar quarter whether or not electronic services have been supplied. The return shall be submitted within 20 days following the end of the reporting period to which the return refers.

   The value added tax return shall set out the identification number and, for each Member State of consumption where tax has become due, the total value, less value added tax, of supplies of electronic services for the reporting period and total amount of the corresponding tax. The applicable tax rates and the total tax due shall also be indicated.

6. The value added tax return shall be made in euro. Member States which have not adopted the euro may require the tax return to be made in their national currencies. If the supplies have been made in other currencies, the exchange rate valid for the last date of the reporting period shall be used when completing the value added tax return. The exchange shall be done following the exchange rates published by the European Central Bank for that day, or, if there is no publication on that day, on the next day of publication.

7. The non-established taxable person shall pay the value added tax when submitting the return. Payment shall be made to a bank account denominated in euro, designated by the Member State of identification. Member States which have not adopted the euro may require the payment to be made to a bank account denominated in their own currency.

8. Notwithstanding Article 1(1) of Directive 86/560/EEC, the non-established taxable person making use of this special scheme shall, instead of making deductions under Article 17(2) of this Directive, be granted a refund according to Directive 86/560/EEC. Articles 2(2), 2(3) and 4(2) of Directive 86/560/EEC shall not apply to the refund related to electronic supplies covered by this special scheme.

9. The non-established taxable person shall keep records of the transactions covered by this special scheme in sufficient detail to enable the tax administration of the Member State of consumption to determine that the value added tax return referred to in paragraph 5 is correct. These records should be made available electronically on request to the Member State of identification and to the Member State of consumption. These records shall be maintained for a period of 10 years from the end of the year when the transaction was carried out.
10. Article 21(2)(b) shall not apply to a non-established taxable person who has opted for this special scheme.'

Article 2

Article 22, contained in Article 28h of Directive 77/388/EEC, is hereby amended as follows:

1. in paragraph 1, point (a) shall be replaced by the following: '(a) Every taxable person shall state when his activity as a taxable person commences, changes or ceases. Member States shall, subject to conditions which they lay down, allow the taxable person to make such statements by electronic means, and may also require that electronic means are used.'
2. in paragraph 4, point (a) shall be replaced by the following: '(a) Every taxable person shall submit a return by a deadline to be determined by Member States. That deadline may not be more than two months later than the end of each tax period. The tax period shall be fixed by each Member State at one month, two months or a quarter. Member States may, however, set different periods provided that they do not exceed one year. Member States shall, subject to conditions which they lay down, allow the taxable person to make such returns by electronic means, and may also require that electronic means are used.'
3. in paragraph 6, point (a) shall be replaced by the following: '(a) Member States may require a taxable person to submit a statement, including all the particulars specified in paragraph 4, concerning all transactions carried out in the preceding year. That statement shall provide all the information necessary for any adjustments. Member States shall, subject to conditions which they lay down, allow the taxable person to make such statements by electronic means, and may also require that electronic means are used.'
4. in paragraph 6, the second paragraph in point (b) shall be replaced by: 'The recapitulative statement shall be drawn up for each calendar quarter within a period and in accordance with procedures to be determined by the Member States, which shall take the measures necessary to ensure that the provisions concerning administrative cooperation in the field of indirect taxation are in any event complied with. Member States shall, subject to conditions which they lay down, allow the taxable person to make such

statements by electronic means, and may also require that electronic means are used.'

Article 3

1. Member States shall bring into force the laws, regulations and administrative provisions necessary to comply with this Directive on 1 July 2003. They shall forthwith inform the Commission thereof.
   When Member States adopt these measures, they shall contain a reference to this Directive or shall be accompanied by such reference on the occasion of their official publication. Member States shall determine how such reference is to be made.
2. Member States shall communicate to the Commission the text of the provisions of domestic law which they adopt in the field covered by this Directive.

Article 4

Article 1 shall apply for a period of three years starting from 1 July 2003.

Article 5

The Council, on the basis of a report from the Commission, shall review the provisions of Article 1 of this Directive before 30 June 2006 and shall either, acting in accordance with Article 93 of the Treaty, adopt measures on an appropriate electronic mechanism on a non-discriminatory basis for charging, declaring, collecting and allocating tax revenue on electronically supplied services with taxation in the place of consumption or, if considered necessary for practical reasons, acting unanimously on the basis of a proposal from the Commission, extend the period mentioned in Article 4.

Article 6

This Directive shall enter into force on the day of its publication in the Official Journal of the European Communities.

Article 7

This Directive is addressed to the Member States.
Done at Brussels, 7 May 2002.
For the Council The President R. De Rato Y Figaredo

ANNEX L

ILLUSTRATIVE LIST OF ELECTRONICALLY SUPPLIED SERVICES REFERRED TO IN ARTICLE 9(2)(e)

1. Website supply, web-hosting, distance maintenance of programmes and equipment.
2. Supply of software and updating thereof.
3. Supply of images, text and information, and making databases available.
4. Supply of music, films and games, including games of chance and gambling games, and of political, cultural, artistic, sporting, scientific and entertainment broadcasts and events.
5. Supply of distance teaching.

Where the supplier of a service and his customer communicates via electronic mail, this shall not of itself mean that the service performed is an electronic service within the meaning of the last indent of Article 9(2)(e).

Appendix II

Council Directive 2008/8/EC of 12 February 2008 Amending Directive 2006/112/EC as Regards the Place of Supply of Services, O.J. 20 February 2008, L 44/11

Selected excerpts:

(...)

Article 2

From 1 January 2010, Directive 2006/112/EC is hereby amended as follows:
(...)

Section 2

General rules

Article 44

The place of supply of services to a taxable person acting as such shall be the place where that person has established his business. However, if those services are provided to a fixed establishment of the taxable person located in a place other than the place where he has established his business, the place of supply of those services shall be the place where that fixed establishment is located. In the absence of such place of establishment or fixed establishment, the place of supply of services shall be the place where the taxable person who receives such services has his permanent address or usually resides.

Article 45

The place of supply of services to a non-taxable person shall be the place where the supplier has established his business. However, if those services are provided from a fixed establishment of the supplier located in a place other than the place where he has established his business, the place of supply of those services shall be the place where that fixed establishment is located. In the absence of such place of establishment or fixed establishment, the place of supply of services shall be the place where the supplier has his permanent address or usually resides.

Section 3

Particular provisions
(...)

Subsection 8

Supply of electronic services to non-taxable persons

Article 58

The place of supply of electronically supplied services, in particular those referred to in Annex II, when supplied to non-taxable persons who are established in a Member State, or who have their permanent address or usually reside in a Member State, by a taxable person who has established his business outside the Community or has a fixed establishment there from which the service is supplied, or who, in the absence of such a place of business or fixed establishment, has his permanent address or usually resides outside the Community, shall be the place where the non- taxable person is established, or where he has his permanent address or usually resides.
Where the supplier of a service and the customer communicate via electronic mail, that shall not of itself mean that the service supplied is an electronically supplied service.

Subsection 9

Supply of services to non-taxable persons outside the Community

Article 59

The place of supply of the following services to a non- taxable person who is established or has his permanent address or usually resides outside the Community, shall be the place where that person is established, has his permanent address or usually resides:

(a) transfers and assignments of copyrights, patents, licences, trade marks and similar rights;
(b) advertising services;

(c) the services of consultants, engineers, consultancy firms, lawyers, accountants and other similar services, as well as data processing and the provision of information;
(d) obligations to refrain from pursuing or exercising, in whole or in part, a business activity or a right referred to in this Article;
(e) banking, financial and insurance transactions including reinsurance, with the exception of the hire of safes;
(f) the supply of staff;
(g) the hiring out of movable tangible property, with the exception of all means of transport;
(h) the provision of access to, and of transport or trans- mission through, natural gas and electricity distribution systems and the provision of other services directly linked thereto;
(i) telecommunications services;
(j) radio and television broadcasting services;
(k) electronically supplied services, in particular those referred to in Annex II.

Where the supplier of a service and the customer commu- nicate via electronic mail, that shall not of itself mean that the service supplied is an electronically supplied service.

Subsection 10

Prevention of double taxation or non- taxation

Article 59a

In order to prevent double taxation, non-taxation or distortion of competition, Member States may, with regard to services the place of supply of which is governed by Articles 44, 45, 56 and 59:

(a) consider the place of supply of any or all of those services, if situated within their territory, as being situated outside the Community if the effective use and enjoyment of the services takes place outside the Community;
(b) consider the place of supply of any or all of those services, if situated outside the Community, as being situated within their territory if the effective use and enjoyment of the services takes place within their territory.

However, this provision shall not apply to the electronically supplied services where those services are rendered to non- taxable persons not established within the Community.

Article 59b

Member States shall apply Article 59a(b) to telecommunications services and radio and television broadcasting services, as referred to in point (j) of the first paragraph of

Article 59, supplied to non-taxable persons who are established in a Member State, or who have their permanent address or usually reside in a Member State, by a taxable person who has established his business outside the Community or has a fixed establishment there from which the services are supplied, or who, in the absence of such a place of business or fixed establishment, has his permanent address or usually resides outside the Community.';
(...)

Article 5

From 1 January 2015, Directive 2006/112/EC is hereby amended as follows:

1. in Section 3 of Chapter 3 of Title V, Subsection 8 shall be replaced by the following:

'Subsection 8

Supply of telecommunications, broadcasting and electronic services to non-taxable persons

Article 58

The place of supply of the following services to a non- taxable person shall be the place where that person is established, has his permanent address or usually resides:

(a) telecommunications services;
(b) radio and television broadcasting services;
(c) electronically supplied services, in particular those referred to in Annex II.

Where the supplier of a service and the customer communicate via electronic mail, that shall not of itself mean that the service supplied is an electronically supplied service.';

2. in Article 59, points (i), (j) and (k) of the first paragraph and the second paragraph shall be deleted;
3. Article 59a shall be replaced by the following:

'Article 59a

In order to prevent double taxation, non-taxation or distortion of competition, Member States may, with regard to services the place of supply of which is governed by Articles 44, 45, 56, 58 and 59:

(a) consider the place of supply of any or all of those services, if situated within their territory, as being situated outside the Community if the effective use and enjoyment of the services takes place outside the Community;

(b) consider the place of supply of any or all of those services, if situated outside the Community, as being situated within their territory if the effective use and enjoyment of the services takes place within their territory.';

4. Article 59b shall be deleted;
5. in Article 204(1), the third subparagraph shall be replaced by the following:

   'However, Member States may not apply the option referred to in the second subparagraph to a taxable person not established within the Community, within the meaning of point (1) of Article 358a, who has opted for the special scheme for telecommunications, broadcasting or electronic services.';

6. in Title XII, the heading of Chapter 6 shall be replaced by the following:

   'Special schemes for non-established taxable persons supplying telecommunications services, broadcasting services or electronic services to non-taxable persons.';

7. Article 357 shall be deleted;
8. Article 358 shall be replaced by the following:

'Article 358

For the purposes of this Chapter, and without prejudice to other Community provisions, the following definitions shall apply:

1. "telecommunications services" and "broadcasting services" mean the services referred to in points (a) and (b) of the first paragraph of Article 58;
2. "electronic services" and "electronically supplied services" mean the services referred to in point (c) of the first paragraph of Article 58;
3. "Member State of consumption" means the Member State in which the supply of the telecommunications, broadcasting or electronic services is deemed to take place according to Article 58;
4. "VAT return" means the statement containing the information necessary to establish the amount of VAT due in each Member State.';
9. in Chapter 6 of Title XII, the heading of Section 2 shall be replaced by the following:
   'Special scheme for telecommunications, broadcasting or electronic services supplied by taxable persons not established within the Community';
10. in Section 2 of Chapter 6 of Title XII, the following Article shall be inserted:

'Article 358a

For the purposes of this Section, and without prejudice to other Community provisions, the following definitions shall apply:

1. "taxable person not established within the Community" means a taxable person who has not established his business in the territory of the Community and who has no fixed establishment there and who is not otherwise required to be identified for VAT purposes;
2. "Member State of identification" means the Member State which the taxable person not established within the Community chooses to contact to state when his activity as a taxable person within the territory of the Community commences in accordance with the provisions of this Section.';

11. Articles 359 to 365 shall be replaced by the following:

'Article 359

Member States shall permit any taxable person not established within the Community supplying telecommunications, broadcasting or electronic services to a non- taxable person who is established in a Member State or has his permanent address or usually resides in a Member State, to use this special scheme. This scheme applies to all those services supplied within the Community.

Article 360

The taxable person not established within the Community shall state to the Member State of identification when he commences or ceases his activity as a taxable person, or changes that activity in such a way that he no longer meets the conditions necessary for use of this special scheme. He shall communicate that information electronically.

Article 361

1. The information which the taxable person not established within the Community must provide to the Member State of identification when he commences a taxable activity shall contain the following details:
   (a) name;
   (b) postal address;
   (c) electronic addresses, including websites;
   (d) national tax number, if any;
   (e) a statement that the person is not identified for VAT purposes within the Community.
2. The taxable person not established within in the Community shall notify the Member State of identification of any changes in the information provided.

Article 362

The Member State of identification shall allocate to the taxable person not established within the Community an individual VAT identification number and shall notify him of that number by electronic means. On the basis of the information used for that identification, Member States of consumption may have recourse to their own identification systems.

Article 363

The Member State of identification shall delete the taxable person not established within the Community from the identification register in the following cases:

(a) if he notifies that Member State that he no longer supplies telecommunications, broadcasting or electronic services;
(b) if it may otherwise be assumed that his taxable activities have ceased;
(c) if he no longer meets the conditions necessary for use of this special scheme;
(d) if he persistently fails to comply with the rules relating to this special scheme.

Article 364

The taxable person not established within the Community shall submit by electronic means to the Member State of identification a VAT return for each calendar quarter, whether or not telecommunications, broadcasting or electronic services have been supplied. The VAT return shall be submitted within 20 days following the end of the tax period covered by the return.

Article 365

The VAT return shall show the identification number and, for each Member State of consumption in which VAT is due, the total value, exclusive of VAT, of supplies of telecommunications, broadcasting and electronic services carried out during the tax period and total amount per rate of the corresponding VAT. The applicable rates of VAT and the total VAT due must also be indicated on the return.';

12. Article 366(1) shall be replaced by the following:

> '1. The VAT return shall be made out in euro.
> Member States which have not adopted the euro may require the VAT return to be made out in their national currency. If the supplies have been made in other currencies, the taxable person not established within the Community shall, for the purposes of completing the VAT return, use the exchange rate applying on the last day of the tax period.';

13. Articles 367 and 368 shall be replaced by the following:

'Article 367

The taxable person not established within the Community shall pay the VAT, making reference to the relevant VAT return, when submitting the VAT return, at the latest, however, at the expiry of the deadline by which the return must be submitted.

Payment shall be made to a bank account denominated in euro, designated by the Member State of identification. Member States which have not adopted the euro may require the payment to be made to a bank account denominated in their own currency.

Article 368

The taxable person not established within the Community making use of this special scheme may not deduct VAT pursuant to Article 168 of this Directive. Notwithstanding Article 1(1) of Directive 86/560/EEC, the taxable person in question shall be refunded in accordance with the said Directive. Articles 2(2) and (3) and Article 4(2) of Directive 86/560/EEC shall not apply to refunds relating to telecommunications, broadcasting or electronic services covered by this special scheme.';

14. Article 369(1) shall be replaced by the following:

> '1. The taxable person not established within the Community shall keep records of the transactions covered by this special scheme. Those records must be sufficiently detailed to enable the tax authorities of the Member State of consumption to verify that the VAT return is correct.';

15. in Chapter 6 of Title XII, the following Section shall be inserted:

'Section 3

Special scheme for telecommunications, broadcasting or electronic services supplied by taxable persons established within the Community but not in the Member State of consumption

Article 369a

For the purposes of this Section, and without prejudice to other Community provisions, the following definitions shall apply:

1. "taxable person not established in the Member State of consumption" means a taxable person who has established his business in the territory of the Community or has a fixed establishment there but has not established his business and has no fixed establishment within the territory of the Member State of consumption;
2. "Member State of identification" means the Member State in the territory of which the taxable person has established his business or, if he has not established his business in the Community, where he has a fixed establishment.
2. Where a taxable person has not established his business in the Community, but has more than one fixed establishment therein, the Member State of identification shall be the Member State with a fixed establishment where that taxable person indicates that he will make use of this special scheme. The taxable person shall be bound by this decision for the calendar year concerned and the two calendar years following.

Article 369b

Member States shall permit any taxable person not established in the Member State of consumption supplying telecommunications, broadcasting or electronic services to a non-taxable person who is established or has his permanent address or usually resides in that Member State, to use this special scheme. This special scheme applies to all those services supplied in the Community.

Article 369c

The taxable person not established in the Member State of consumption shall state to the Member State of identification when he commences and ceases his taxable activities covered by this special scheme, or changes those activities in such a way that he no longer meets the conditions necessary for use of this special scheme. He shall communicate that information electronically.

Article 369d

A taxable person making use of this special scheme shall, for the taxable transactions carried out under this scheme, be identified for VAT purposes in the Member State of identification only. For that purpose the Member State shall use the individual VAT identification number already allocated to the taxable person in respect of his obligations under the internal system.
On the basis of the information used for that identification, Member States of consumption may have recourse to their own identification systems.

Article 369e

The Member State of identification shall exclude the taxable person not established in the Member State of consumption from this special scheme in any of the following cases:

(a) if he notifies that he no longer supplies telecommunications, broadcasting or electronic services;
(b) if it may otherwise be assumed that his taxable activities covered by this special scheme have ceased;
(c) if he no longer meets the conditions necessary for use of this special scheme;
(d) if he persistently fails to comply with the rules relating to this special scheme.

Article 369f

The taxable person not established in the Member State of consumption shall submit by electronic means to the Member State of identification a VAT return for each calendar quarter, whether or not telecommunications, broadcasting or electronic services have been supplied. The VAT return shall be submitted within 20 days following the end of the tax period covered by the return.

Article 369g

The VAT return shall show the identification number referred to in Article 369d and, for each Member State of consumption in which VAT is due, the total value, exclusive of VAT, of supplies of telecommunications, broadcasting or electronic services carried out during the tax period and the total amount per rate of the corresponding VAT. The applicable rates of VAT and the total VAT due must also be indicated on the return.
Where the taxable person has one or more fixed establishments, other than that in the Member State of identification, from which the services are supplied, the VAT return shall in addition to the information referred to in the first paragraph include the total value of supplies of telecommunications, broadcasting or electronic services covered by this special scheme, for each Member State in which he has an establishment, together with the individual VAT identification number or the tax reference number of this establishment, broken down by Member State of consumption.

Article 369h

1. The VAT return shall be made out in euro.
Member States which have not adopted the euro may require the VAT return to be made out in their national currency. If the supplies have been made in other currencies, the taxable person not established in the Member State of consumption shall, for the purposes of completing the VAT return, use the exchange rate applying on the last date of the tax period.
2. The conversion shall be made by applying the exchange rates published by the European Central Bank for that day, or, if there is no publication on that day, on the next day of publication.

Article 369i

The taxable person not established in the Member State of consumption shall pay the VAT, making reference to the relevant VAT return, when submitting the VAT return, at the latest, however, at the expiry of the deadline by which the return must be submitted.
Payment shall be made to a bank account denominated in euro, designated by the Member State of identification. Member States which have not adopted the euro may require the payment to be made to a bank account denominated in their own currency.

Article 369j

The taxable person not established in the Member State of consumption making use of this special scheme may not, in respect of his taxable activities covered by this scheme, deduct VAT pursuant to Article 168 of this Directive. Notwithstanding Article 2(1) and

Article 3 of Directive 2008/9/EC, the taxable person in question shall be refunded in accordance with the said Directive.
If the taxable person not established in the Member State of consumption making use of this special scheme also carries out in the Member State of consumption activities not covered by this scheme in respect of which he is obliged to be registered for VAT purposes, he shall deduct VAT in respect of his taxable activities which are covered by this scheme in the VAT return to be submitted pursuant to Article 250.

Article 369k

1. The taxable person not established in the Member State of consumption shall keep records of the transactions covered by this special scheme. Those records must be sufficiently detailed to enable the tax authorities of the Member State of consumption to verify that the VAT return is correct.
2. The records referred to in paragraph 1 must be made available electronically on request to the Member State of consumption and to the Member State of identification.

Those records must be kept for a period of 10 years from 31 December of the year during which the transaction was carried out.';
(...)

APPENDIX III

Council Implementing Regulation (EU) No 282/2011 of 15 March 2011 Laying Down Implementing Measures for Directive 2006/112/EC on the Common System of Value Added Tax (Recast), O.J. 23 March 2011, L77/1 (Recast of Council Regulation (EC) No 1777/2005 of 17 October 2005 Laying Down Implementing Measures for Directive 77/388/EEC on the Common System of Value Added Tax)

Selected excerpts:

(...)

CHAPTER IV

TAXABLE TRANSACTIONS

(...)

Article 7

1. 'Electronically supplied services' as referred to in Directive 2006/112/EC shall include services which are delivered over the Internet or an electronic network

and the nature of which renders their supply essentially automated and involving minimal human intervention, and impossible to ensure in the absence of information technology.

2. Paragraph 1 shall cover, in particular, the following:
   (a) the supply of digitised products generally, including software and changes to or upgrades of software;
   (b) services providing or supporting a business or personal presence on an electronic network such as a website or a webpage;
   (c) services automatically generated from a computer via the Internet or an electronic network, in response to specific data input by the recipient;
   (d) the transfer for consideration of the right to put goods or services up for sale on an Internet site operating as an online market on which potential buyers make their bids by an automated procedure and on which the parties are notified of a sale by electronic mail automatically generated from a computer;
   (e) Internet Service Packages (ISP) of information in which the telecommunications component forms an ancillary and subordinate part (i.e. packages going beyond mere Internet access and including other elements such as content pages giving access to news, weather or travel reports; play grounds; website hosting; access to online debates etc.);
   (f) the services listed in Annex I.
3. Paragraph 1 shall not, in particular, cover the following:
   (a) radio and television broadcasting services;
   (b) telecommunications services;
   (c) goods, where the order and processing is done electronically;
   (d) CD-ROMs, floppy disks and similar tangible media;
   (e) printed matter, such as books, newsletters, newspapers or journals;
   (f) CDs and audiocassettes;
   (g) video cassettes and DVDs;
   (h) games on a CD-ROM;
   (i) services of professionals such as lawyers and financial consultants, who advise clients by e-mail;
   (j) teaching services, where the course content is delivered by a teacher over the Internet or an electronic network (namely via a remote link);
   (k) offline physical repair services of computer equipment;
   (l) offline data warehousing services;
   (m) advertising services, in particular as in newspapers, on posters and on television;
   (n) telephone helpdesk services;
   (o) teaching services purely involving correspondence courses, such as postal courses;
   (p) conventional auctioneers' services reliant on direct human intervention, irrespective of how bids are made;

(q) telephone services with a video component, otherwise known as videophone services;
(r) access to the Internet and World Wide Web;
(s) telephone services provided through the Internet.
(...)

CHAPTER V

PLACE OF TAXABLE TRANSACTIONS

SECTION 1

Concepts

Article 10

1. For the application of Articles 44 and 45 of Directive 2006/112/EC, the place where the business of a taxable person is established shall be the place where the functions of the business's central administration are carried out.
2. In order to determine the place referred to in paragraph1, account shall be taken of the place where essential decisions concerning the general management of the business are taken, the place where the registered office of the business is located and the place where management meets.
   Where these criteria do not allow the place of establishment of a business to be determined with certainty, the place where essential decisions concerning the general management of the business are taken shall take precedence.
3. The mere presence of a postal address may not be taken to be the place of establishment of a business of a taxable person.

Article 11

1. For the application of Article 44 of Directive 2006/112/EC, a 'fixed establishment' shall be any establishment, other than the place of establishment of a business referred to in Article 10 of this Regulation, characterised by a sufficient degree of permanence and a suitable structure in terms of human and technical resources to enable it to receive and use the services supplied to it for its own needs.
2. For the application of the following Articles, a 'fixed establishment' shall be any establishment, other than the place of establishment of a business referred to in Article 10 of this Regulation, characterised by a sufficient degree of

permanence and a suitable structure in terms of human and technical resources to enable it to provide the services which it supplies:

(a) Article 45 of Directive 2006/112/EC;
(b) from 1 January 2013, the second subparagraph of Article 56(2) of Directive 2006/112/EC;
(c) until 31 December 2014, Article 58 of Directive 2006/112/EC;
(d) Article 192a of Directive 2006/112/EC.

3. The fact of having a VAT identification number shall not in itself be sufficient to consider that a taxable person has a fixed establishment.

Article 12

For the application of Directive 2006/112/EC, the 'permanent address' of a natural person, whether or not a taxable person, shall be the address entered in the population or similar register, or the address indicated by that person to the relevant tax authorities, unless there is evidence that this address does not reflect reality.

Article 13

The place where a natural person 'usually resides', whether or not a taxable person, as referred to in Directive 2006/112/EC shall be the place where that natural person usually lives as a result of personal and occupational ties.

Where the occupational ties are in a country different from that of the personal ties, or where no occupational ties exist, the place of usual residence shall be determined by personal ties which show close links between the natural person and a place where he is living.
(...)

SECTION 4

Place of supply of services

(...)

Article 17

1. If the place of supply of services depends on whether the customer is a taxable or non-taxable person, the status of the customer shall be determined on the basis of Articles 9 to 13 and Article 43 of Directive 2006/112/EC.
2. Anon-taxable legal person who is identified or required to be identified for VAT purposes under point (b) of Article 214(1) of Directive 2006/112/EC because his intra-Community acquisitions of goods are subject to VAT or because he has exercised the option of making those operations subject to VAT shall be a taxable person within the meaning of Article 43 of that Directive.

Article 18

1. Unless he has information to the contrary, the supplier may regard a customer established within the Community as a taxable person:
   (a) where the customer has communicated his individual VAT identification number to him, and the supplier obtains confirmation of the validity of that identification number and f the associated name and address in accordance with Article 31 of Council Regulation (EC) No 904/2010 of 7 October 2010 on administrative cooperation and combating fraud in the field of value added tax;
   (b) where the customer has not yet received an individual VAT identification number, but informs the supplier that he has applied for it and the supplier obtains any other proof which demonstrates that the customer is a taxable person or a non-taxable legal person required to be identified for VAT purposes and carries out a reasonable level of verifi cation of the accuracy of the information provided by the customer, by normal commercial security measures such as those relating to identity or payment checks.
2. Unless he has information to the contrary, the supplier may regard a customer established within the Community as a non-taxable person when he can demonstrate that the customer has not communicated his individual VAT identification number to him.
3. Unless he has information to the contrary, the supplier may regard a customer established outside the Community as a taxable person:
   (a) if he obtains from the customer a certificate issued by the customer's competent tax authorities as confirmation that the customer is engaged in economic activities in order to enable him to obtain a refund of VAT under Council Directive 86/560/EEC of 17 November 1986 on the harmonization of the laws of the Member States relating to turnover taxes – Arrangements for the refund of value added tax to taxable persons not established in Community territory;
   (b) where the customer does not possess that certificate, if the supplier has the VAT number, or a similar number attributed to the customer by the country of establishment and used to identify businesses or any other proof which demonstrates that the customer is a taxable person and if the supplier carries out a reasonable level of verification of the accuracy of the information provided by the customer, by normal commercial security measures such as those relating to identity or payment checks.
   (...)

Article 20

Where a supply of services carried out for a taxable person, or a non-taxable legal person deemed to be a taxable person, falls within the scope of Article 44 of Directive 2006/112/EC, and where that taxable person is established in a single country, or, in

the absence of a place of establishment of a business or a fixed establishment, has his permanent address and usually resides in a single country, that supply of services shall be taxable in that country.
The supplier shall establish that place based on information from the customer, and verify that information by normal commercial security measures such as those relating to identity or payment checks.
The information may include the VAT identification number attributed by the Member State where the customer is established.

Article 21

Where a supply of services to a taxable person, or a non-taxable legal person deemed to be a taxable person, falls within the scope of Article 44 of Directive 2006/112/EC, and the taxable person is established in more than one country, that supply shall be taxable in the country where that taxable person has established his business.

However, where the service is provided to a fixed establishment of the taxable person located in a place other than that where the customer has established his business, that supply shall be taxable at the place of the fixed establishment receiving that service and using it for its own needs.

Where the taxable person does not have a place of estab lishment of a business or a fixed establishment, the supply shall be taxable at his permanent address or usual residence.

Article 22

1. In order to identify the customer's fixed establishment to which the service is provided, the supplier shall examine the nature and use of the service provided.
   Where the nature and use of the service provided do not enable him to identify the fixed establishment to which the service is provided, the supplier, in identifying that fixed establishment, shall pay particular attention to whether the contract, the order form and the VAT identification number attributed by the Member State of the customer and communicated to him by the customer identify the fixed establishment as the customer of the service and whether the fixed establishment is the entity paying for the service.
   Where the customer's fixed establishment to which the service is provided cannot be determined in accordance with the first and second subparagraphs of this paragraph or where services covered by Article 44 of Directive 2006/112/EC are supplied to a taxable person under a contract covering one or more services used in an unidentifiable and non-quantifiable manner, the supplier may legitimately consider that the services have been supplied at the place where the customer has established his business.
2. The application of this Article shall be without prejudice to the customer's obligations.

Article 23

1. From 1 January 2013, where, in accordance with the first subparagraph of Article 56(2) of Directive 2006/112/EC, a supply of services is taxable at the place where the customer is established, or, in the absence of an establishment, where he has his permanent address or usually resides, the supplier shall establish that place based on factual information provided by the customer, and verify that information by normal commercial security measures such as those relating to identity or payment checks.
2. Where, in accordance with Articles 58 and 59 of Directive 2006/112/EC, a supply of services is taxable at the place where the customer is established, or, in the absence of an establishment, where he has his permanent address or usually resides, the supplier shall establish that place based on factual information provided by the customer, and verify that information by normal commercial security measures such as those relating to identity or payment checks.

Article 24

(...)

2. Where services covered by Articles 58 and 59 of Directive 2006/112/EC are supplied to a non-taxable person who is established in more than one country or has his permanent address in one country and his usual residence in another, priority shall be given to the place that best ensures taxation at the place of actual consumption when determining the place of supply of those services.

(...)

CHAPTER X

OBLIGATIONS OF TAXABLE PERSONS AND CERTAIN NON- TAXABLE PERSONS

(...)

Article 53

1. For the application of Article 192a of Directive 2006/112/EC, a fixed establishment of the taxable person shall be taken into consideration only when it is characterised by a sufficient degree of permanence and a suitable structure in terms of human and technical resources to enable it to make the supply of goods or services in which it intervenes.
2. Where a taxable person has a fixed establishment within the territory of the Member State where the VAT is due, that establishment shall be considered as

not intervening in the supply of goods or services within the meaning of point (b) of Article 192a of Directive 2006/112/EC, unless the technical and human resources of that fixed establishment are used by him for transactions inherent in the fulfilment of the taxable supply of those goods or services made within that Member State, before or during this fulfilment.
Where the resources of the fixed establishment are only used for administrative support tasks such as accounting, invoicing and collection of debt-claims, they shall not be regarded as being used for the fulfilment of the supply of goods or services.
However, if an invoice is issued under the VAT identification number attributed by the Member State of the fixed establishment, that fixed establishment shall be regarded as having intervened in the supply of goods or services made in that Member State unless there is proof to the contrary.

Article 54

Where a taxable person has established his place of business within the territory of the Member State where the VAT is due, Article 192a of Directive 2006/112/EC shall not apply whether or not that place of business intervenes in the supply of goods or services he makes within that Member State.
(...)

CHAPTER XI

SPECIAL SCHEMES

(...)

Article 58

Where, in the course of a calendar quarter, a non-established taxable person using the special scheme for electronically supplied services provided for in Articles 357 to 369 of Directive 2006/112/EC meets at least one of the criteria for exclusion laid down in Article 363 of that Directive, the Member State of identification shall exclude that non-established taxable person from the special scheme. In such cases the non-established taxable person may subsequently be excluded from the special scheme at any time during that quarter.
In respect of services supplied electronically prior to exclusion but during the calendar quarter in which exclusion occurs, the non-established taxable person shall submit a VAT return for the entire quarter in accordance with Article 364 of Directive 2006/112/EC. The requirement to submit this return shall have no effect on the requirement, if any, to be identified for VAT purposes in a Member State under the normal rules.

Article 59

Any return period (calendar quarter) within the meaning of Article 364 of Directive 2006/112/EC shall be a separate return period.

Article 60

Once a VAT return has been submitted as provided for under Article 364 of Directive 2006/112/EC, any subsequent changes to the figures contained therein may be made only by means of an amendment to that return and not by an adjustment to a subsequent return.

Article 61

Amounts on VAT returns made under the special scheme for electronically supplied services provided for in Articles 357 to 369 of Directive 2006/112/EC shall not be rounded up or down to the nearest whole monetary unit. The exact amount of VAT shall be reported and remitted.

Article 62

A Member State of identification which receives a payment in excess of that resulting from the VAT return submitted for electronically supplied services under Article 364 of Directive 2006/112/EC shall reimburse the overpaid amount directly to the taxable person concerned.
Where the Member State of identification has received an amount pursuant to a VAT return subsequently found to be incorrect, and that Member State has already distributed that amount among the Member States of consumption, those Member States shall directly reimburse the overpayment to the non-established taxable person and inform the Member State of identification of the adjustment to be made.

Article 63

Amounts of VAT paid under Article 367 of Directive 2006/112/EC shall be specific to the VAT return submitted pursuant to Article 364 of that Directive. Any subsequent amendments to the amounts paid may be effected only by reference to that return and may not be allocated to another return, or adjusted on a subsequent return.

APPENDIX IV

Council Implementing Regulation (EU) No 1042/2013 of 7 October 2013 Amending Implementing Regulation (EU) No 282/2011 as Regards the Place of Supply of Services, O.J. 26 October 2013, L284/1

Selected excerpts:

Article 1

Implementing Regulation (EU) No 282/2011 is amended as follows:
(...)

(2) Chapter V is amended as follows:

(a) in Section 1, the following Articles are inserted:

'*Article 13a*

The place where a non-taxable legal person is established, as referred to in the first subparagraph of Article 56(2) and Articles 58 and 59 of Directive 2006/112/EC, shall be:

1. (a) the place where the functions of its central administration are carried out; or
2. (b) the place of any other establishment characterised by a sufficient degree of permanence and a suitable structure in terms of human and technical resources to enable it to receive and use the services supplied to it for its own needs.
   (...)

(b) in Article 18(2), the following subparagraph is added:

> 'However, irrespective of information to the contrary, the supplier of telecommunications, broadcasting or electronically supplied services may regard a customer established within the Community as a non-taxable person as long as that customer has not communicated his individual VAT identification number to him.';

(c) Article 24 is replaced by the following:

'Article 24

Where services covered by the first subparagraph of Article 56(2) or Articles 58 and 59 of Directive 2006/112/EC are supplied to a non-taxable person who is established in more than one country or who has his permanent address in one country and his usual residence in another, priority shall be given:

(a) in the case of a non-taxable legal person, to the place referred to in point (a) of Article 13a of this Regulation, unless there is evidence that the service is used at the establishment referred to in point (b) of that article;
(b) in the case of a natural person, to the place where he usually resides, unless there is evidence that the service is used at his permanent address.';

(d) Section 4 is amended as follows:

(i) the following subsections are inserted:

Subsection 3a

Presumptions for the location of the customer

Article 24a

1. For the application of Articles 44, 58 and 59a of Directive 2006/112/EC, where a supplier of telecommunications, broadcasting or electronically supplied services provides those services at a location such as a telephone box, a telephone kiosk, a wi-fi hot spot, an internet café, a restaurant or a hotel lobby where the physical presence of the recipient of the service at that location is needed for the service to be provided to him by that supplier, it shall be presumed that the customer is established, has his permanent address or usually resides at the place of that location and that the service is effectively used and enjoyed there.
2. If the location referred to in paragraph1of this Article is on board a ship, aircraft or train carrying out a passenger transport operation effected within the Community pursuant to Articles 37 and 57 of Directive 2006/112/EC,

the country of the location shall be the country of departure of the passenger transport operation.

Article 24b

For the application of Article 58 of Directive 2006/112/EC, where telecommunications, broad casting or electronically supplied services are supplied to a non-taxable person:

(a) through his fixed land line, it shall be presumed that the customer is established, has his permanent address or usually resides at the place of installation of the fixed land line;
(b) through mobile networks, it shall be presumed that the place where the customer is established, has his permanent address or usually resides is the country identified by the mobile country code of the SIM card used when receiving those services;
(c) for which the use of a decoder or similar device or a viewing card is needed and a fixed land line is not used, it shall be presumed that the customer is established, has his permanent address or usually resides at the place where that decoder or similar device is located, or if that place is not known, at the place to which the viewing card is sent with a view to being used there;
(d) under circumstances other than those referred to in Article 24a and in points (a), (b) and (c) of this Article, it shall be presumed that the customer is established, has his permanent address or usually resides at the place identified as such by the supplier on the basis of two items of non-contradictory evidence as listed in Article 24f of this Regulation.

Article 24c

For the application of Article 56(2) of Directive 2006/112/EC, where the hiring, other than short-term hiring, of means of transport is supplied to a non-taxable person, it shall be presumed that the customer is established, has his permanent address or usually resides at the place identified as such by the supplier on the basis of two items of non- contradictory evidence as listed in Article 24e of this Regulation.

Subsection 3b

Rebuttal of presumptions

Article 24d

1. Where a supplier supplies a service listed in Article 58 of Directive 2006/112/EC, he may rebut a presumption referred to in Article 24a or in

point (a), (b) or (c) of Article 24b of this Regulation on the basis of three items of non-contradictory evidence indicating that the customer is established, has his permanent address or usually resides else where.

2. A tax authority may rebut presumptions that have been made under Article 24a, 24b or 24c where there are indications of misuse or abuse by the supplier.

Subsection 3c

Evidence for the identification of the location of the customer and rebuttal of presumptions

Article 24e

For the purposes of applying the rules in Article 56(2) of Directive 2006/112/EC and fulfilling the requirements of Article 24c of this Regulation, the following shall, in particular, serve as evidence:

1. (a) the billing address of the customer;
2. (b) bank details such as the location of the bank account used for payment or the billing address of the customer held by that bank;
3. (c) registration details of the means of transport hired by the customer, if registration of that means of transport is required at the place where it is used, or other similar information;
4. (d) other commercially relevant information.

Article 24f

For the purpose of applying the rules in Article 58 of Directive 2006/112/EC and fulfilling the requirements of point (d) of Article 24b or Article 24d(1) of this Regulation, the following shall, in particular, serve as evidence:

(a) the billing address of the customer;
(b) the internet Protocol (IP) address of the device used by the customer or any method of geolocation;
(c) bank details such as the location of the bank account used for payment or the billing address of the customer held by that bank;
(d) the Mobile Country Code (MCC) of the Inter national Mobile Subscriber Identity (IMSI) stored on the Subscriber Identity Module (SIM) card used by the customer;
(e) the location of the customer's fixed land line through which the service is supplied to him;
(f) other commercially relevant information.';

Article 2

For telecommunications, radio and television broadcasting or electronically supplied services supplied by a supplier established within the Community to a non-taxable person who is established, has his permanent address or usually resides there, the following shall apply:

(a) the place of supply in respect of each chargeable event that occurs before 1 January 2015 shall be the place where the supplier is established, as provided for in Article 45 of Directive 2006/112/EC, regardless of when the supply, or continuous supply, of those services is completed;
(b) the place of supply in respect of each chargeable event that occurs on or after 1 January 2015 shall be the place where the customer is established, has his permanent address or usually resides, regardless of when the supply, or continuous supply, of those services commenced;
(c) where the chargeable event occurred before 1 January 2015 in the Member State where the supplier is established, no tax shall become chargeable in the Member State of the customer on or after 1 January 2015 in relation to the same chargeable event.

APPENDIX V

Explanatory Notes on the EU VAT Changes to the Place of Supply of Telecommunications, Broadcasting and Electronic Services That Enter into Force in 2015 (Council Regulation 1042/2013)

The full text of the explanatory note is available at http://ec.europa.eu/taxation_customs/resources/documents/taxation/vat/how_vat_works/telecom/explanatory_notes_2015_en.pdf. Clarifications concerning customer identification and the presumptions for customer location can be found at p. 45 to 74.

APPENDIX VI

Council Regulation 967/2012 of 9 October 2012 Amending Implementing Regulation (EU) No 282/2011 as Regards the Special Schemes for Non-established Taxable Persons Supplying Telecommunications Services, Broadcasting Services or Electronic Services to Non-taxable Persons

Full text:

THE COUNCIL OF THE EUROPEAN UNION,
Having regard to the Treaty on the Functioning of the European Union,
Having regard to Council Directive 2006/112/EC of 28 November 2006 on the common system of value added tax[(1)], and in particular Article 397 thereof,
Having regard to the proposal from the European Commission,
Whereas:

(1) Directive 2006/112/EC provides that as from 1 January 2015, all telecommunications, broadcasting and electronic services are to be taxed in the Member State in which the customer is established or has his permanent address or usual residence (hereinafter the 'Member State of consumption') regardless of where the taxable person supplying those services is established.

(2) In order to facilitate compliance with fiscal obligations where such services are supplied to non-taxable persons, a special scheme has been put in place for taxable persons established within the Community but not in the Member

(1) OJ L 347, 11.12.2006, p. 1.

State where the services are supplied (hereinafter the 'Union scheme'). The other special scheme, for taxable persons not established within the Community (hereinafter the 'non-Union scheme') currently in place, has been extended to cover all of those services. This will enable non-established taxable persons to designate a Member State of identification as a single point of electronic contact for value added tax (VAT) identification and VAT declarations.

(3) A taxable person with establishments in more than one Member State should, under the Union scheme, be able to designate any of the Member States concerned as the Member State of identification, unless he has his place of business within the Community. In that case the Member State of identification is where the taxable person has his place of business.

(4) In order to avoid disproportionate burdens for taxable persons using the Union scheme, it should be clarified how a change of the Member State of identification can be effected where the taxable person changes his fixed establishment or business establishment in such a way that a change in the Member State of identification is necessary in order for him to continue using the scheme.

(5) Telecommunications, broadcasting and electronic services supplied in Member States where the taxable person has established his business or has a fixed establishment are not covered by either of the special schemes. It should be made clear that such supplies should be declared directly to the Member State concerned.

(6) Since both of the special schemes are optional, a non-established taxable person is able to decide at any time to cease using them. It is necessary to clarify when such decisions take effect.

(7) However, to avoid unnecessary burdens for tax authorities, a taxable person who decides to cease using one of the special schemes should, for a certain period, be refused re-entry into that scheme.

(8) To keep the registration details in its database up-to-date, the Member State of identification relies on the information received from the taxable person. In order to ensure that databases are updated without delay, it is necessary to lay down a time limit within which the taxable person using the special schemes should communicate any relevant information on ceasing or changing activities and on changes to any relevant information already supplied.

(9) A VAT identification number needs to be allocated to a non-established taxable person who wants to make use of a special scheme. To prevent unintended retroactive use by taxable persons who are already identified for VAT purposes, it is necessary to clarify from which moment the special schemes should apply.

(10) To avoid doubt as to which Member State has jurisdiction, the Member State which may exclude a taxable person from using a special scheme should be specified. The circumstances in which that Member State is to

take its decision on exclusion should also be specified, as should the time from which that decision takes effect.

(11) The concept of a non-established taxable person's cessation of activities eligible for one of the special schemes should be clarified, as should the concept of persistent failure on the part of a non-established taxable person.

(12) To promote compliance and avoid unnecessary burdens for tax authorities, a taxable person who is excluded from one of the special schemes due to persistent failure, should, for a certain period, be refused entry to any of the special schemes.

(13) It should be made clear that where a taxable person ceases to use one of the special schemes, is excluded from one of the special schemes, or changes the Member State of identification, all tax obligations regarding return periods prior to that cessation, exclusion or change are to be discharged with the Member State which was the Member State of identification prior to the cessation, exclusion or change.

(14) Each return period should be treated separately so as to facilitate control by the Member States of consumption and amendments should be made only to the VAT return concerned.

(15) It is appropriate, for reasons of control, to require non-established taxable persons to submit VAT returns to Member States of identification, even where no services have been supplied during the return period. It should also be clarified that the exact amount of VAT must be stated without any rounding up or down.

(16) It is necessary, in respect of amendments to VAT returns, to establish a time limit within which returns can be submitted electronically to the Member State of identification. Member States of consumption should, in any event, be able to accept or request relevant information directly from the taxable person and process VAT assessments according to their national rules.

(17) Where the Member State of identification does not have the euro as its currency, non-established taxable persons should be bound by the decision of that Member State as to the currency in which all VAT returns under the special schemes should be made.

(18) Without affecting the national rules of Member States of consumption on offsetting excess payments and for the sole purpose of ensuring efficient administration of the special schemes by the Member State of identification and avoiding an excessive administrative burden on both that Member State and the Member States of consumption, it should be ensured that taxable persons cannot allocate amounts of VAT paid to more than one return, whether from the outset or by subsequent adjustment.

(19) In the case of non-payment, underpayment or payment in excess made by non-established taxable persons and with regard to interest, penalties and other incidental charges, it is important to specify the respective obligations

of the Member State of identification and the Member States of consumption so as to facilitate the collection of VAT and to ensure that the right amount is paid in respect of the services supplied under the special schemes.

(20) The records kept by non-established taxable persons need to be sufficiently detailed to enable the tax authorities of Member States of consumption to verify that the VAT return is correct. What information is, as a minimum, required to be kept in such records should therefore be specified.

(21) To facilitate the implementation of the special schemes and with a view to enabling services supplied as of 1 January 2015 to be covered by those schemes, it should be possible for non-established taxable persons to submit their registration details to the Member State which is designated by them as Member State of identification as from 1 October 2014.

(22) Council Implementing Regulation (EU) No 282/2011[2] should therefore be amended accordingly,

HAS ADOPTED THIS REGULATION:

Article 1

In Implementing Regulation (EU) No 282/2011, Section 2 of Chapter XI is replaced by the following:

'SECTION 2

Special schemes for non-established taxable persons supplying telecommunications services, broadcasting services or electronic services to non-taxable persons (Articles 358 to 369k of Directive 2006/112/EC)

Subsection 1

Definitions

Article 57a

For the purposes of this Section, the following definitions shall apply:

(1) "non-Union scheme" means the special scheme for telecommunications services, broadcasting services or electronic services supplied by taxable persons not established within the Community provided for in Section 2 of Chapter 6 of Title XII of Directive 2006/112/EC;

(2) "Union scheme" means the special scheme for telecommunications services, broadcasting services or electronic services supplied by taxable persons established within the Community but not established in the Member State of

(2) OJ L 77, 23.3.2011, p. 1.

consumption provided for in Section 3 of Chapter 6 of Title XII of Directive 2006/112/EC;

(3) "special scheme" means the "non-Union scheme" and/or the "Union scheme" as the context requires;

(4) "taxable person" means a taxable person not established within the Community as defined in point (1) of Article 358a of Directive 2006/112/EC, or a taxable person not established in the Member State of consumption, as defined in point (1) of the first paragraph of Article 369a of that Directive.

Subsection 2

Application of the Union scheme

Article 57b

Where a taxable person using the Union scheme has established his business within the Community, the Member State in which his place of business is established shall be the Member State of identification.
Where a taxable person using the Union scheme has established his business outside the Community, but has more than one fixed establishment in the Community, he may choose any Member State in which he has a fixed establishment as the Member State of identification, in accordance with the second paragraph of Article 369a of Directive 2006/112/EC.

Subsection 3

Scope of the Union scheme

Article 57c

The Union scheme shall not apply to telecommunications, broadcasting or electronic services supplied in a Member State where the taxable person has established his business or has a fixed establishment. The supplies of those services shall be declared to the competent tax authorities of that Member State in the VAT return as provided for under Article 250 of Directive 2006/112/EC.

Subsection 4

Identification

Article 57d

When a taxable person informs the Member State of identification that he intends to make use of one of the special schemes, that special scheme shall apply as from the first day of the following calendar quarter.

However, where the first supply of services to be covered by that special scheme takes place before the date referred to in the first paragraph, the special scheme shall apply as from the date of that first supply, provided the taxable person informs the Member State of identification of the commencement of his activities to be covered by the scheme no later than the tenth day of the month following that first supply.

Article 57e

The Member State of identification shall identify the taxable person using the Union scheme by means of his VAT identification number as referred to in Articles 214 and 215 of Directive 2006/112/EC.

Article 57f

1. Where a taxable person using the Union scheme ceases to meet the conditions of the definition laid down in point (2) of the first paragraph of Article 369a of Directive 2006/112/EC, the Member State in which he has been identified shall cease to be the Member State of identification. Where that taxable person still fulfils the conditions for using that special scheme, he shall, to continue using that scheme, indicate as the new Member State of identification the Member State in which he has established his business or, if he has not established his business in the Community, a Member State where he has a fixed establishment.
2. Where the Member State of identification changes in accordance with paragraph 1, that change shall apply as from the date on which the taxable person ceases to have a business establishment or a fixed establishment in the Member State previously indicated as the Member State of identification.

Article 57g

A taxable person using a special scheme may cease using that special scheme regardless of whether he continues to supply services which can be eligible for that special scheme. The taxable person shall inform the Member State of identification at least 15 days before the end of the calendar quarter prior to that in which he intends to cease using the scheme. Cessation shall be effective as of the first day of the next calendar quarter.
VAT obligations relating to supplies of telecommunications, broadcasting or electronic services arising after the date on which the cessation became effective shall be discharged directly with the tax authorities of the Member State of consumption concerned.
Where a taxable person ceases using a special scheme in accordance with the first paragraph, he shall be excluded from using that scheme in any Member State for two calendar quarters from the date of cessation.

Subsection 5

Reporting obligations

Article 57h

1. A taxable person shall, no later than the tenth day of the next month, inform the Member State of identification by electronic means of:
   — the cessation of his activities covered by a special scheme,
   — any changes to his activities covered by a special scheme whereby he no longer meets the c conditions necessary for using that special scheme, and
   — any changes to the information previously provided to the Member State of identification.
2. Where the Member State of identification changes in accordance with Article 57f, the taxable person shall inform both relevant Member States of the change no later than the tenth day of the month following the change of establishment. He shall communicate to the new Member State of identification the registration details required when a taxable person makes use of a special scheme for the first time.

Subsection 6

Exclusion

Article 58

Where at least one of the criteria for exclusion laid down in Article 363 or Article 369e of Directive 2006/112/EC applies to a taxable person using one of the special schemes, the Member State of identification shall exclude that taxable person from that scheme. Only the Member State of identification can exclude a taxable person from using one of the special schemes.
The Member State of identification shall base its decision on exclusion on any information available, including information provided by any other Member State.
The exclusion shall be effective as from the first day of the calendar quarter following the day on which the decision on exclusion is sent by electronic means to the taxable person.
However where the exclusion is due to a change of place of business or fixed establishment, the exclusion shall be effective as from the date of that change.

Article 58a

A taxable person using a special scheme who has, for a period of eight consecutive calendar quarters, made no supplies of services covered by that scheme in any Member State of consumption, shall be assumed to have ceased his taxable activities within the meaning of point (b) of Article 363 or point (b) of Article 369e of Directive 2006/112/EC respectively. This cessation shall not preclude him from using a special scheme if he recommences his activities covered by either scheme.

Article 58b

1. Where a taxable person is excluded from one of the special schemes for persistent failure to comply with the rules relating to that scheme, that taxable person shall remain excluded from using either scheme in any Member State for eight calendar quarters following the calendar quarter during which the taxable person was excluded.
2. A taxable person shall be regarded as having persistently failed to comply with the rules relating to one of the special schemes, within the meaning of point (d) of Article 363 or point (d) of Article 369e of Directive 2006/112/EC, in at least the following cases:
   (a) where reminders pursuant to Article 60a have been issued to him by the Member State of identification, for three immediately preceding calendar quarters and the VAT return has not been submitted for each and every one of these calendar quarters within 10 days after the reminder has been sent;
   (b) where reminders pursuant to Article 63a have been issued to him by the Member State of identification, for three immediately preceding calendar quarters and the full amount of VAT declared has not been paid by him for each and every one of these calendar quarters within 10 days after the reminder has been sent, except where the remaining unpaid amount is less than EUR 100 for each calendar quarter;
   (c) where following a request from the Member State of identification or the Member State of consumption and one month after a subsequent reminder by the Member State of identification, he has failed to make electronically available the records referred to in Articles 369 and 369k of Directive 2006/112/EC.

Article 58c

A taxable person who has been excluded from one of the special schemes shall discharge all VAT obligations relating to supplies of telecommunications, broadcasting or electronic services arising after the date on which the exclusion became effective directly with the tax authorities of the Member State of consumption concerned.

Subsection 7

VAT return

Article 59

1. Any return period within the meaning of Article 364 or Article 369f of Directive 2006/112/EC shall be a separate return period.
2. Where, in accordance with the second paragraph of Article 57d, a special scheme applies from the date of the first supply, the taxable person shall submit a separate VAT return for the calendar quarter during which the first supply took place.
3. Where a taxable person has been registered under each of the special schemes during a return period, he shall submit VAT returns and make the corresponding payments to the Member State of identification for each scheme in respect of the supplies made and the periods covered by that scheme.
4. Where the Member State of identification changes in accordance with Article 57f after the first day of the calendar quarter in question, the taxable person shall submit VAT returns and make corresponding payments to both the former and the new Member State of identification covering the supplies made during the respective periods in which the Member States have been Member State of identification.

Article 59a

Where a taxable person using a special scheme has supplied no services in any Member State of consumption under that special scheme during a return period, he shall submit a VAT return indicating that no supplies have been made during that period (a nil-VAT return).

Article 60

Amounts on VAT returns made under the special schemes shall not be rounded up or down to the nearest whole monetary unit. The exact amount of VAT shall be reported and remitted.

Article 60a

The Member State of identification shall remind, by electronic means, taxable persons who have failed to submit a VAT return under Article 364 or Article 369f of Directive 2006/112/EC, of their obligation to submit such a return. The Member State of identification shall issue the reminder on the tenth day following that on which the return should have been submitted, and shall inform the other Member States by electronic means that a reminder has been issued.

Any subsequent reminders and steps taken to assess and collect the VAT shall be the responsibility of the Member State of consumption concerned.

Notwithstanding any reminders issued, and any steps taken, by a Member State of consumption, the taxable person shall submit the VAT return to the Member State of identification.

Article 61

1. Changes to the figures contained in a VAT return shall, after its submission, be made only by means of amendments to that return and not by adjustments to a subsequent return.
2. The amendments referred to in paragraph 1 shall be submitted electronically to the Member State of identification within three years of the date on which the initial return was required to be submitted.
   However, the rules of the Member State of consumption on assessments and amendments shall remain unaffected.

Article 61a

If a taxable person:

(a) ceases to use one of the special schemes;
(b) is excluded from one of the special schemes; or
(c) changes the Member State of identification in accordance with Article 57f;

he shall submit his final VAT return and the corresponding payment, and any corrections to or late submissions of previous returns, and the corresponding payments, to the Member State which was the Member State of identification at the time of the cessation, exclusion or change.

Subsection 8

Currency

Article 61b

Where a Member State of identification whose currency is not the euro determines that VAT returns are to be made out in its national currency, that determination shall apply to the VAT returns of all taxable persons using the special schemes.

Subsection 9

Payments

Article 62

Without prejudice to the third paragraph of Article 63a, and to Article 63b, a taxable person shall make any payment to the Member State of identification.

Payments of VAT made by the taxable person under Article 367 or Article 369i of Directive 2006/112/EC shall be specific to the VAT return submitted pursuant to Article

364 or Article 369f of that Directive. Any subsequent adjustment to the amounts paid shall be effected by the taxable person only by reference to that return and may neither be allocated to another return, nor adjusted on a subsequent return. Each payment shall refer to the reference number of that specific return.

Article 63

A Member State of identification which receives a payment in excess of that resulting from the VAT return submitted under Article 364 or Article 369f of Directive 2006/112/EC shall reimburse the overpaid amount directly to the taxable person concerned.

Where a Member State of identification has received an amount in respect of a VAT return subsequently found to be incorrect, and that Member State has already distributed that amount to the Member States of consumption, those Member States of consumption shall each reimburse their respective part of any overpaid amount directly to the taxable person.

However, where overpayments relate to periods up to and including the last return period in 2018, the Member State of identification shall reimburse the relevant portion of the corresponding part of the amount retained in accordance with Article 46(3) of Regulation (EU) No 904/2010 and the Member State of consumption shall reimburse the overpayment less the amount that shall be reimbursed by the Member State of identification.

The Member States of consumption shall, by electronic means, inform the Member State of identification of the amount of those reimbursements.

Article 63a

Where a taxable person has submitted a VAT return under Article 364 or Article 369f of Directive 2006/112/EC, but no payment has been made or the payment is less than that resulting from the return, the Member State of identification shall, by electronic means on the tenth day following the latest day on which the payment should have been made in accordance with Article 367 or Article 369i of Directive 2006/112/EC, remind the taxable person of any VAT payment outstanding.

The Member State of identification shall by electronic means inform the Member States of consumption that the reminder has been sent.

Any subsequent reminders and steps taken to collect the VAT shall be the responsibility of the Member State of consumption concerned. When such subsequent reminders have been issued by a Member State of consumption, the corresponding VAT shall be paid to that Member State.

The Member State of consumption shall, by electronic means, inform the Member State of identification that a reminder has been issued.

Article 63b

Where no VAT return has been submitted, or where the VAT return has been submitted late or is incomplete or incorrect, or where the payment of VAT is late, any interest, penalties or any other charges shall be calculated and assessed by the Member State of consumption. The taxable person shall pay such interests, penalties or any other charges directly to the Member State of consumption.

Subsection 10

Records

Article 63c

1. In order to be regarded as sufficiently detailed within the meaning of Articles 369 and 369k of Directive 2006/112/EC, the records kept by the taxable person shall contain the following information:
   (a) the Member State of consumption to which the service is supplied;
   (b) the type of service supplied;
   (c) the date of the supply of service;
   (d) the taxable amount indicating the currency used;
   (e) any subsequent increase or reduction of the taxable amount;
   (f) the VAT rate applied;
   (g) the amount of VAT payable indicating the currency used;
   (h) the date and amount of payments received;
   (i) any payments on account received before the supply of service;
   (j) where an invoice is issued, the information contained on the invoice;
   (k) the name of the customer, where known to the taxable person;
   (l) the information used to determine the place where the customer is established or has his permanent address or usually resides.
2. The information referred to in paragraph 1 shall be recorded by the taxable person in such a way that it can be made available by electronic means without delay and for each single service supplied.'

Article 2

This Regulation shall enter into force on the twentieth day following that of its publication in the Official Journal of the European Union.

It shall apply from 1 January 2015.

However, Member States shall allow non-established taxable persons to submit the information required under Article 360 or Article 369c of Directive 2006/112/EC for registration under the special schemes for non-established taxable persons supplying

telecommunications services, broadcasting services or electronic services to non-taxable persons as from 1 October 2014.
This Regulation shall be binding in its entirety and directly applicable in all Member States.

Done at Luxembourg, 9 October 2012. For the Council The President V. SHIARLY

APPENDIX VII

European Commission - Tax Administration and Fight against Tax Fraud: Information for Businesses Signing Up for the MOSS: Additional Guidelines on Auditing under the MOSS

Full text:

A. New rules: from 1 January 2015

Supplies of telecoms/broadcasting/electronic services to consumers will be taxed in the country where the customer is established (the 'member state of consumption' or MSC).

Businesses can designate a country, a 'member state of identification' (MSI), to be their single contact point for VAT identification, submitting VAT returns and paying the VAT due in all MSCs (via a website in their MSI).

To make MOSS as straightforward and easy as possible for businesses to register and use, guidelines in relation to the audit of MOSS-data will complement the practical guide mentioned above (especially for SMEs and non-EU businesses).

B. Guidelines for audits

As MOSS VAT returns will include tax due in a number of MSCs, it is important for national tax authorities to agree on:

- how best to contact businesses as part of an audit;
- the method businesses should use to provide the information required by an audit;

To this end, we have developed some guidelines for standard audit and control activities (*these are recommendations only – they are not binding over national rules*). For each guideline, there is a list of those countries that have agreed to apply them.

C. How to contact taxable persons as part of an audit

a. Initial contact with taxable persons should, where possible, be routed through the MSI. Once initial contact is made, a case by case approach is advisable as in some circumstances direct contact between the MSC and business could be necessary. The recommendation above is without prejudice to the right of a MSC tax authority to make direct contact with the taxable person to obtain the information listed in Article 63(c) of Regulation (EU) 967/2012 and in some circumstances it may even be necessary for an MSC to make direct contact with the business for related purposes (e.g. for additional clarification relating data already received).

   Countries that will apply this recommendation: BE, BG, DK, EE, ES, FI, HR, IE, LT, LU, LV, NL, PL, PT, RO, SE, SI, UK.
b. MSI should use their normal national procedures when contacting taxable persons registered for the EU scheme in the MSI. They should use e-mail for an initial contact with non-EU scheme users registered in the MSI.

   Countries that will apply this recommendation: BE, BG, CZ, DK, EE, ES, HR, HU, IE, LU, LV, MT, NL, PL, PT,RO, SE, SI, SK, UK.
c. Where there is contact from the MSC, this should be initiated via the taxable person's contact e-mail address (for both EU and non-EU businesses). As this is an electronic system and the main contact information is the taxable person's email address, this should be used to initiate contact if the taxable person is not established in the Member State making contact.

   Countries that will apply this recommendation: BE, BG, CZ, DK, EE, ES, HR, HU, IE, LT, LU, LV, MT, NL, PL, PT, SE, SI, SK, UK

D. How to request information from traders as part of an audit

d. The best method for the exchange of information should be agreed between taxable person and the tax authority and should depend on what electronic means is available to both. One possibility is to use a standard audit file for MOSS (SAF-MOSS), in xml format. Member States will accept the SAF-MOSS format (in XML) if a business chooses to use it to supply the requested information.

   Countries that will apply this recommendation: AT, BE, BG, CZ, DK, EE, ES, FI, HR, HU, IE, LT, LU, MT, NL, PL, PT, SE, SI, SK, UK

Bibliography

Th. S. Adams (1921): 'Fundamental Problems of Federal Income Taxation' 35 Quarterly Journal of Economics at p. 527.

C. Amand and K. Boucquez (2011): 'A New Defence for Victims of EU Missing-Trader Fraud?', 22 International VAT Monitor of July/August 2011 at 234.

S. P. Anderson, J. J. Gabszewicz (2005): 'The Media and Advertising: A Tale of Two-Sided Markets', CORE Discussion Paper 2005/88.

C. Anderson (2009): 'The Future of a Radical Price: The Economics of Abundance and Why Zero Pricing Is Changing the Face of Business', Random House, 2009.

C. Arena (1947): 'Principi di Scienza delle Finanze e Statistica Economica', 3rd ed. of 1947.

M. Armstrong (2006): 'Competition in Two-Sided Markets', 37 RAND Journal of Economics 3 of Autumn 2006 at 668–691.

Ph. Baker (1999): 'Transnational Enforcement of Tax Liabilities', British Tax Law Review of 1999 at 313–318.

A. Bal (2012): 'Tax Implications of Cloud Computing – How Real Taxes Fit into Virtual Clouds', 66 Bulletin for International Taxation 6 of June 2012 at 335–339.

A. Bal (2014): 'The Myth of Taxing Cloud Computing under EU VAT', 25 International VAT Monitor of November/December 2014 at 343–349.

A. Bal (2015): 'Taxing Virtual Currency: Challenges and Solutions', 43 Intertax 5 of 2015 at 388.

S. Basu (2007): 'Global Perspectives on E-Commerce Taxation Law', Ashgate Publishing, 2007.

U. Bernitz (2012): 'Europarättens genomslag', Norstedts Juridik 2012.

R. Bird (2005): 'Taxing Electronic Commerce: The End of the Beginning', Paper 0502 University of Toronto series International Tax Program Papers.

F. Bolkestein (2003): 'Fiscalité européenne: la Convention fait fausse route', Le Monde of 12 June 2003 Horizons-Débats at 16.

Boston Consulting Group (2011): 'Turning Local: From Madrid to Moscow, the Internet Is Going Native', September 2011.

Boston Consulting Group (2012): 'The Connected World: The Internet Economy in the G-20', March 2012.

M. Casanegra de Jantscher (1990): 'Administering the VAT', in M. Gillis, C.S. Shoup, G.P. Sicat, (eds.) (1990): 'Value Added Taxation in Developing Countries', Washington: World Bank, 1990 at 171–179.

O. Castendyk, E.J. Dommering, A. Scheuer (2008): 'European Media Law', Wolters Kluwer Law & Business, 2008 at 105.

P. Centore (1998): 'Prestazioni gratuite di servizi fra normativa comunitaria e nazionale', GT – Rivista di giurisprudenza tributaria 3 of 1998 at 220.

P. Centore (2002): 'Niente IVA in entrata e niente IVA in uscita: il principio dell "only once"', Corriere tributario 28 of 2002 at 2556.

P. Centore (2009): 'Enti non commerciali: profili iva nazionali e comunitari', Enti non profit 11 of 2009.

P. Centore (2011): 'Il campione gratuito in bilico fra imponibilità e non soggezione IVA, GT', Rivista di giurisprudenza tributaria 2 of 2011 at 97.

P. Centore and M. T. Sutich (2014): 'Taxation and Digital Economy: Europe Is Ready', 42 Intertax 12 of 2014 at 785.

A. Christians (2007): 'Hard Law & Soft Law in International Taxation', University of Wisconsin Law School, Legal Studies Research Paper Series, Paper No. 1049 of May 2007.

E. Cintolesi, G. Mocci (2001): 'Web economy: aspetti di natura tributaria nella permuta di banners o per lo scambio di link', Il Fisco 26 of 2001.

S. Claessens, T. Corbette (2014): 'Intermediary Delivery and Third Party Billing: Implications for the Operation of VAT Systems Around the World', conference 'The Future of VAT in a Digital Global Economy' Vienna, 24–26 September 2014 (to be published).

S. Claessens (2015): 'Levelling the location debate: introducing the Digital Single Market for small value consignments', PwC World in beta blog of 25 June 2015 at http://www.worldinbeta.com.

A.J. Cockfield (2000): 'Should We Really Tax Profits From Computer Servers? A Case Study in E-Commerce Taxation', 21 Tax notes Int'l of 2000 at 2407.

A. Cockfield, W. Hellerstein, R. Millar and Ch. Waerzegers (2013): 'Taxing Global Digital Commerce', Kluwer

P. Collin, N. Colin (2013): 'Mission d'expertise sur la fiscalité de l'economie numérique', 2013 at 49 (available at: http://www.hadopi.fr/observation/documentation/rapport-dexpertise-sur-la-fiscalite-de-leconomie-numerique).

C. Cornia (2007): 'Operazioni di finanziamento infragruppo e detraibilità dell'Iva', Rassegna tributaria 5 of 2004 at 1866.

F. Dittmar and H-J Selling (1998): 'How to Control Internet Transactions? A Contribution from the Point of View of German Tax Inspectors', 26 Intertax 3 of 1998 at 88.

R. Doernberg and L. Hinnekens (1999): 'Electronic Commerce and International Taxation', Kluwer Law International.

T. Eisenmann, G. Parker, M.W. Van Alstyne (2006): 'Strategies for Two-Sided Markets', 84 Harvard Business Review 10 of 2006 at 92.

Ecommerce Europe (2014): 'Western Europe B2C E-commerce Report 2014'.

J. Englisch (2009): 'VAT/GST and Direct Taxes: Different Purposes', in M. Lang, P. Melz, E. Kristoffersson (Eds.) (2009): 'Value Added Tax and Direct Taxation, Similarities and Differences', IBFD 2009 at pp. 14–15.

J. Farmer (2014): 'Web 2.0 and Two-sided Markets', at http://20bits.com/ 2008. Accessed 2 September 2014.

R. de la Feria (2014): 'Finance Act 2014 Notes...', British Tax Review 4 of 2014.

A. Ferrand, L. Torrigiani, A. Camps i Povill (2007): 'Handbook of Sports Sponsorship: Successful Strategies', Routledge, 2007 at 135.

Gaoua (2014): 'Taxation of the Digital Economy: French Reflections', 54 European Taxation 1 of January 2014 at 10.

B. Gasparotto (2013): 'TVA: focus sur l'actualité jurisprudentielle communautaire 2010-2013', Kluwer 2013.

M. Gianni (2014): 'The OECD'S Flawed and Dated Approach to Computer Servers Creating Permanent Establishments', Vanderbilt Journal of Entertainment & Technology Law of 2014 at 5.

Goldman Sachs (2015): 'B2C e-commerce as percentage of global GDP from 2009 to 2018'.

D. Graeber (2011): 'Debt: the first 5,000 Years', Melville House Publishing, 2011.

A.T. Guzman, T. L. Meyer (2010): 'International Soft Law', 2 Journal of Legal Analysis 1 of 2010 at 171–225.

A.T. Guzman (2014): 'A Compliance Based Theory of International Law', 90 California Law Review 6 at 1823.

R. Heinen (2014): 'Le régime de TVA applicable au commerce électronique', Le Code Fiscal of March 2014 at 26–27.

W. Hellerstein, Ch. Mc Lure (2001): 'Sales Taxation of Electronic Commerce: What John Due Knew All Along', Tax Analysts of January 2001.

W. Hellerstein (2003): 'Jurisdiction to Tax Income and Consumption in the New Economy: A Theoretical and Comparative Perspective,' 38 Georgia Law Review 1 of 2003 at 1–70.

W. Hellerstein, and Jon Sedon (2012): 'State Taxation of Cloud Computing: A Framework for Analysis', 117 Journal of Taxation 1 of 2012 at 11–31.

J.R. Hellerstein, W. Hellerstein, J.A. Swain (2015): 'State Taxation', Vol. II (3d ed. 2015 rev.)

O. Henkow (2008): 'Financial Activities in European VAT', Kluwer Law International, 2008.

Charlène Herbain (2015): 'VAT Neutrality', Promoculture-Larcier, 2015.

L. Hinnekens (1998): 'The Challenges of Applying VAT and Income Tax Territoriality Concepts and Rules to International Electronic Commerce' in 26 Intertax 3 at 54.

M. Iavagnilio (2007): 'I soggetti passive', L'IVA 2 of 2007 at 17.

P. Jenkins (1995): 'VAT and Electronic Commerce: The Challenges and Opportunities', 10 International VAT Monitor of January/February 1995 at 3.

P. Kavelaars (2013): 'EU and OECD: Fighting against Tax Avoidance', 41 Intertax 10 of 2013 at 507.

E. Kleinbard (2011): 'Stateless Income', 11 Florida Tax Review of 2011 at 699.

G. Kofler, M. Poiares Maduro, P. Pistone (éd.) (2011): 'Human Rights and Taxation in Europe and the World', Amsterdam, IBFD Publications, 2011.

E. Kristoffersson, M. Lang, P. Pistone, J. Schuch, C. Staringer, and A. Storck (eds.)(2013): 'Tax Secrecy and Tax Transparency: The Relevance of Confidentiality in Tax Matters', Peter Lang, Frankfurt, 2013.

M. Lamensch (2012): 'Are Reverse Charging and the One-Stop-Scheme Efficient Ways to Collect VAT on Digital Supplies?', 1 WJOVL 1 of 2012 at 1.

M. Lamensch (2014): 'The Treatment of Digital Products and Other E-Services under VAT', conference 'The Future of VAT in a Digital Global Economy', Vienna, 24–26 September 2014, to be published in 2015.

M. Lamensch (2015): 'European Value Added Tax in the Digital Era: A Critical Analysis and Proposals for Reform', IBFD Amsterdam, Doctoral series (expected volume 36).

I. Lejeune, E. Cortvriend and D. Accorsi (2011): 'Implementing Measures Relating to EU Place-of-Supply Rules: Are Business Issues Solved and Certainty Provided?' 22 International VAT Monitor 3 of 2011 at 144.

E.H. Levi (1949): 'An Introduction to Legal Reasoning' (Chicago: University of Chicago Press 1949.

J. Li (2003): 'International Taxation in the Age of Electronic Commerce: A Comparative Study', Canadian Tax Foundation, 2003 at 1-28N.

Ph. Malherbe, E.Traversa (2014): 'Du secret en droit fiscal' in V. Cassiers/ S. Gilson (coord.) (2014): 'L'entreprise et le secret' Larcier, 2014.

P. Martin, T. Valletti (2005): 'Content and Advertising in the Media: Pay-TV versus Free-to-Air', Mimeo, Imperial College, London, CEPR working paper 4771 of 2005.

M. Massbaum, K. Eicker (2001): 'The Proposal for an EC Council Directive regarding the VAT Arrangement Applicable to Services Supplied by Electronic Means', 29 Intertax 3 of 2001 at 91–97.

McKinsey Global Institute (2011): 'Sizing the Internet Economy', May 2011.

Ch. Mc Lure (2002): 'Thinking Straight About the Taxation of Electronic Commerce: Tax Principles, Compliance Problems, and Nexus', National Bureau of Economic Research (Tax Policy and the Economy), MIT Press, p. 122.

Ch. E. McLure Jr., W. Hellerstein (2004): 'Congressional Intervention in State Taxation: A Normative Analysis of Three Proposals', 31 State Tax Notes 9 of 2004 at 721–735.

R. Minor, C. Gartner (2012): 'VAT on Electronically Supplied Services to EU Consumers - A Practical Compliance Guide for Cross-Border Suppliers', Spitze Publishing 2012.

OECD (2010): 'Tax Policy Reform and Economic Growth', OECD Tax Policy Studies, No. 20, OECD Publishing. http://dx.doi.org/10.1787/9789264091085-en.

D.M. Parrilli (2008): 'Grid and Taxation: The Server as Permanent Establishment in International Grids', in J. Altmann and others (eds) (2008): 'Grid Economics and Business Models: 5th International Workshop, GECON 2008', Springer Verlag 2008 at 89–102.

D.M. Parrilli (2009): 'Tax Treatment of Companies Providing Grid Services: Direct v Indirect Taxation' in M. Lang, P. Melz, et al (eds) (2009): 'Value Added Tax and Direct Taxation, Similarities and Differences', IBFD 2009.

P. Pistone, Ph. Baker (2015): 'General Report - Subject 2: Practical Protection of Taxpayers' Fundamental Rights', IFA Cahiers de droit fiscal international, Volume 100B, Sdu at 21–74.

D. Raponi (2000): 'VAT Treatment of Electronically Delivered Services', 9 EC Tax Review 3 at 188.

P. Rendahl (2009): 'Cross-Border Consumption Taxation of Digital Supplies', IBFD Doctoral Series No 18.

P. Rendahl (2011): 'Imposing EU VAT on Unlawful Digital Supplies?', EC Tax Rev. 4 of 2011 at 192–2020.

F. Roccatagliata, P. Valente (2001): 'Internet – Classificazione del reddito e delle prestazioni di servizi', Il Fisco 32 of 2001.

A. Schenk, O. Oldman (2007): 'Value Added Tax: A Comparative Approach', Cambridge Tax Law Series, Cambridge University Press, 2007.

A. Semeta (2012): 'The Mini-One-Stop-Shop for VAT – The Start of Something Big!', World Commerce Review of June 2012.

A. Sinyor (2002): 'EU VAT on E-commerce: The Practical Implications', 13 International Tax Review 6 of 2002 at 32.

Adam Smith (1776), 'An Inquiry Into the Nature and Causes of the Wealth of Nations'.

J. Stanley-Smith (2015): 'VAT MOSS Losing Momentum with Smaller Businesses but Working Well for Multinationals', International Tax Review of 23 July 2015.

D. F. Spulber (2009): 'The Map of Commerce: Internet Search, Competition, and the Circular Flow of Information', 5 Journal of Competition Law and Economics 4 of 2009 at 649.

D.J.B. Svantesson (2007): 'E-Commerce Tax: How the Taxman Brought Geography to the Borderless Internet', 17 Revenue Law Journal 1 of 2007.

D.J.B. Svantesson (2008): 'How Does the Accuracy of Geo-location Technologies Affect the Law?', 2 Masaryk University Journal of Law and Technology, 1 of 2008 at 11–21.

A. Tait (1988): 'Value-Added-Tax: International Practices and Problems', IMF.

B. Terra (1998): 'The Place of Supply in European VAT', Kluwer Law International, 1998 at p. 5.

B. Terra, J. Kajus (2014): 'A Guide to the European VAT Directives', 2014.

F. Thépot (2013): 'Market Power in Online Search and Social Networking: A Matter of Two-Sided Markets', 36 World Competition 2 of 2013 at 195–221.

V. Thuronyi (2000): 'Drafting Tax Legislation' in V. Thuronyi (ed.) (2000): 'Tax Law Design and Drafting', International Monetary Fund, Kluwer Law International 2000 at 71–94.

E. Traversa and G. D'Angelo (2010): 'Diritto tributario e privacy: un binomio critico' in L. Bolognini, D. Fulco, P. Paganini (eds.) (2010) 'Next privacy: Il futuro dei nostri dati nell'era digitale', RCS ETAS of 2010 at 230–249.

E. Traversa (2014): 'Prevention of Evasion, Avoidance and Abuse in EU VAT Law', in M. Lang, P. Pistone, J. Schuch, C. Staringer, D. Raponi (Eds.) (2014): 'ECJ - Recent Developments in Value Added Tax: The Evolution of European VAT Jurisprudence and Its Role in the EU Common VAT System', Viena, Linde Verlag, at 48–53.

C. Trenta (2013): 'VAT in Peer-to-Peer Content Distribution: Towards a Tax Proposal for Decentralized Networks', Jönköping University, Jönköping International Business School, JIBS Dissertation Series, 2013.

R. Van Brederode (2009): 'Sales Taxation', Kluwer.

W. van den Corput (2008): 'Amendments to the EU VAT System', 19 International VAT Monitor 1 of 2008 at p. 6–12.

B.A.Van der Merwe (2004): 'VAT in the European Union and Electronically Supplied Services to Final Consumers' 16 SA Tydskrif vir Handelsreg 4 at p. 577–588.

M. E. Van Hilten (1999): 'The Legal Character of VAT', in 'Selected Issues in European Tax Law. The Legal Character of VAT and the Application of General Principles of Justice', Foundation for European Fiscal Studies, Erasmus University Rotterdam, Kluwer Law International, 1999.

S. van Thiel (Ed.) (2008): 'VAT Harmonisation in the EU and Unfinished Business', Conféderation Fiscale Europeenne, Brochure on Taxation 3 of April 2008.

A.Vega (2012): 'International Governance through Soft Law: The Case of the OECD Transfer Pricing Guidelines', Max Planck Institute for Tax Law and Public Finance, Working Paper 2012-05 of July 2012.

K. Vogel (2000): 'The Influence of the OECD Commentaries on Treaty Interpretation', Bulletin 2000 at 617–618.

A. von Bogdandy (2008) D. Bently (2004): 'Tax Law Drafting: The Principled Method', 14 Revenue Law Journal 1 of 2004 at 1–4.

C.F. von Siemens (1919): 'Veredelte Umasatzsteuer' (published in 'Siemenstadt').

D. A. Ward et.al. (2005): 'The Interpretation of Income Tax Treaties with Particular Reference to the Commentaries on the OECD Model', IFA and IBFD 2005.

S. Weinstein (2001): 'Copyright, Patents and the Internet' in C. Wild, N. MacEwan, S. Weinstein, N. Geach (Eds.) (2011): 'Electronic and Mobile Commerce Law, An Analysis of Trade, Finance, Media and Cybercrime in the Digital Age', University of Hertfordshire Press, 2011.

B. Westberg (2014): 'Taxation of the Digital Economy: An EU Perspective', 54 European Taxation 12 of December 2014 at 541.

L. Woods (2004): 'Free Movement of Goods and Services within the European Community', Ashgate Publishing, 2004 at 165.

Table of Cases

A. Court of Justice of the European Union (available at http://curia.europa.eu/juris/recherche.jsf)

B. USA

C. UK

Index

EUCOTAX Series on European Taxation

(1) Peter HJ Essers, Guido JME de Bont & Eric CCM Kemmeren (eds), *The Compatibility of Anti-Abuse Provisions in Tax Treaties with EC Law,* 1998 (ISBN 90-411-9678-1).
(2) Gerard TK Meussen (ed.), *The Principle of Equality in European Taxation,* 1999 (ISBN 90-411-9693-5).
(3) Michael Lang (ed.), *Tax Treaty Interpretation,* 2001 (ISBN 90-411-9857-1).
(4) Pasquale Pistone, *The Impact of Community Law on Tax Treaties: Issues and Solutions,* 2002 (ISBN 90-411-9860-1).
(5) René Offermanns, *The Entrepreneurship Concept in a European Comparative Tax Law Perspective,* 2002 (ISBN 90-411-9887-3).
(6) Michael Lang & Mario Züger, *Settlement of Disputes in Tax Treaty Law,* 2002 (ISBN 90-411-9904-7).
(7) Carlo Pinto, *Tax Competition and EU Law,* 2003 (ISBN 90-411-9913-6).
(8) Michael Lang, Hans-Jörgen Aigner, Ulrich Scheuerle & Markus *Stefaner, CFC Legislation, Tax Treaties and EC Law,* 2004 (ISBN 90-411-2284-2).
(9) Mattias Dahlberg, *Direct Taxation in Relation to the Freedom of Establishment and the Free Movement of Capital,* 2005 (ISBN 90-411-2363-6).
(10) Michael Lang, Judith Herdin & Ines Hofbauer, *WTO and Direct Taxation,* 2005 (ISBN 90-411-2371-7).
(11) Dennis Weber, *Tax Avoidance and the EC Tray Freedoms: A Study of the Limitations under European Law for the Prevention of Tax Avoidance,* 2005 (ISBN 90-411-2402-0).
(12) Félix Alberto Vega Borrego, *Limitations on Benefits Clauses on Double Taxation Conventions,* 2005 (ISBN 90-411-2370-9).
(13) Michael Lang, Josef Schuch & Claus Staringer, *ECJ-Recent Developments in Direct Taxation,* 2006 (ISBN 90-411-2509-4).
(14) Reuven S. Avi-Yonah, James R. Hines Jr. & Michael Lang, *Comparative Fiscal Federalism. Comparing the European Court of Justice and the US Supreme Court's Tax Jurisprudence,* 2007 (ISBN 978-90-411-2552-1).
(15) Christiana HJI Panayi, *Double Taxation, Tax Treaties, Treaty-Shopping and the European Community,* 2007 (ISBN 978-90-411-2658-0).
(16) Dennis Weber, *The Influence of European Law on Direct Taxation: Recent and Future Developments,* 2007 (ISBN 978-90-411-2667-2).
(17) Michael Lang & Pasquale Pistone, *The EU and Third Countries: Direct Taxation,* 2007 (ISBN 978-90-411-2665-8).
(18) Oskar Henkow, *Financial Activities in European VAT: A Theoretical and Legal Research of the European VAT System and Preferred Treatment of Financial Activities,* 2007 (ISBN 978-90-411-2703-7).
(19) Michael Lang (ed.), *Tax Compliance Costs for Companies in an Enlarged European Community,* 2008 (ISBN 978-90-411-2666-5).

(20) Michael Lang (ed.), *Source versus Residence. Problems Arising from the Allocation of Taxing Rights in Tax Treaty Law and Possible Alternatives,* 2008 (ISBN 978-90-411-2763-1).

(21) Ioanna Mitroyanni, *Integration Approaches to Group Taxation in the European Internal Market,* 2008 (ISBN 978-90-411-2779-2).

(22) Rolf Eicke, *Tax Planning with Holding Companies. Repatriation of US Profits from Europe:Concepts, Strategies, Structures,* 2008 (ISBN978-90-411-2794-5).

(23) Peter Essers et al. (ed.), *The Influence of IAS/IFRS on the CCCTB, Tax Accounting, Disclosure and Corporate Law Accounting Concepts: 'A Clash of Cultures',* 2008 (ISBN 978-90-411-2819-5).

(24) Tonny Schenk-Geers, *International Exchange of Information and the Protection of Taxpayers,* 2009 (ISBN 978-90-411-3142-3).

(25) Raymond Adema, *UCITS and Taxation: Towards Harmonization of the Taxation of UCITS,* 2009 (ISBN 978-90-411-2839-3).

(26) Michael Lang, Jianwen Liu & Gongliang Tang (eds), *Europe–China Tax Treaties,* 2010 (ISBN 978-90-411-3216-1).

(27) Michael Lang, Pasquale Pistone, Josef Schuch & Claus Staringer (eds), *Procedural Rules in Tax Law in the Context of European Union and Domestic Law,* 2010 (ISBN 978-90-411-3376-2).

(28) Sjaak J.J.M. Jansen, *Fiscal Sovereignty of the Member States in an Internal Market: Past and Future,* 2011 (ISBN 978-90-411-3403-5).

(29) Dennis Weber & Bruno da Silva, *From Marks & Spencer to X Holding: The Future of Cross-Border Group Taxation,* 2011 (ISBN 978-90-411-3399-1).

(30) Claus Bohn Jespersen, *Intermediation of Insurance and Financial Services in European VAT,* 2011 (ISBN 978-90-411-3732-6).

(31) Sabine Heidenbauer, *Charity Crossing Borders: The Fundamental Freedoms' Influence on Charity and Donor Taxation in Europe,* 2011 (ISBN 978-90-411-3813-2).

(32) Michael Lang, et al., *The Future of Indirect Taxation: Recent Trends in VAT and GST Systems around the World,* 2012 (ISBN 978-90-411-3797-5).

(33) Harm van den Broek, *Cross-Border Mergers within the EU: Proposals to Remove the Remaining Tax Obstacles,* 2012 (ISBN 978-90-411-3824-8).

(34) Michael Lang, et al. (eds), *Tax Treaty Case Law around the Globe – 2011,* 2012 (ISBN 978-90-411-3876-7).

(35) Dennis Weber (ed.), *CCCTB: Selected Issues,* 2012 (ISBN 978-90-411-3872-9).

(36) Daniël Smit, *EU Freedoms, Non-EU Countries and Company Taxation,* 2012 (ISBN 978-90-411-4041-8).

(37) Rita de la Feria, *VAT Exemptions: Consequences and Design Alternatives,* 2013 (ISBN 978-90-411-3276-5).

(38) Karin Simader, *Withholding Taxes and the Fundamental Freedoms,* 2013 (ISBN 978-90-411-4842-1).

(39) Madeleine Merkx, *Establishments in European VAT,* 2013 (ISBN 978-90-411-4554-3).

(40) Carla De Pietro, *Tax Treaty Override,* 2014 (ISBN 978-90-411-5406-4).

(41) G.K. Fibbe & A.J.A. Stevens (eds), *Hybrid Entities and the EU Direct Tax Directives*, 2015 (ISBN 978-90-411-5942-7).
(42) Gerard Staats, *Personal Pensions in the EU*, 2015 (ISBN 978-90-411-5953-3).
(43) Michael Lang & Ine Lejeune (eds), *VAT/GST in a Global Digital Economy*, 2015 (ISBN 978-90-411-5952-6).
(44) Massimo Basilavecchia, Lorenzo del Federico & Pietro Mastellone (eds), *Tax Implications of Environmental Disasters and Pollution*, 2015 (ISBN 978-90-411-5611-2).
(45) Cristina Trenta, *Rethinking EU VAT for P2P Distribution*, 2015 (ISBN 978-90-411-6137-6).
(46) Marie Lamensch, Edoardo Traversa & Servaas van Thiel (eds), *Value Added Tax and the Digital Economy: The 2015 EU Rules and Broader Issues* 2016 (ISBN 978-90-411-6612-8).